ECHOES FROM THE HILLS

Memoirs of a Bradford lad, born 1907

Richard at his trusty typewriter

ECHOES FROM THE HILLS

Memoirs of a Bradford lad, born 1907

RICHARD TEMPEST

First Edition published 2025 by Richard William Tempest
Shelf, Halifax HX3 7TH

Photography Richard Tempest collection and Pepper Hill Unitarian Chapel.

Typesetting and cover design by Charlotte Mouncey www.bookstyle.co.uk

Printed in Great Britain by Print2Demand

A CIP catalogue record for this book is available from the British Library

ISBN - 978-1-0369-2087-6

CONTENTS

INTRODUCTION

My father Richard Tempest born in Bradford in 1907, grew up to become a quite imposing figure, being six feet three inches tall, with the proud bearing of an ex-army man. He was largely self-educated, having left full-time education at twelve years old to be a 'half-timer', spending half of each day at school and the other half working in the mill – a situation that could not come soon enough for him.

His lifelong thirst for knowledge led to him buying many books, mostly second-hand, to satisfy his curiosity. He had many interests: literature, poetry, Yorkshire dialect, the Brontë sisters, Haworth, the Yorkshire Dales, America, and many more. Perhaps his greatest love, though, was music: from barrel organs to brass bands, *Oklahoma* to Sibelius, he loved the lot.

In the mid 1950s he started writing short stories (based on his experiences) and poems, many of them in Yorkshire dialect. Then, in the 1960s, he approached the BBC, and the result was that many of these writings were featured on its long-running radio programme *The Northcountryman*, narrated by Richard himself in the Manchester or Leeds studios.

For the last twenty years of his working life he was in the employ of John Mackintosh, the confectionery company; every day he would walk the best part of a mile down from his beloved 'House on a Hill' to Stone Chair, to catch a bus to work in Halifax. Gales, driving rain, blizzards made no difference; this was his routine. Down in the morning, back at night. A hard man.

His health had been a problem since he was invalided out of the army while serving in India in the early 1930s, and later he developed arthritis which badly affected his hands. This did not slow him down one jot, however; in a further testament to his determination, he continued typing and walking to his heart's content. In the years leading up to his retirement, he 'bowt a bit o' land aht back'. This was a small plot, part of a larger rough grass field, which he fenced off, dug over and turned into his dream garden: roses and an immaculate lawn. He spent many happy hours there, sitting listening to his beloved music on his transistor radio with the ever-present pint pot of tea by his side.

Richard passed away in his 'House on a Hill' in November 1975. This memoir is his legacy.

Richard William Tempest 2025

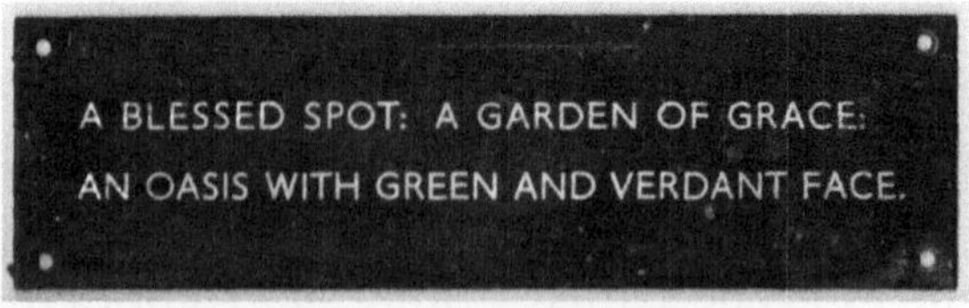

Plaque from Richard's garden.

CHAPTER ONE

FIRST IMPRESSIONS

To me, glimpses of my early days are accorded by a puckish imp whose antics are to be compared to the caprices of the perverse mists on our West Riding moorlands that drop like a blanket, then roll away in a few minutes; so with my memories: some years are a complete blank whilst others, as though brought to light with a sudden bright shaft of mental sunshine, loom large and crystal-clear. Nothing at all emerges of the first three years, and then remembrances start filtering through of childhood's days in far-off South Wales. It isn't really far off in distance in these space-devouring times, but Wales and what happened there seem to be at the back of beyond; indeed, everything seems so far away now as to suggest its having happened to somebody else. Not that anything extraordinary or noteworthy came my way, but I suppose the stuff called history is the ordinary of life piled up on end and interlarded with upheavals to make legends, and going on for ever and a day.

The consciousness of recollection starts in some small mining village of South Wales. It may have been Cwm, Ynysybwl, or Waunlydd – any one of these for I don't know which – but what I do know is that brother Bill and sister Edie, both younger then myself, were born in two of these places, and that I was born some time before, in 1907, in a small back-to-back house in Yorkshire's Bradford, within sight and sound of great double-decker electric trams that clattered, grated, and clanged their way down into town, or upwards to Tong cemetery, or Drighlington, 'out into the country' as out there was called right up to some forty years ago. That was before the building booms; before spiderwebs of scaffolding and cement mixers and mobile cranes and the craze for away-from-the-city bungalows with coloured tiles and large garages made naught of distinction between town and country, city and suburb.

I do not remember being taken from Bradford at the age of two, nor Bill being born within the next twelve months, but I have a clear picture of red-coated soldiers lining thronged streets, and of martial music, and of celebrating that must surely have signified the coronation of King George in 1911, and most probably seen in Cardiff for, during our traipsing about in Wales, I'm told we had a brief stay in the capital. Probably, this short interlude spent from coalfields was yet another breakaway effort on Dad's part because, for the rest of the time we were in Wales, we kept to the mining villages.

The term 'breakaway effort' is used firmly, for Dad was like that all his life: a roamer with no deep roots or loyalties, and with a disastrous addiction to beer. Yet he was well liked and not afraid of work, and he could always get a job, even in industry's darkest days. Excepting this South Wales adventure, he generally favoured the building trade; this, in all probability, was because in the trade a man could draw, every evening, a goodly amount of the money he'd earned. This privilege was called 'subbing' and suited Dad down to the ground, for one thing he liked was a bob or two in his pocket for a drink. He had been known to refuse jobs where the boss did not allow 'sub' and, altogether, paydays were not blessed events for my mother; many bitter tears followed much-depleted pay packets. Perhaps it was one of these disagreeable scenes that led Dad to try his hand in South Wales… and, without more ado, he had upped and gone – and not for the last time!

He left Mam to struggle on some months, with infant me on her hands, before he eventually sent money for her to join him for what proved a four-year spell down south. Knowing Mam for the all too short time for which I was privileged to do so, I marvel how she ever got involved with Dad – but she did, and never knew a settled life again. Yet – and this can't be emphasised too much – he was a popular chap; he was impeded in his speech, yet he could hold a conversation in the work cabin, or taproom, and in the house with us in the early years. He was fascinating with his tales, generally with a one-upmanship theme, but he was never a bore. I've been agreeably surprised at the high regard many people had for him and it may have been, as Mam jokingly put it, that 'Folks that only half half-knew your dad thought the sun shone from his backside.'

He had a hasty temper, however, and could be a terrible man in wrath and suffer terrible hurts, as we saw at times when he limped home savagely beaten about in some drunken brawl with his fellows, for the men he associated with were rough boys to play with. Yet, after licking his wounds for a few hours, he'd be out and about again, either seeking revenge or drinking with them, all depending on the mood of the moment – same old unpredictable Arthur – and what with this attitude and the wanderlust, he played many varied and unenviable roles in his rough life, which probably explains many things that came to pass for us Tempests, especially in the years when we were all together as a young family.

When we lived in pit villages, we always seemed to share a house with others – though not the same rooms, for one family would live entirely upstairs and another lot wholly downstairs – and it was in these houses that I seemed fated to lead the most hazardous days of my whole life. I bear scars yet of a bad burning received when lighting a kitchen fire – doing Mam a surprise good turn early one morning whilst still clad only in a little shirt, a lighted candle to hand – and of a severe cut under my right foot, caused through my running wild in the backyard in my bare feet and treading on a broken cup. And I remember falling through a low ironwork bridge that spanned a shallow stream at the rear of our house, and which served a nearby colliery. Luckily, I fell into the stream when it was at its lowest and quickly scrambled out, bellowing loudly home to Mam and to anxious, exploratory hands looking for hurt, a rough towelling, then a cuff on the ear from Dad, for those were the days when any child running home in tears was most likely met with a request from Father to straighten its face, under threat of further reason for crying. And all these things, and many more, happened in the tender formative years of life, yet I don't remember any of them disturbing me unduly above a few minutes – but then, that was the usual lot of us youngsters. Gosh! I tremble to think about how I ever survived, for I was not cast in a tough or heroic mould.

Starting school in one of the villages comes back to me clearly, for this school commanded a grand view of a hillside along which, at a gradual incline, a long wire rope hauled tubs to and from a distant pithead, and this fascinating distraction caused me to suffer several minor chastisements at the hands of the teacher before the novelty wore off. It was in this tiny infants' classroom I learned my first song, 'Land of my Fathers', and I never hear it now without being stirred, not by sadness or hurt, but by some proud emotion I find it hard to analyse. And talking of school reminds me of another sort: a Sunday afternoon one, though non-religious, that took place without fail on a well-wooded hillside overlooking our houses. We children were barred from going there that one afternoon in the week, for then it became alive with groups of clean-scrubbed, best-clothed miners earnestly engaged in games of chance, of which pitch-and-toss was the favourite. They had little fear of police intervention, for impecunious mates watched from spots where they could see a policeman hundreds of yards away. And this cameo in turn prompts a reminder, in some other place, of big, rough men pitching horseshoes into well-wetted clay, and uttering great oaths of glee, or frustration, all according to how they threw. Of course, Dad had to be in at all these things, always approaching them full of optimism and using every portent of good luck, to return sometimes gay and verbose, at other times surly and very much out of temper.

This ill temper didn't usually last long and then, resigned to his misfortune of being broke, he would play with us, and have Mam and myself singing, with Mam showing off her sketchy acquisition of a few snatches of Welsh ditties she'd picked up in the valleys. It was all so simply joyous at those moments, for even the place names down there were a poetry of sound: Ynysybwl, Waunlydd, Cwm, Cwmvellanbach – all these and others now lost in a limbo of hazy memory.

But it was not all poetry and simplicity – this same haziness blurs a picture of trouble at one pit; of lots of angry miners and grim-looking policemen; and of Mam fearful of Dad getting into something he knew only one solution for, the violent hard way. Mam well knew Dad was a law unto himself, given to sudden, drastic action with no attempt at finesse or subtlety. His decisions were never a result of deep thought, being mostly taken on the spur of the moment, dictated by the present, and generally going from one extreme to the other and heightened (as I suspected when I got older) by a fierce desire to bolster up his own resolve, for he knew, deep inside him, that he was his own worst enemy and so easily won over by others.

Symptomatic of this was his totally unexpected decision to take the pledge of total abstinence from beer. 'Going teetotal' was the phrase he used, and he didn't do so with any discreet keeping-it-dark, or affecting a quiet falling-off in his habit; no, he had to commit himself hook, line and sinker when he was reeling drunk. He staggered to a Salvation Army Citadel and offered himself to the welcoming open arms of a beaming officer, in front of a small congregation who must, in strict confidence, have had a quiet chuckle when such as Dad came into their midst seeking redemption, and of such there were not a few. However, whilst the blood-and-fire flame of salvation warmed him, he took Mam – with Bill wrapped closely to her side in a huge shawl, and me – many times to the tin-hut Citadel, excursions which provided many quiet, happy hours for Mam, though she knew in her heart this era wouldn't last.

When Dad's noble venture ended in abject failure through him letting down the army right, left, and centre, he yet, regardless of their estimation of him, bore them a great respect and admiration which was manifest on the many occasions, in later life, when he stood and listened to their Sunday-evening service on Bradford's Market Street. Some there were who suspected his motive and scoffed he was only really passing the time on until the pubs would open at seven. The army, perhaps not wholly ignorant, ended their service very opportunely; with brass blaring and banner proudly floating before, the good people marched away to the Citadel; most of the thin crowd (the ones who watched from a safe distance as though fearfully affected by the army's much-sniggered-at powers of persuasion!) melted away into the side streets with now only a few minutes to kill before opening time, before the demon drink beckoned them with a power more to their liking.

After Dad's fall from favour, I was sent elsewhere to Sunday school, for Mam fair shamed, she confessed, any of us 'facing them good folks agen on their own midden'. I never knew what brand of Christianity this new place taught, but then Mam didn't bother about any obscure, academic distinction of creed so long as going to worship implanted some seed that might later take root: of goodness, of tolerance, and love of others. And, though most of that seed fell on stony ground, I do know the difference between right and wrong, for if this first essay into spiritual things taught me anything, it taught me to feel deeply ashamed of many sins I have compulsively committed since then.

I cherish thoughts of wintry Sunday afternoons sat in a small chapel amongst the Welsh hills, the dying sun sinking and seen through a high window above the preacher's head. We kiddies believed every word of the hymns we sang; there was one began 'there's a friend for little children…' and I really thought Jesus was out there, somewhere out in that sky far, far away – where the red sun drowned in seas of fire and black and gold, and the last rays of sunset streamed through a rift in the black, beetling hills. Yes, away up there was Heaven and forgotten the old, wheezing harmonium, the hard forms, the tattered books, until the deepening gloom dictated the lighting of gas jets, and the magic of the promised Heaven faded in the harsh, hissing glare, and we bent over our heads in prayers of dismissal.

On the second day of one new year, I was playing in a copse filled with small fir trees when a neighbour came to take me home, a few hundred yards away. I was puzzled why, but utterly surprised when I got inside, for there was Mam smiling so happily at Bill and me as we gaped open-mouthed at her, lying in bed (having been very active only a short time before) with a little baby in her arms. I cried, Bill followed suit, and Mam had both of us lifted up and had us caress our new sister, Edie. I was short of six years old.

Another time – and this must have been in Cardiff – I was taken to a dockside to look on a ship with sails, and Dad told me it was used for polar expeditions. He painted a glowing picture of the deeds of this wonderful ship, and I think he called it the *Fram*.[1] But then, he painted equally glowing pictures of wrestlers and rugby men who thrived in every pit down there, and how fervently I did wish I was one of these. Mam often laughed when Dad was in full swing with his tales; she said of him, 'Dad could charm a bird out of a tree, then sell it for the price of a pint if he wanted,' and I believe he could, for he had the knack of making you laugh, and cry, or tremble in fear, and, altogether, he was a mighty man in my eyes, in those days.

So life went on, with every year or so us, like the Arabs, folding up our tent and quietly making for pastures, or pits, new. I should hate to think this may have been because we didn't pay our rent, though a suspicion lingers, for I never heard an adequate reason for the many migrations. Then, one eventful day, travelling light, we left South

1 The *Fram* was used by Norwegian explorers on voyages to the Arctic and Antarctic, including Roald Amundsen's 1912 expedition to the South Pole.

Wales for ever and, as evidence of Dad's quixotic nature, we left so unprepared for what faced us – we walked to Bradford! There were five of us, with Edie about twelve months old. I don't know how long it took us on the trek, but we slept and fed in a variety of places. In my sketchy recollections, what I now know to be the workhouses were the best, for then we had jam and bread, basins of gruel, hot tea and cocoa, nice beds, and a great compassion shown from others probably worse off than us. Mostly we walked, though Dad gave Bill and I piggybacks at times, and poor Mam carried Edie and told me, long after, that I was quite ill part of the way – though, mercifully, I can't recall this distressing phase.

However, at long last we neared our Mecca, dear old Bradford again, and did the last mile or so in style, travelling in on a tramcar. Arrived, Dad promptly foisted us all on Mam's sister and took himself off to bachelor quarters at a Salvation Army hostel, until after a few days of looking around, a house was found and we settled in. It was whilst we were here that the First World War started. To a seven-year-old's ears, it all sounded so exciting, and we Britons so gallant and righteous in going to the rescue of brave, outraged Belgium. I recall listening with eyes and ears wide open whilst a lad much older then me regaled us younger end with frightful tales – of the Queen of the Belgians weltering in her own gore, of Belgian babes being tossed about on long German bayonets – and I took it all in. Still, I've always remained like a pawnshop in that respect; that is, taking anything in.

THE GOLDEN AGE

Then, we were young and time was on tap,
And most of our ills fled in Mother's lap.
Then, white was white and black jet black,
And a so-gentle Jesus stood at our back.
Trust was a simple, unwavering thing,
And a truth always bore the genuine ring.

But that was ere growing-up sprang its trap,
And no one on hand now with consoling lap.
Time's turned hot night and harsh-shrilling day,
And black and white has merged into grey.
Trust has become but a relative term,
Truth, ugh! An ambiguous bit-of-a-worm.

Yet, through the dross of the baser years,
Scratch hard and a bright silver gleam appears,
And thereon, sparkling like jewels arrayed,
Are graven the names of friends we made,
And spirit and resolve again grow bold
To flout this sad business of one's getting old.

POP BOB

'Pop Bob' had a one-man business. He put onions to steep and pickle in big stone jars; he sold lumps of yellow scouring-stone, of which article Bradford housewives used more than their fair share on faithfully-scrubbed-once-a-week front doorsteps; and he also took round bottles of pop, which had gotten him his nickname in the first place. Everybody knew him as 'Pop Bob', but his proper name was Robert Robinson and, at the time I come into his story, he was bodging along, minding his own business in the second year of the Great War; that is, the one that was to end all wars, the '14–'18 one. Both of us were living, for the time being, in a district that bore a highfalutin note of quality; at least it did on paper, for I dwelt in Pen Street, and Pop's establishment was in Quill Street[2], where also stood a certain Shakespeare Inn for the delectation of the many who took a drop.

Pop was a spare, red-faced, middle-aged chap of very uncertain temper that flared out in rude, unprintable words, mostly when we youngsters got under his feet – which was almost daily, for we found his stores a very fascinating place, a veritable Aladdin's cave of dark mystery, acrid with vinegar fumes, and gained by uttering some magic password such as 'I've browt some pickle jars back, Mr Robinson' if he looked cross, or 'please can I rub yer hoss down, Bob?' if he beamed at you. His premises were a high-walled yard with a crude wooden roof laid across from wall to wall; they were dark and ill-lit with paraffin lamps and, so rumour had it, infested with rats, though I never saw any – and I looked hard and fearfully enough behind barrels and crates, and drums and sacks were moved gingerly whenever there was

2 Pen Street and Quill Street were off Bowling Back Lane and have since been demolished

need to do so. Also, at one end of the yard, away from the work and store places, and behind a thin board partition, he housed an old nag and a weathered flat cart on four wheels that stood very high from the floor.

Beside himself there were two small ladies – so old and shrivelled, they looked to us lads – who wore an external air of being blue with cold; in fact, one could have imagined them being pickled, long ago, in the all-pervading atmosphere of vinegar, with brine added for good measure, and to the total exclusion of sun and fresh air from their stunted lives.

None of us ever knew where the women slept or lived, for they seemed to be there at dawn, and they were still at it in the late evening, peeling and pickling and bottling those small onions without ever an eyelid fluttering in damp sympathy. Straight away, it always became evident to any lad getting a tentative foot inside Bob's that he was not welcome, leastways not by those two, and we lads, by common consent, gave them the cold shoulder, being more than a little convinced these two unusual ladies were not far removed from witches; indeed, one lad had it – bitches.

Whenever we could escape the venomous glare of the little women – and not forgetting the redoubtable Pop Bob himself, who boasted he had eyes in his rear – we thought it real smart to mouth an onion and bolt it without giving ourselves away, for the onions were so sharp one almost involuntarily screwed one's face up, and then got a sharp reproof to 'keep thy ruddy hand aht'. Another thing with them: if you went the whole hog and ate a few, they tended to dry the roof of the mouth into hard corrugations, though the cure for this was not far away with a quick swig of Bob's celebrated pop, and a lad was back to normal again.

But Bob's big day was Saturday, and on this morning we youngsters could always rely on him taking one of us along with him on the Saturday round, and there was keen rivalry to go with him, more especially in the nice weather, for winter was not a popular season for perching on the high open cart as it made its long way round mean city streets and rutted country lanes. No, we were pretty ungrateful little beasts come frost or snow, being then more inclined for a penn'orth at the Saturday afternoon picture, with its appealing warmth and laughter.

Yet, except in the very worst weather, he never lacked a lad to help fetch and carry the jars and bottles and big lumps of scouring-stone to the many houses he called on regularly, and every lad knew that at midday Bob would stop at a coffee tavern and stand treat to a pint of scalding tea and a fat teacake stuffed with lean meat. And there we'd sit, eating and supping noisily like the rest, and listen dead quiet to the menfolk talking. It was so novel and fascinating hearing them, for they peopled a strange, altered world from ours. A world of beer and betting, and football and fighting, women and dirt – and when they got to that last subject, Pop Bob would grimace in disgust, suck noisily at the tea leaves in the bottom of his pot, grunt a short 'Away, lad!' to his youthful companion, then hasten away on the long afternoon round, muttering a half-apology for the muck men talk. It might be well past teatime when he got home, though he would still be another hour unloading the cart and seeing to his horse, long after he'd sent his youthful helps home, with a mutual promise of seeing each other again on the morrow, though Bob would only be in on Sunday to see his 'galluwur', as he called his ancient horse.

And that was the way, and the day, of the one-man outfit, when chaps earned a living off a proverbial shoestring and were quite happy doing so. Now Pop Bob is no more, his old shed and traps and 'galluwur' are gone; the two ladies took their broomsticks and flew away this many year since, left without any trace, one might say. Though they are not without a little remembrance now and then, for they, and Pop Bob, always spring readily to mind whenever casual talk turns to unusual, stodgy jobs and, as talk so casually turns, I find myself telling of the quaint affinity of scouring-stone to pop, and pop to pickles, and so on.

GONE TO THE WAR

When Dad enlisted, it was sometime in 1915. He had tried before – indeed, had served an inglorious few months as a Scots Guardsman at the turn of the century – but the impediment in his speech worsening over the years had proved a stumbling block to getting back when the Great War came along. Then, after some months chafing at the reins of the dull, the ordinary, whilst hell was loose across the Channel, he realised in a flash of inspiration how much more fluent his speech was when he was merry and bright with ale. So, what more to his liking than to get a bellyful of beer, make his'unsteady way to a recruiting station, and be accepted, with the result that a day or two later he was on his way to a transit, and a few days away from his goal, France.

Arthur Tempest in the Scot's Guards about 1900

He left Mam and three bairns with a laugh, and an oath, and with a couple of his cronies oiling him up before he went. Though, for one, I was proud of my dad going to be a soldier, even though he was in a Labour Battalion – and Mam wasn't exactly heartbroken when he went, for he had threatened and fumed, every time he got some drink, about getting into the army and, altogether, had made Mam's life pretty miserable over it, so it was a sort of mixed relief to us all when he did go. Another thing: Mam was now assured of a weekly income, small though it might be, and governed by acts of indiscipline that meant loss of pay, and docking of Mam's army allowance; yet it was there, she got something, and regular, which was more than when Dad was at home with his constant 'subbing', or heartless cadging, or deliberate spending of what should have been Mam's housekeeping money.

Richard (back), Bill, Edith and baby Arthur

On the whole, we were a happy little crew over those four years when Dad was away in France, especially after Arthur was born in 1916. This was the time Mam leaned ever more on me, and I liked it, though many times I was found wanting; yet I tried mostly to be a good lad, for I did realise how miserable her life had been with Dad, and I tried to make up to her a bit. She always filled me with a sense of awareness of responsibilities devolving on an eldest, and she would tell me how the young 'uns looked to me for example and, aye, in proof were sure to follow like imitative little monkeys anything I did wrong.

These were the years of resumed Sunday school, and pleasant surprises on Mam's part; the biggest being when Arthur came like a bolt out of the blue to delight us all. And she bought us all small, blue-ringed basins for our now regular feeds of stew and dumpling (how these memories surge back!), and for lots of Sunday teas after Sunday school there was a wee apple dumpling in each basin. Mam also made an excellent pasty that I told the others was made from tea leaves but, in reality, was a delicacy made from currants and chopped mint leaves, and they were long enough before they knew better, marvelling at its goodness. As the oldest, Mam would let me have a wee sip of her bottle of Whitbread's, which luxury was only available if she was flush, which was not very often. Whenever I was sent to the off-licence for a bottle, I fair swelled with importance, as when I went for our family's supper repast of 'Two penn'orth o' tripe bits, with plenty o' vinegar, please,' or 'Ha'porth of each, four times' from the fried-fish shop, for it was well into 1916 before the practice ceased of chopping a fish in two and serving plenty of chips for the price of a penny. Which all sounded pretty remarkable cheap living until one discovered a labourer had to work fifteen minutes for that small coin – if he was in work.

However, to something less grim. We were then living in Pen Street, in the Pop Bob era, at the time of a long winter that was very cold and snowy, and we sledged down our short street on an old armchair, turned upside-down and minus the arms; we even had a snowman right up until Easter that year. And all this time, Mam was getting short, rough-scribbled letters from Dad; now and then, some fancy-laced postcard to mark one of our birthdays; and, once, a photo of some people in old-fashioned dress who Dad said were a French farming family. He told us that their dad was in the front line, and he was looking after them. It was a long time later when it came home to me that Dad may not have been the good old Samaritan he made out to be in those days, with his talk of scrounged blankets, rations, clothing, etc., for Madame was a fine-looking woman and Dad was no puritan.

The first time he came home on leave was in late '16, and he came without a word of warning. One morning, very early, there was a loud drumming on the front door; I stirred uneasily, then became aware of Mam moving next door and her hurrying downstairs, to be quickly followed by myself, and Bill, and Edie. There was a huge khaki-clad figure looming in the small doorway who was almost overwhelmed by weeping, laughing youngsters in shirt and shift, and he was crying out to let him in and get his things off. And what things he got off – a tangle of webbing equipment that took my immediate fancy, a khaki greatcoat, a vast kitbag with its muddle of underclothes and puttees, and hospital-smelling packs of bandage, and loose, tough army biscuits which we kids had to start testing straight away, and issue cigs, and a couple of small tins of bully beef, and a rash of brushes and polish, and needles and thread, and soiled socks, and a few French coins and trinkets. That kitbag was a veritable lucky dip and well worthy of all the months we had asked, 'When is Dad coming home?' and 'What will he bring us?'.

But he was not in with us often; his chief port of call was the Horse and Jockey out on the main road, and we were in bed when he used to get home, though I would hear him and Mam come upstairs and go into their little room, and I'd fall asleep and dream of soldiers and the war in France as told me by my dad – and how confused my dreams were, conflicting as they did with what we were told in school of this noble war of such high principle. And how long seemed that war; it lasted a lifetime, surely! I was a child when it started, but I was a serious young lad when it finished, aware of many things: the sad, and the glad, and the simply happy, and the inevitability of poverty amongst such as my family. I was well aware of my having to start work at the very first opportunity – though I must confess I faced that with much eagerness, for it was a new horizon, where one actually got money for doing a little bit of work. I was enabled to handle the magic stuff that seemed so tied up with happiness, and cleanliness, and the creature comforts of life. It seemed, to my young mind, that all who had access to money were happy – or didn't look quite as drawn and perpetually worried as the great host, then very evident, of the 'have-nots'.

TALKING THEATRE

My first recollection of any music hall was the time I saw a diminutive comedian, white of face, baggy of clothes, and facing up to a formidable female of uncertain age and crowned with a monstrous wig of flaming red hair. I know not where it was, or when; all I know is that they followed a silent, moving picture of the Battle of Waterloo, a very exciting affair that seemed to fill the screen with smoke and fire, augmented by concussing thumps and rat-tattings from drums in a black hole below the screen that was right up my youthful street. Then, after a decent interval to clear away the noise and smoke of titanic battle, the incongruous comedy pair were on stage. What they were funny about, I have not the slightest idea, but what did stick was the song they sang. It has stuck in my memory ever since, constantly bringing back the odd pair whenever I hear it again, which isn't very often – just rarely, but it has a tremendous impact on my emotions. I don't know why, but straight away it struck a chord of sympathy, of something pathetic, though the couple were singing it for laughs, if their gestures were aught to go by. It was called 'If I Should Plant A Tiny Seed Of Love (In The Garden Of Your Heart)'.

However, the place most in my affections is the now demolished Palace Theatre, Bradford. If ever a place merited the name of 'fleapit', this surely was it but, amongst the less savoury odours, it did, to me, reek of magical atmosphere – a make-believe place, it was. Before one got in, whilst waiting in a long Monday-night queue (Monday being a tradition among our class) on a narrow street of tall, deserted wool warehouses, there was a blind man hawking song sheets and intoning all the titles in a singsong voice, and also a little chap with a great basket and an apologetic whine that told us he was offering lovely oranges and bags of monkey nuts – and if the state of the floor in the fourpennies at the end of a house was aught to go by, he had a good living. One gained admittance by means of a large square, metal check paid for at a paybox and surrendered to an old codger at the bottom of a short flight of very steep steps – steps that led into the rear of the hall, and the popular fourpenny area.

Typical of Dad, he had the old man squared; quickly he would dodge past the paybox, whose good lady was too preoccupied by a milling half-dozen round her box to notice the slippers-in, of whom there were more than a fair proportion, and he would slip the aged attendant a couple of coppers, sufficient for the price of a gill[3], at that time. I used to quake when he took me and we ran the gauntlet, and down the steps (for I was more sensitive than Dad) but, once inside and sat safely in a crowd on long wooden seats with backs to twine one's arms round, all my nervousness fled, and I would occupy the minutes still to run, whilst the orchestra filtered in and scraped into tune, by staring hard at the huge safety sheet on the stage, reading for the many-eth time all the small local adverts: 'Joe Jaggers, Family Butcher, Home-Fed Bacons and Hams' – how attractive that 'home-fed' touch always read to me – and a local pub advertising its 'wines from the woods' and me daftly asking Dad, 'What woods?' and him telling me not to be so daft – though he never enlightened. Then, without any preliminary fuss or warning, the safety curtain would rise, silent as a ghost, the lights would dim – though an illuminated number would appear in frames sidestage, for the sole benefit of those few who bought programmes – the orchestra would saw away into a popular march, the curtains would part, and some acrobat or juggler would smilingly start the unenviable task of warming the house for later, more important, turns.

I loved Dad to take me to the Palace, though he didn't do so every time he went. He knew how to punish any wrongdoing on my part,

3 A gill is a unit of liquid measure, equal to a quarter of a pint.

and knew nothing hurt more than to see him setting off for the Palace and me left behind, even though it did only cost the same twopence for us both to get in. It was a treat, and a real privilege I considered it, with the added joy at the interval of Dad presuming to stretch his legs by retiring to a long beer bar at the rear, and later bringing me a meat pie, and a lingering smell of yeasty beer whenever he spoke. Mostly, the programmes were variety, although revues were rearing their unpopular heads; for, to me, variety was, indeed, the spice of life. As hinted, the Palace was only a third-rate place, with the top stars going on at the posh Alhambra, across town; so we were entertained by alcoholic has-beens, ageing never-was-ers, and eager up-and-comers just starting out. Gracie Fields came to the Palace in a revue called 'Mr Tower of London', though I never saw her. Anyway, the sensational acts were the ones for me: the newly arrived 'sawing a woman in half', and there was an Egyptian magician who used to cut his own head off, twice nightly. He would hold it high, though he himself was in utter darkness – and I used to marvel at the absence of mess, and shiver with delicious spasms of fear at this sinister act, not quite believable, yet there for all to see.

But best of all was a turn billed as 'Professor Walford Bodie', who told of his prowess as a mind-over-matter man – handsomely moustached, and immaculate in evening dress with a beautiful cloak thrown carelessly back over his shoulders and looking, to my young eyes, very much like the devil. But far more fearsome was his gimmick on a stage crammed with electrical equipment that flashed and sputtered, and emitted jagged spikes of lightning. To make this more authentic, there was a lady, looking fresh and antiseptic in full nurse regalia, in attendance. She would act as receptionist, as we now regard such a person, when Walford Bodie – after a few preliminary skirmishes with the dangerous monsters he held leashed with his many switches – would ask for a few volunteers from the audiences; he would put these halfwits (for they generally looked half-baked) into a trance and have them make asses of themselves. Then, in a mounting atmosphere brought on by him dismissing all but one of the dupes, and with a serious shaking of hand, he would get down to the real job of work. Firstly, the nurse would ensure the stooge was in a fit state to stand what might transpire (though, if one were going to fry, that would hardly have mattered), the stooge would dumbly shake his head when Bodie absolved himself from any mishap that may happen, and with dramatic gestures the good professor would hypnotise the hapless 'volunteer'.

It was then, in a silence in which one could have heard a pin drop, that Walford Bodie came to the front of the stage, told us he was going to pass many thousands of volts (a lot, I know!) through the stooge; he also added – with tongue in cheek, I'm sure – that he challenged anybody in the audience to doubt its genuineness. Needless to say, nobody ever got up to challenge him, for Walford Bodie could slay with a very witty, sarcastic tongue, besides that paraphernalia standing to do his bidding. Yet, once more, would the lights in the hall go low, the stage become alive with cracklings and sputterings and vivid flashes, the drums would roll, the bewitched man's hair stand on end; then, with a crash, Walford Bodie would bring it all to an end. For a minute the poor stooge would stand bemused after the professor had brought him back to normal and, with a pat of hand on back and the good nurse to steady him down the steps, the 'volunteer' would come down amongst us again, the cynosure of all eyes. On stage, the curtain would slowly start to drop whilst Walford Bodie took his dues of terrific applause, a very tempest of stamping, clapping, whistling. Dad would try to decry it by saying he knew the stooge who, in his cups[4], was unwise enough to tell a chosen few it was all a fiddle, but I never would have this, though I did not say so; somehow, I did not want to believe it was so disappointingly ordinary as Dad hinted.

Besides the Palace and the Alhambra, Bradford was, or had been, well served with theatres. There was the Theatre Royal, later surrendered to the moving pictures; it was on the stage there that Henry

4 *In his cups* meaning under the influence of alcohol

Irving made his last appearance, before dying suddenly a few hours later at the Midland Hotel. There was the Empire, another that went to the movies – but not before, paradoxically, Charlie Chaplin graced its stage with a gang of Fred Karno's comedians, amongst whom was another yet to achieve fame in far away, then unheard-of, Hollywood: a long-faced young chap by the name of Stan Laurel. And there was the Prince's, last home of the 'legit' in Bradford, with 'The Face at the Window', 'Man from the Klondyke'[5] and 'East Lynne', to mention but a few of the old-fashioned melodramas that moved us to tears and every emotion on the card. Yet it was said by a famous actor – and repeated often, with a touch of venom, by others who didn't come off – that Bradford was the graveyard of showbusiness. 'One had to break an arm to get a clap, or a laugh' was the substance of many rehashes attributed to the unnamed. I'm sure it wasn't as bad as that, but undoubtedly one had to be good to get good Bradford brass, and applause as well.

5 'The Klondyke Nugget' made its first appearance at the Palace Theatre in the summer of 1900.

A MONTH AT GRANDMA'S

Long before the tall, slim television mast dominated Emley Moor – yes, even before the BBC itself started up in business – I was taken on a month's holiday to a small pithead village between Wakefield and Huddersfield, away to my Grandma Tempest's at Emley.

I never knew why I was chosen for this signal honour – none of us had gone before, none of us went again – and I was not keen, for it was the back end of October and dark early, and that spelled early bed, for Grandma was by way of being a martinet, not like my own mam, now constantly badgered by three young 'uns and another on the way in this bloody year of 1915. Unlike the usual run of our family, Grandma was a little body, but stern, austere, with authority in every inch of her short stature. She was a widow, had been for long years, Granddad having been killed in a pit accident over Morley way when my dad was a little boy, and she had been left to fend with two girls and two boys, the oldest being ten when Granddad went.[6]

Yet she managed. Aunty Ciss and Aunty Emma went into nursing, emigrated to America early in the century, married and did quite well for themselves, and settled down in San Diego where, eventually, they died. Uncle Sam followed his dad's calling down the pit. My father was put to being a joiner but, sad to relate, he promptly made himself a nuisance and finished up as a soldier, even though but for a very short spell, before starting a long chequered career in scores of jobs that always ended when Dad looked too deep into a pint glass to the detriment of work. At the time I went to Emley Moor, Grandma lived in a cottage out of the village of Emley – one of a row of three,

6 Richard Tempest senior (b. July 1843) was killed in a roof fall at Morley Main Colliery on 16th September 1886.

still there, that abutted on a muck road which joined the main road to the village. She'd gone there because Uncle Sam, then a bachelor and living with her, had got work in the local colliery and, like Ruth, where he went, so did she.

I can well remember the morning Uncle Sam came to Bradford for me. Mam and the youngsters fussed round me, making sure I had everything – which must have been precious little, for I had to deliberately set off light because Uncle Sam was to buy me a new suit in town. I got my suit, straight off a peg, and put it on there and then, and the things I took off, rough corduroys, were parcelled up to stand service as my play clothes at Grandma's.

We got to the station (and how vast and important Exchange Station then seemed!) some little time before the Wakefield train came in, so Uncle San parked me on a bench whilst he went and bought two huge meat pies. And, whilst I stuffed, Uncle Sam bade me have a care of spilling the rich, warm gravy down my new suit, or woe betide if she, the daunting fount of us both, saw any telltale spots when we got to Emley. What little I had seen of Grandma made me mind this caution, and I managed to keep clean. Besides, no lad ever felt prouder in a strange aura of newness, although it was tinctured by the painful fact that a pair of boots, bought specially by Mam against this going-away and worn for the first time, nipped my feet and gave me gyp. It was whilst we sat waiting for the train that Uncle Sam asked, 'Hah much spending brass does thi ma gi' thee?'

'Three ha'pence. Evvry Satdi. Penny for pictures, ha'penny for spice,' I answered truthfully, filling with a lovely glow that something pleasant was about to happen.

It did. 'Aw…' speculated my uncle. 'We-ell, Ah'll gi' thee thri'pence ivvry Satdi while th'art wi' us. Hah's that suit?' And every Saturday at noon, I got my three pence, of which sum Grandma insisted I put a penny a week away for my brothers and sister, much to my chagrin.

She stood in a small doorway when we fronted the houses from the muck road. She greeted us – 'Nah then!' – surveyed me keenly, then turned to Uncle Sam with, 'Ee! Isn't he getting a big lad, Sam? And just like his dad, isn't he? Come here, doy.' She embraced me, then had to spoil it with 'But he wants a good crop. It is thick an' untidy… Sam, tek him to t'barber's when y've time.' She pushed me in front of her into the cottage, Uncle Sam following hard on; and my misgivings were a little allayed by a warm, welcoming smell of home baking.

At first, I was forever doubting the wisdom of Mam ever letting me go to Emley, for Grandma was a regular tartar in the house and, coming as I did from a humbler home – though when I look back, how much humbler than Grandma could we possibly have been? – it struck me my slackest ways were not to her liking, and I was a regular sitting target for her hourly corrections in the first few days. At times, I fair groaned when she lifted her eyes to me, for it tokened a chiding from this small woman with stern face and eyes so uncompromising, whose word was absolute law on this domestic hearth. Yet, she could thaw, as when she talked to me about her daughters – my aunts, models of correctitude and spotless mien, and now grown married women in strange California. And she would speak of Arthur, my dad, with a sigh of regret, for Dad was the off-white sheep of the family. He was one she had never succeeded with but I knew, though I was only eight, that she loved him dearest, the way she behaved.

The first night, I saw an old wooden cradle in the corner of the small bedroom where Uncle Sam and I were to sleep. She saw me looking and remarked, 'Aye, tha's slept i' there, Dick, lad.' She sighed heavily, then went on, 'And thi Dad. He wor the bonniest babby ivver. But, by, he did used to roar, and all aht o' temper. Wanted all t'attention, did thi Dad, even i' them days.'

Grandma slept downstairs in an old-fashioned shut-up bed; I slept upstairs, in the same bed as Uncle Sam, and everything was so oppressively quiet, upstairs, downstairs, outside. I can't quite convey how, but if I say it was all fields around, with even the pithead in a field, it might stroke a chord. It was so different from the streets in dear old

Bradford, with their mills and smoke-vomiting big chimneys, and the mill buzzers and clatter of tramcars. Even the going to bed was so vastly different. I had been used to a noisy tumbling into a huge bed besides Bill and young Edie, with a fratching or giggling session before we all finally drifted into deep sleep. Here, I was tucked into a lone bed with an admonition: 'Nah, mind! Straight off to sleep, an' noa tossing abaht – an' Ah doan't want to hear a muff.' The first night, after Grandma went downstairs, I started crying, very softly so as not to attract attention. I was still at it when Uncle Sam dropped into bed beside me. He heard my stifled sobs and asked, 'What's ta crying abaht?'

'I want me mam,' I burst out.

'Gerraway wi' thee! Doan't be a big softie – 'sides, tha's got thi granma.'

But I was not to be easily stayed. 'Can I go home, Uncle Sam? Please,' I pleaded. 'In the morning, please.'

For reply, Uncle Sam turned round to me, cuddled me into his big body and muttered, sleepily, 'Come on, mate, play the white man… Thi Dad'd noan want thee to roar, wod he? Well, then, get to sleep, an' we'll see what t'morning brings.'

I always liked Uncle Sam, with his rugged face, and hands gnarled and blackened with hewing coal – he was always so decent to all he came in contact with – a kind of natural gentleman.

Oh, I loved Grandma, in a different way, but she inspired fear. I always feared I was not doing the right thing; many times I feared I wasn't pleasing her, feared often she was not taking to me, which would hurt Mam if she ever knew. It seemed so very hard to get under her skin, to get right inside, through the garb of long, unrelieved black garments and bonnet she wore when dressed up. At these times, my grandma looked so very old to my young eyes, her yellowing skin a network of deep lines, and her not given to a lot of smiling. About the house she wore, over some old black dress, a drab sacking apron which just allowed a peep of black, buttoned-up boots, very small and very shapely.

This sacking she wore was very common in West Riding homes in those days. It was a hessian, but we called it 'hardin', which might have been after the village named Harden? It had many uses, the commonest being for aprons, oven cloths, or for backing home-made rugs, though I must not forget one useful function, as a rough towelling. Every day, when Uncle Sam came from the pit he would have a 'top-and-tail' wash, knelt before a big tin tub on the kitchen hearth, and dry himself on a square of hardin, rubbing until his arms, face, body, shone with healthy glow – a big, strong man – indeed, a very Hercules in my eyes. Then, whilst Grandma took the tin tub away, Uncle Sam would don his clean vest and his second-best trousers and sit himself in patience at the kitchen table, its plush cloth gone, an American-cloth covering in its place, and knives and forks set forth for our main meal, with a mouthwatering smell of fresh cooking issuing from the big oven always on the go, for Uncle Sam got free coals from the colliery. And, only then when Uncle Sam had bathed, dressed, and rested, would dinner be put out, with my ever-ready belly fair screaming its impatience.

Though much of my stay is blurred, I can still savour Grandma's flat, delicate Yorkshire pudding, the batter poured into a large meat tin, straight following the meat roasting, and done in the fat. Cor! what a start! For we always ate our Yorkshire as a first dish, all by itself on a plate swimming with rich gravy that made golden islands of the freshly-cut squares. Grandma never complained I did not appreciate her good cooking. I loved it and, like Oliver Twist, I'd ask for more and have Uncle Sam chuckle, 'By, Mother, this lad o' thine can eyt!' 'Let him, Sam, let him,' she'd reply, with a hint of a pleased smile on her face. 'He's t'mekkings of a big lad, same as his dad.'

I got pally with a young chap who came to Grandma's house with a laundry van. He used to take me with him on his round, out along the muck road, out to lots of other houses and cottages on remote lanes, then he would drop me off home on his way back to the laundry. At times we came home in the gloomy dusk, a big candled lamp at each side of the covered-in cart throwing a dim light along the unlit lanes. I can still smell the antiseptic of the laundered bundles, the hot whiff from the lamps, the strong exciting smell of the horse jogging at a half-trot homewards.

Talking of horses reminds me of a time when I was in deep disgrace – I blush to this day when I think of what I did! Grandma had a greengrocer's cart come along every day, and once, in a moment of crass lunacy, I threw a stone at his old horse as he passed me on a slight hill by our house. Straight away, the man jumped from his cart, picked up his long whip and, in his righteous rage, gave me a couple of licks round my buttocks with the vicious, stinging lash. In reality I was more frightened than hurt, but I set up a great howling and dashed off home to Grandma, to pour my tears on her lap as she hurriedly examined my still-hot bottom.

The poor man had, perforce, to come back our way, and Grandma was waiting for him. She gave him hell for ten minutes whilst he vainly protested the justice of his summary punishment. I stood by, secretly sorry I had ever started this rotten business, whilst Grandma waded in with, 'A gurt men like thee wading into a little lad like him' – pointing to discomfited me – 'When he needs the whip Ah'll see he gets it, not thee. Oooh! Ah wish ahr Sam wur here, Ah do.' The poor man couldn't get a word in edgewise, and I felt ashamed, though I wisely steered clear of him for the rest of my stay. After her session with the hapless greengrocer, Grandma gave me a real dressing-down, and told Uncle Sam later. His sole comment was, 'Aye, well, that's what comes of hevving nowt to do. Find him some wark, Mother. Oh, owt – running errands, an' suchlahk.' I got plenty of the 'suchlahk', which included emery-papering knives and forks, tidying Uncle Sam's pit clothes away, and cleaning his walking-out boots, which one did by applying polish wet, though Grandma took a dim view of my first attempt, when she caught me spitting in the polish. I was found plenty of errands to run, but these I liked, for they afforded me time to stand and stare at the great pithead wheels spinning hundreds of tubs of coal to the surface every shift, and run in the erstwhile-oppressive fields, and wonder what lay along the next lane and over the hill.

Whilst I was there, Plot Night came along and, the weekend before, Uncle Sam bought me a few fireworks, comprising some strings of Chinese crackers, rip-raps, cannons… Oh! the lot of that day. I was delighted as I stared round-eyed at the treasure he spilled on the kitchen table. I even danced round until Grandma, coming in from the scullery, put a stop to that. 'What's this abaht, Sam?' she demanded. 'What's ta bowt him theas for? He'll blaw hissen up, tha knaws that.'

'Nay, Mother!' protested Uncle Sam. 'Let t'lad hev his bit o' fun. Lewk, he's as suited as a dog wi' two tails… Nay, leave him be, he's noan gormless, Ah'm sure.'

Alas, I was to prove them both wrong. For I didn't get 'blawn up', but I was gormless.

Grandma was really the unwitting cause of the Plot Night fiasco for, in her zeal for my well-being, she had me put my fireworks in a large cocoa tin, for safety's sake round the fire. These I clutched very tightly as Uncle Sam took me along to a huge, prepared bonfire in a field away from the village; then, having got me 'bedded-in' with the other youngsters, left me whilst he slipped away to the local for a quiet hour. Of course, it wasn't long before my native self came to the fore, and I was one in with the others, yelling, rushing round the now fiercely blazing fire, my precious tin clutched to my chest as I was pushed, and retaliated, in childish play.

Imagine my horror when I put my hand to remove the lid for my first cracker. It wasn't there! I gasped, thrust scrabbling fingers into the tin. It was empty! Oh, the agony of that awful moment. In anguish I yelled my plight to the others, and soon we were all scraping in the long wet grass; me, in a fever of hope that something, if only a few, would turn up. But I scraped in vain, long after the others had given up the search; nothing was found, and I spent the rest of Plot Night wistfully watching other fireworks going up in delicious fire and smoke. I was a sad little boy that night. Of course, somebody felt they must tell Uncle Sam when, at long last, he came back to take me home, and he felt he must tell Grandma, though I wished he hadn't. Her comment was, 'Aye, well, he'd nobbut hev set fire to summat, so it wur perhaps for t'best.'

I cried when I left Emley – when Uncle Sam started back with me to Bradford, and Grandma waving, with eyes I swear were slightly wet, us right out of sight. Yet when I savoured the unmistakeable woolly smell of our streets from afar, my spirits soared again, and I eagerly anticipated the open-mouthed wonder of the young 'uns at home when I told them the highlights of my month in the country, and how they would roar with laughter at some of the things I'd tell. But we all cried when they brought her home – to her birthplace, to Birkenshaw – for she went before us into the church, then out into a corner of the churchyard, there to lie beside her long-departed husband. She was in her sixties when she died, yet, to me, she had always been as old, and as wise, as the world – the founthead of life; that is, our life, our family. Sadly enough, only Uncle Sam, of her children, was at the graveside, with Aunty Emma and Aunty Ciss in America, and Dad still in France.

From where I now live, and on a very clear day – autumn days are best – I can see the so-tall television mast away to the south and, in my mind's eye, the huddle of three small cottages that are not above four hundred yards away from the mast. And I see again the small, trim figure of Grandma Tempest standing at her low door as she did the day I left, so many years ago, waving, but ever feebler as the image dies away and I turn around to re-enter my low doorway.

IN PRAISE OF POP SHOPS

When I was born I was heir, theoretically, to a proud national heritage for Britannia, with several battle fleets ruling the waves and none, as yet, caring to dispute her sway; her many overseas garrisons saw to it the Union Jack flew high and proud with only the bugle call 'Retreat', sounding on instruments every evening and all over the world, to bring it slowly, majestically to earth until each new dawn. The immaculate sun-helmets were doffed at dusk, the jingoists chanted 'The Recessional' (more widely known as 'Lest We Forget'), and it was roses – specially cultured for the climate – all the way, in tropical gardens fenced with pickets of British bayonets and displaying notices, in several languages for the enlightenment of covetous neighbours, stating 'Keep Off The Grass'.

The English lorded it abroad as though we were the chosen of God but, at home, things were not so rosy, stripped of the exotic, the mumming and sorcery, the power displays that made us omnipotent in balmier climes. True, self-respecting housewives bought their flour by the stone to do their own twice-a-week baking; they could fill a pillowcase, as many did, with the week's groceries for a few shillings; houses, of a kind, stood always available to let all over the country; rail travel was cheap; tobacco was but a copper or two an ounce; and beer flowed at negligible cost – all day. Yet it was possible for a child to go to school in bare feet and not cause a sensation; it was possible for a half-time worker of eleven or twelve to lapse into deep sleep across a desk and not earn a reproof from teacher; a man could be sacked without reason, or notice; an outdoor man could be in employment yet not work for long periods throughout a bad winter by reason of being 'snowed off', 'frosted off', or merely 'rained off', without any pay to compensate for the vagaries of the English climate – to which could be added two more items of the labourer's own choosing: 'browned off' and 'boozed off'.

Given a shilling, a chap could, at any hour of the day, avail himself of the hospitality of mine host in the local pub, who also provided free eats to keep the whole shilling in his house, such was the competition for money that was very hard to come by. Unhappily, these stout landlords did not also provide beef sandwiches and pickled onions for the drinker's wife and kiddies, to stay their pangs of easily awakened keening hunger, in many cases further sharpened by Dad's unendearing habit of raiding the already slender family purse for his beer money. Dad, at the least excuse, would up and out, in high dudgeon, to his special oasis of peace, the local, with an indignant burst of 'getting aht of it' – 'it' being a small back-to-back housing a flurry of quickly gotten kiddies and a worried-looking Mam pulled to bits, physically and mentally, and looking anything but happy and glorious with her share of the national heritage.

What more natural, then, but for Mam to seek a way of relieving her desperate plight? To raise the wind, to find a couple of shillings that would at least keep body and soul of the family going for a few days. A couple of bob went a long way then in broths and stews and 'tattiehash' – but then, florins were mighty hard to come by! There was one way, provided the situation found possessions that would realise hard cash; that is, if Dad's drinking rants were too depressingly often and keeping him from finding work, and the poverty grown chronic and not to be allayed otherwise, by an isolated visit to the pawnshops – or 'pop shops', as they were commonly called. Your guess is as good as mine how some families, sunk low in the trough of despond, managed finance. It never occurred to me to start guessing, being but a child when the pop shop started figuring in our economic reckonings. Mam did all the guessing for our family; after all, isn't that what mams were for? That's what I thought in my childish mind, for Mam was in the same category as faith, and could work minor miracles.

Though pawnshops went hand in hand with grinding poverty, grim distress, and less-publicised tragedies, everybody held them in a humorous light, from the men in the street to the music-hall comedian and the newspapers. There was a Valentine displayed in a York museum that had, long ago, been sent to a certain young lady employed in a pawnshop in Woolshops, in Halifax. Heaven knows down there was no atmosphere to encourage romance, or levity, with its smelly noisome proximity of a vegetable market in posh-sounding Piece Hall, its lodging houses, and a teeming, dowdy square. Nevertheless, this dainty missive was addressed to a maiden in the seedy pop shop – but who sent it? Was he a regular? Another of her kind in some other pawnshop? That will probably never be known. Later, there was a ribald song of the First World War period that ran 'She's a ragtime soldier's wife... Every Monday morning at the pop shop door... With rings on her fingers and bells on her toes – all on a shilling a day.'

Any serious student of those times can rest assured this was not the devil-may-care lot of my mam, left to fend with four young 'uns and Dad away in France. 'Bells on her toes'– ugh! It didn't even run to a bell on the door, and Mam's plight – not to be wholly blamed on the war, I would add – was no rare, localised complaint. This highly contagious state of 'hard-upness' spread far from our streets; it raced out and up to the very hilltops surrounding our fair city, for fresh air did not stay it, and many there were from the heights came down into the smoke and grime in search of temporary financial easement, it was said, and this by a gentleman well versed to speak. He was an old tramcar man, a conductor who noted well all that passed.

'Ee, it wor funny!' he started. 'Ivvry Monday morning, an' under the steps o' yond ten-to-nine into tahn, it used to be fair packed aht wi' parcels being tekken dahn to t'pop shops. An' all of 'em reckoning' – he chuckled – 'not to let on where they wor going. It wor really an eddication to see 'em sneaking off, bundles under arms, to their hole-and-corner pop shops. Ee, it wor funny!'

Most often, the Pledge Department of a pawnbroking establishment was to be gained by an unobtrusive entry into a side or back door, as opposed to the big windows on the main road that were laid out with fascinating displays of unredeemed goods. There would be gold pieces, row on row of silver watches, chains, seals, medals, lockets and bangles, opera glasses, and loads of rings. How many have got wed with pop shop rings? For all the things in the windows seemed so wondrous cheap – if one only had money, had a win, had a windfall. No one ever did have a windfall, leastways not within shouting distance of where we lived, and where these windfalls came from was something so vague as to be never seriously thought about. Pools had not then raised their attractive heads with alluring Saturday teatime mirages to buoy one up for a few minutes, and Lady Luck was a jade who seemed to studiously cold-shoulder the have-nots. It was always somebody who had a bob or two who had luck so that, if one of our ilk did suddenly acquire money, it was a ninety-day wonder – or a matter that didn't bide looking into, for it might end in the police, then very unpopular men on our street. A chap had only to have half a crown on a big race winner at long odds to be hailed throughout the streets as a poor man's Lord Derby, as a confidante of trainer Alec Taylor, as on nodding terms with the peerless pigskin artiste Steve Donoghue.

Incidentally, our wealthiest neighbours were always the street bookies, who never stooped to hard work, not even during the bitterest moments of truth, those occasioned by some popular fancy coming in first at twenty to one and everybody being on, to a man. Following these rare catastrophes, the bookie would sneak along some narrow snicket or round a sharp corner to the saviour of all in distress, Uncle in his pawnshop, going with the very gold watch he had bought there earlier in a high summer of dizzy successes, when all he had touched had turned to gold, in every sense of that glittering word.

It was a touch of delicacy, or perhaps genius, on the pawnbroker's part to have his needy clients come to the back door. We folks might not have been unduly sensitive and were mostly in the same money-shy boat from Sunday to Friday pay-time, yet we were loath to have others see us on our pop shop expeditions. We couldn't have felt much worse being caught shamefully naked. Aught but that! This studied privacy was a sop to our tattered, bruised dignity that dictated a very human hiding of ostrich-like heads en route to Uncle's. Which was all rather quaint, for our neighbours and ourselves well knew each other's affairs, habits, and shortcomings, and we were decent enough to make an allowance for almost anything – we practised an acquiescing attitude that made life tolerable for all, the rogue and the decent. And, if folks were ultra-shy of personally attending the pop shop, there was always an elderly – generally widowed – lady to take one's parcel along, for a consideration, say a penny in the bob. One such lady amongst us gloried in the nickname of 'Snuffy Emma' by virtue of the fact of her using the stuff so very much that her upper lip always bore the gingery telltale smudge. Thus were the conventions kept.

Yet woe betide them when open warfare blazed across the street, as was quite regular and could be both entertaining and informative; then the beans were spilled, piping hot: moral depredations, child neglect, one's visits to the pawnshop, all became the common property of those within earshot. Confidences, given but yesterday in dear friendship's intimacy, were flagrantly betrayed as tongues, sharpened and tempered in the heat of battle, darted in and out in telling thrust and parry, with the deadliest to the effect of 'who got her kids a new suit apiece for Whit – an' then popped 'em straight after – an' them got on a club cheque, an' all!' Oh, that was a dig about the club cheque, ever the poor man's promissory note, to obtain clothing, etc., and then to repay weekly at a shilling per pound. The confronted (unless she had the cheek of the devil to brazen it out) would hastily break off the wordy engagement and slam her door shut in the other's face – surely a tacit admission of defeat, if ever there was one!

Our pawnshop had two definite, differing periods – black IN and bright OUT – and Monday morning the busiest period for the INs.

On this dourest, most sober morning, the hapless seekers of ready cash would creep along with their parcels: big, little, according to one's reserves or convertibles. If the time was the height of summer, a parcel might run to a blanket, lately washed and taken from the line; if winter, a watch and chain, or a ring; but always a good insurance, summer or winter, were kiddie Sunday suits. To digress, I once had a little pal who had a *Saturday* suit, to boot. But then, his parents kept a flourishing coffee tavern, and were never without a bob or two, and counted amongst the elite of us, and were pillars of their chapel. We young 'uns were inclined to snigger at the fact he wore a pinny to his dinner at home, and laughed loud at his amazing ignorance of the most ordinary things. He didn't know a pawnbroker would have no truck with a drunken man, and that folks were not allowed to send young 'uns to pop stuff, although we could get it out. Nor did he know that tools of trade were not, really, things to be put in pawn – lots of craftsmen were also birds-of-passage in those days, and Uncle could soon have had his windows stuffed with plumb lines, planes, saws, and even brick hods!

In most cases folks put things in as a temporary measure to tide them through the week for, after all, it was mostly stuff not needed on weekdays. Besides, it would have been a very black mark against a mother to leave her children's clothes in pop over the weekend and have them run about threadbare on the Sunday. During the week, it didn't matter about scruffiness, but all strove to have their kids decent on the Sabbath, probably owing to the fact we were a predominantly Catholic community with the priest insisting on seeing, at least once a week and at Mass, the youngsters clad respectably. Also, Dad took a dim view if his best shirt was not forthcoming for his Saturday night in the taproom; that is, a best shirt as distinct from the rough union one he wore on weekdays.

Generally speaking, a person's economic status could be gauged by their parcel, for whilst the financial embarrassment was temporary and buoyed up by a prospect of relief if there was something worth pawning, if the position deteriorated the hunter-watch and ring and best suit would be followed by boots and shoes, looking suspiciously thin-soled, or perhaps some bedding or curtains, and the odds shortening all the time on how much more could be brought forth to stem the breech in dire straits. The end of the line had surely been reached, on both sides of the counter, when an old linen collar-and-front, dingy and yellowing, or some crinkled chemise, was pushed under the pawnbroker's sensitive nostrils, to be firmly pushed back with a cold air and a single word of negativity. Yet every Monday morning some well-known hard-up would spring a surprise with something definitely brand new, and you could bet a bright shilling the club cheque man had got a caning, especially some new, still-green agent from some other part of town.

The more cheerful side, OUT, started flowing directly after Friday teatime and continued all the next day, right into Saturday night. We kiddies would then have a chance to earn ourselves a copper or two, chiefly by going to redeem some old dear's precious parcel, and being told in a fierce whisper to mind and not let our mother know where we'd been and for whom. The cash tide was now coming in fast, and on it rode now less lugubrious pop shop assistants, far removed from Monday's cynical, heartless men of stone – men now even allowing themselves a smile and small talk, and using miles of new string, pink sheets of shining new pins, acres of new stiff brown paper, shining and crackly (though it all added a copper more). And the customer was also far removed from Monday's timorous creature, chattering away and going home with broad beam of face and neat new parcel carried boldly to the fore, for a change!

Thus for a few hours on the Sunday we youngsters were vouchsafed the privilege of wearing our best apparel – though late afternoon, after all the Sunday-schooling, saw us stripping and our suits being examined for tears and rough usage, then brushed and folded against the morrow's visit to Uncle's. This much was to be said for the habit of pawning: its incentive bonus of a bob or two more to be gained 'on' a well-kept suit taught one to care for clothes and inculcated tidy habits. Never since, I swear, have young ones been urged to have a care with such earnestness, and implied threat, as we were. One reckless half-hour larking, on a Sabbath, in the nearby derelict brickfield, could wreck a household economy, based as this was on the bartering values of what we stood in. But our mothers were not easily beaten; there would be a vigorous application to sponging with wet flannel and a neater than usual show of needle and cotton, the old-fashioned fire-heated iron would press the harder, and Monday would find the refurbished suit pushed hopefully, and with poker face, across the high counter with the time-aged request, 'Same as last week, please.'

There was one high counter with a two-shilling piece, a blatant dud, screwed down on its dull surface. Whether this was a warning to customers not to try it on or a horrible reminder to assistants about relaxing vigilance, I leave it to others to decide. Suffice to say, it got fingered very covetously by all, and no doubt if the coast had been clear but a few moments, attempts would have been made to give it a separate existence, for money, good or dud, commanded our great respect.

If one was a newcomer to the pawnshop, it was fatal to betray this fact, though it was equally hard to hide it from the gimlet eyes over the counter, eyes grown cunning and jaundiced across the years.

'How much?' the voice would ask, automatic, whilst the hands opened the parcel and pretended to be unfavourably impressed.

'Could you give me, er, five shillings?' might come the first halting probe, and the assistant would allow himself a suspicion of a sneer, and one short demoralising phrase: 'Half a crown.' He would be pushing the parcel back ere the shocked customer gathered his wits and quickly mumbled, 'All right,' and saw his goods whipped away and pushed back on to some deep shelf, and a ticket and the precious half-crown handed over.

As a contrast, the old-timer would go in, chirp brightly, 'Same again, Mr Blank... Been nice, hasn't it?' and that personal touch might just make the difference between 'same again' and a sickening downgrading. As well, the man behind the counter knew the old-timer (except he get pinched, go in the workhouse, die) would be back in again on Friday, whereas the new client might never be seen again, and it would be a long time before the unredeemed goods could go in the front window.

There are some towns nowadays seem to manage quite well without pawnshops, and it is becoming increasingly hard to find, in my native city where they formerly flourished, any of the truly hung trios of golden balls. This distinctive trademark was brought to England, I'm told, by Huguenot moneylenders, but I bet they had not the shabby clientele our pop shops had. Dear old pop shops! Now almost gone, along with the all-day beerhouses and enticing beef-and-pickles, and half-time juvenile labour and barefoot children. In their strictly business way, they rendered a goodly service – they filled many an empty belly when plenty, from a few street-lengths away, seemed to mock and do no more about it. Many good people, reconciled to short commons, were heartened by the comforting thought that Uncle and his three brass balls were never very far away; in fact, were just around that next corner and along a dark, all-concealing passage. They always knew they had a fair chance of coming out with a jingle in their pockets, and its implied promise of some coals to put in the dusty grate and something heating in the pan for dinner. Even the not-so-good sparked warm at the nice thought of the ever-welcoming taproom, with its foaming pint of beer, the eats, the congenial company, and a soothing smoke. Yes, Uncle – skeleton in the cupboard, derided, maligned – was the best, kindest, relation some of them ever had.

WHEN MAM CRIED

One time – I know Dad wasn't at home, though whether he was in France or on one of his many perambulations, I don't know – Mam went to work in a wool-combing shed.

This same shed was to draw her back a time or two more and was to prove a deadly allurement with its very hot, debilitating atmosphere, but on this special occasion Mam had to stop working there only because we young 'uns didn't behave very well with the folks in whose care we were left whilst she worked; they gave us up as a bad job. Mam then started taking in washing, which job was a terrible extra business for her in those times of peggy sticks and rubbing boards, and clumsy iron wringing machines with vast turning handles. And all this washing was done in the one room, the kitchen-dining-parlour.

I still smile over the washday I rushed into the house (for we always rushed either in or out, with no happy medium of walking) having dashed all the way from school, arrived hot and thirsty, saw a drinking pot on the bared kitchen table, hastily perceived it was filled, then swigged fully half of it before the odd taste made itself felt on my palate – it was s-s-soapy water! Brrh! I spat and sputtered and coughed, and cried in vexation, whilst Mam laughed heartily. Bill and Edie also laughed, and even baby Arthur beamed up to me whilst Mam now reproved, a chuckle still in her throat, 'Serves you right!' Her arms waved expressive of my silly haste as she went on, 'You rush in here like somebody not right, with never a word of by your leave… Oh, oh! Perhaps you'll ask next time.'

In vain I asked then, 'Well, what was the pot doing on the table filled with soapy water? Eh, Mam?'

Although the family income was always meagre, even in the best of times, my mother had a bad habit, so I thought, of leaving odd coins on the high shelf above the large, blackleaded fireplace. There might be a shilling, from the washings, in the tea caddy, a few halfpence rubbing shoulders with a much-chipped pot dog who guarded – not very well as all turned out – one end of the shelf, and another copper or so in a small vase, nominal depository for all buttons riven from our clothing on our many, hourly, tumblings. Mam would tend to forget this small wealth, and it might lay there long enough… and soon, because of this petty fault of hers, terrible seeds of temptation gradually germinated in the grey matter ill-used in my donkey-cropped noddle.

The first time, I filched a halfpenny for some aniseed balls and nothing was said – it was never missed. I grew bolder, and the filching (see how I chose a genteel name for it!) grew in extent, and my range of territory spread, away from the high tempting shelf out of the house and on to the end of the street, to a small grocery shop, a one-man business. The old man here, a nice old chap, sold broken biscuits to us lads, ha'porths and penn'orths, and kept these crumbly titbits – cream, plain, coconut, ginger, currant – in an old tea chest at the shop doorway. We boys always jested that the box was a real oasis for dogs, counting by the number of canine rear legs cocked there. Nevertheless, this did not stay me, grown bold on home success, from now helping myself to a few biscuits whenever I saw the old boy preoccupied with a customer in the dim interior. These I would hastily stuff into a pocket, running away and gasping half-delighted, half-scared at my growing nerve. My only excuse for that effort at this late day is to plead that I saw the older boys doing just this, and with such consummate ease and air of nothing-to-it, and it looked such fun.

It began to dawn on me that the stuff they fed us at Sunday school was feeble fare compared with this strong meat; it was ours for the taking, with never any adult knowing and asking awkward questions, or any comeback in the way of corporal punishment to make a boy feel uncomfortable, body and soul. I saw, clearly, the big boys' point of view during this hectic, short-lived period of wrongdoing. But then, it wasn't wrong to carry out small, unimportant filchings, because nobody ever knew, and what they never knew they never missed, so nobody was ever hurt, and that was the beauty of it all. Here was I, a mere kid, chumming up with all these bigger fellows and not now having, as of yore, to stand at a distance and ache to be making one in with them. The answer to all that had formerly eluded me was to nod eagerly and acquiesce to a shout of 'Let's go pinch some peacods from Jonty,' or 'What say we raid the biscuits?' or, better still, gaily show off with, 'I can get a penny for some chips.'

One morning, I took twopence from the shelf. This was to buy a packet of cigs, of all things! For the big boys had initiated me in one short dizzy-sickly lesson that had not cured. Then, in the early afternoon, cigs gone and friends, and all us kiddies sat quiet a minute or two in the house, I became aware Mam was searching on the shelf. I guessed what she was looking for but, brazen-hard as I had become, I asked what she was looking for.

'Tuppence I put up here.' She looked puzzled and answered very slowly. 'It was for some corned beef for our tea.' She resumed her search, muttered, 'I could swear I put them coppers here,' and pointed an emphatic finger, then gave it up as a bad job. 'Well, that's it,' she sighed. 'No tea… I was going to put the corned beef in a tateyhash for us all. I've naught else till morning, till Mrs Dunn comes with her washing money. Ugh!'

Suddenly I felt horrible. My mouth was wobbling and I wished she wouldn't go on about it. Something was welling up inside me and I knew I had to tell, for I just couldn't deceive Mam any longer.

'Stop it!' I shouted whilst she was still harping on. 'Oh, Mam, stop!' – at the same time jumping up and finding myself looking straight into her dear eyes, now looking perplexed and hurt.

Then, for the first time in my short life, I noticed how dreadfully ill she really looked. And she was going to cry – and that was another first time for me. That did it, for if Mam cried, it must be the end of the world – our world, anyway. Mam was so tough, she never cried… Oh, it was all so bleak and desolating, and everything was lost, it seemed, as the tears burst from my eyes and I blurted, 'Oh, Mam, I t-t-t-' – but the words just would not come, for my mouth wobbled uncontrollably in my acute distress, and there I stood sobbing wildly and clinging to Mam whilst she wound her warm, buxom arms around me and she, too, wept bitter as though her heart was breaking, as I don't doubt it was.

And that was the meanest moment of my whole life, if I lived to be a hundred. Oh, what would I have done to undo my wrong! To have Mam back to her old self and me again in my former position of great trust! But, that's a ready tale, faithfully churned out every time we meet retribution, so I won't pursue further my repentant, making-amends way.

Of course the young 'uns wept, and a very noisy weeping this proved to be, with baby Arthur wailing at the same time as he pummelled at my legs with his pudgy fists, instinctively knowing I was the villain of the piece, and a deep-dyed one, at that. Mam was soothing me, and the others at the same time, with, 'That'll do, for all of you… Now, Dick, stop it, love… Hey, Arthur, stop that kicking, he's going to be black and blue… All right, Dick, I know you'll never do it again, and I'm not writing your dad. Now, give me a kiss – ooh, all right, then, all of you… You little slopot!' – this last to Arthur on offering his open, generously wet mouth. Then she was shooing the young 'uns outside and altogether coming back to her old self, and briskly remarking, 'Hmm… Well, it's tateyhash *without* – Ooh, don't start that all over again, love! I'm sorry I mentioned it – anyway, I've a couple of beef cubes I'll drop in… Come on now, smile!' And smile I did, though I was feeling far from smiley.

I suppose I got away light, and the conclusion should be that I was a good boy ever after. I wasn't – many times, in my inconsiderate way, I cheeked Mam; at times I pulled faces over unpopular errands; sometimes I teased the young 'uns and made her cross – but I was never dishonest with Mam again. That dreadful showdown had opened my eyes to things beyond broken biscuits and purloined coins: to awful burdens borne cheerfully and with little complaining, and to the beauty of my mother – not in looks, fading fast, but in soul. When I clung to her in that naked, desolating moment of truth, I realised how deeply these wrongs of mine had hurt, and hurt with a dreadful wound that would never mend, not below the surface. Mam's cross had been heavy enough before, in all conscience, but she had been greatly comforted by the mutual bond of love and trust that held her and us young 'uns in a mystic oneness; and then I'd gone and spoiled everything.

No, I didn't get away as light as I thought. Ever after, in quiet moments when Mam and I sat alone with the others asleep upstairs – her mending or darning, me reading a second-hand *Penny Pictorial* – I would steal a sidelong glance at her when she was unaware I was so doing. I would earnestly, and searching, look for flowers in her cheeks, fail and feel bleak at the knowledge she was still ill and, silently, ask one small favour for my mam. But, as things transpired, nobody ever heard my humble inward plea.

SANTA CLAUS c/o COOKE'S XMAS CLUB

It was one of those popular question-and-answer sessions on the radio; the time, an evening in early December, and our small household disposed to listening in once in a while, as distinct from watching the television. The speakers had dealt with the problems of juvenile delinquency and motorist versus pedestrian, and now the chairman, in lighter mood, was reading a question, a topical teaser: 'Do Christmas Clubs tend to destroy the legend of Santa Claus?' Slowly, he repeated it, paused, threw out a feeler. 'Mr Perkins – any comment?'

Mr Perkins gave an audible sniff of disdain, asked in his turn, 'What, exactly, is a Christmas Club?' and got the expected good laugh from his fellows. He gave his preliminary view, then the others set to dealing scathingly with the clubs and making no end of an ass of poor old Santa. They harped on about the vulgar touch of commercialism that spoiled the whole show – of clubs starting way back in summer, making a proper nuisance of themselves – of bogus Santas standing on every street corner come the first week in December, men in grimy robes and reeking of ale, and offering lucky-dip sacks of rubbish to starry-eyed youngsters, who parted with precious sixpences and their tender illusions at the hands of these obvious fakers, these spurious, bleary-eyed monsters – and so on the speakers went!

As I sat silent, listening, my thoughts went back, right back, to the time when we still lived in that little crowded street off Wakefield Road, a noisy monster of a highway. On this road, away up the hill, was a second-hand furniture shop with a unique distinction, to me, in that it stood exactly one mile from Bradford Town Hall. It also had a black-and-white painted gable end that told all Cooke's sold furniture, good furniture and all. More to my present point, Mr Cooke also sold toys, and every year, when the streets got colder and the evenings darker, he would put a card in his window inviting all to 'Join our Xmas Club… Pay what you like… When you like… Have what you like.'

Across the counter, for the next three months, would flow a steady dribble of precious sixpences and shillings, after the initial ceremony of Mr Cooke letting the prospective club customer have a good look around his toys. He was a model of charm and patience on all occasions and, when the toys had been earmarked (or something special ordered), Mr Cooke would hint at the wisdom of starting the payments there and then; his point being made and a coin having 'fastened' the deal, he would make a faithful record of payment on a small Christmas Club card, and the bespoke toys were solemnly wrapped in crackly brown paper and put away on a high shelf against the coming of Christmas and, of course, the regular payments being kept up.

I remember one particular year – it was 1916, with Dad away at the war, and myself taking over in his place, or so Mam had it – I was taken along with her, straight following tea one dark evening, to Cooke's to start that year's club and help her pick the toys. First, I prinked and preened amongst the toys I *would* have liked, and the ones the young 'uns would go mad about, but Mam was adamant in her meagre budgeting. All our toys had to conform to a strict price ceiling, so my aim dropped, perforce – dropped appreciably lower – and Mam and I finally chose us each a toy that combined appeal with economy, though with as much attention as though precious jewellery were involved.

After that initial visit, on every Friday evening I was sent along to pay the club: sometimes as low as sixpence, now and then up to a couple of shillings, but always something, or I should have despaired had we actually missed altogether any one week. And, always, my eyes feasted on the big parcel on the high shelf which I knew to be ours. Of course, in all this I was sworn to secrecy as regards the rest of our family, and well I kept my delicious secret. I don't know who got greatest pleasure out of anticipating Christmas – me, knowing what we were getting, or the young 'uns, being fed on my hints of wonders to expect from Santa, and all depending on behaviour and the little ordinaries of life, such as washing oneself clean, eating one's crusts, willingly running Mam's errands.

As always, it was an agony of time waiting for the Eve, especially in the last few days that positively crawled after I brought the big parcel home, with Mr Cooke's kindly benediction, and under a cloak of sleep that enveloped my brothers and sister on the chosen night I crept in and helped Mam find a hiding place, away from young prying eyes. On the Eve, Mam got them to bed again rather early, on the premise that Santa would not start about his business until all young children were in bed. Then, having given them time to bed down, Mam and I took the toys from the hiding place, crept upstairs, and laid them snug on the bedroom floor against stockings of all sizes filled with a few mixed nuts, an apple and orange apiece, and a few sweets. Need I add that I also had a stocking in line with the others? For I was not yet immune to this mounting fever of excited expectancy, not yet staled with these annual occasions of sheer enchantment in childhood.

Baby Arthur got a rattle with a long handle to bite repeatedly with his new, needle-sharp teeth; Edie got a sawdust doll with a pot face and a marked inclination to folding up and lying down; Bill got a small wooden fort with a skeleton garrison of lead soldiers, grossly over-officered; I got a wooden battleship and submarine set. Come to think of it, Mam got nothing! It would have been nice if she had, though it's a bit late in the day now for such grand thoughts! However, the naval set was quite novel and topical, at that time, with the sub housing a spring-loaded torpedo in its bow, this being released sharply when one pulled a wire trigger. The battleship – bigger, more complicated – was built up from about ten small sections, and its hull held a tiny, powerful mousetrap affair. On the trap being set, the rest of the battleship was assembled on top.

One can imagine the fun and games when the torpedo shot out, and how fiercely snapped the trap as the torpedo hit home on the battleship's vulnerable sides. Bits of battleship flew high and littered the table, and all accompanied by excited 'hoorahs' and 'oohs' from Bill and me, depending who worked the sub, with more noise coming from Edie holding an agitated Arthur warily, perched up on a chair for a grandstand view. I say 'warily' advisedly, for Arthur, infected with the excitement, had an irritating habit of shooting out a chubby fist and wrecking the battleship just as we finished assembling. And the ship wasn't the only thing that was touchy when Arthur got his fingers on it; I would yelp out in tearful rage, Bill would add his quota of indignation, but Arthur would howl loudest of all in his alarm, and was only to be quietened by Edie's soothing words as we, very noisily, very annoyed, rebuilt again. Little did we know then of the terrible game being played by bigger subs on the vast Atlantic wastes in this merciless winter of '16–'17; and we were mercifully unaware that one of us, long years after, would be taken away by just such a U-boat.

At times – whenever her sorely tried temper gave out as we screamed and shouted in quarrel – Mam threatened to burn the small navy, but the brave little boats weathered all these storms and lasted a while longer than Bill's fort and soldiers, for his warriors couldn't stand up, forever, to all the knocking-about we gave them, and soon had to be mended with matchsticks pushed strategically into broken arms and legs, and even heads, to keep them in active service long after they suffered grievous injury. Also, from time to time, Arthur's new molars bit deep into his rattle and, finally, found the pea and silenced the lot. These same teeth caused Edie's sawdust doll to leak, though it still withstood weeks of dressing-up and putting to bed at Edie's hands before being dropped from a high chair and shattering its head in a dozen pieces, to be followed by a storm of tears from Edie; and even she couldn't love it any more after that terrible accident of losing its head.

From time to time we got bits of other things, such as the stiff cards of galloping cavalry and infantry soldiers, perforated so as to be pushed out of the card and stood up and arrayed in line of battle countless times before wear and tear rendered them unable to stand any longer; and the threepenny stage-acts, with one particularly standing out in memory – that of 'Little Emily crossing the ice', a touching scene from *Uncle Tom's Cabin*. Yet, above them all, our toys at Christmas were always the dearest, for the magic of Santa always held, choose how humble the toy, choose how it was come by. If Santa Claus had set his seal on it, that glossed over the many imperfections and blemishes inherent in children's toys of that time...

***

Gradually, my ears again paid due attention to the radio, and I became aware the speakers were still on about old Santa and Christmas Clubs. They blinded the image of the poor old man with science and concluded that the over-commercialised Christmas Clubs and Santa Claus, or rather his many seedy counterfeiters, did not mix. Straight away, I grumped my disagreement, for I knew different. Here was I, Christmas-clubbed and HP'ed most of my life, yet I still believed in the grand old man with the white beard – he was a wonderful soul! I tried to rally support, but my wife wasn't having any. 'Give up chuntering on,' she chided. 'You're too old-fashioned by far.'

'What think you?' I pleaded, turning my head in mock despair to my son, seventeen and growing up fast.

'We-e-ell, I wouldn't like to say, Dad,' he chuckled. 'Mmm, I suppose you are a bit, oh, you know.' A wink fluttered across to his mother; he must also have supposed I was a bit blind! 'Anyway, I hope the old man remembers I want a new bike saddle this time.'

ETERNALLY INGRAVED

Sunday's long, luxurious lie-a-bed
And the sizzling, smelly bacon afry.
Shrill laughter of kiddies at play,
And baby's sweet, sloppy first kiss.
Hot fish-and-chips eaten in hand,
The hot-day, thirst-slaking long drink…
And corned-beef-and-pickle sandwiches…
These are the things I'll remember
When very near all else is gone.

The blessed, serene peace of cricket,
That heartbursting run for a try.
The smell of hot rain on dry earth,
And bouquet from gardens at eve.
Sibelius, raging with water and wind,
And Elgar's sweet sadness in flood…
The end of a long day, well spent…
Yes, these are the joys I'll cherish,
Aye, 'til life itself is done.

CHAPTER TWO

THE BRICKFIELD

From the brickfield one might hear the Town Hall clock striking – but only on a Sunday morning, when our wild rushings at soccer paused a moment on a lost ball or a strolling policeman, and when all the varying hums of industry were stilled: the mills stopped, the horses and carts locked in stables, the few lorries and steam wagons stood idle in yards, trams and trains cut down to a minimum on the day of the Sabbath. The tall, graceful campanile tower housing the clock was only ten minutes' walk from our street and the brickfield and, to paraphrase a song then popular, 'We'd have seen the clock quite clearly, if it hadn't been for the warehouses and railway depot in between'. Though to say we could hear the Town Hall's pleasant chimes at this particular era of life might not have been strictly correct, coming as it did in the years of the First War when, I believe, some act or other decreed the clock must not strike. Why, I know not – indeed, it would have been good to hear a bit of music in the time of short commons, for Bradford's Town Hall had always played some popular air at ten, two, and six of a day, which was very pleasantly received by all.

However, to return to our strictly unofficial playing field, the brickfield: it was a large, untidy triangle of waste ground. It was also a misnomer, inasmuch as the nearest proper field was half a mile away, where Ripley's Dyeworks gave way to a patch of scruffy clay and shale where a starved-looking brown-green growth passed for grass. The brickfield couldn't even boast of that, having but a few tall scraggy weeds decorating a banking that dropped sheer for some thirty feet from wooden railings that made one side of a long snicket. Another side was halted by still another long snicket that ran alongside St Dunstan's railway junction, whilst the remaining and lowest boundary was given over to a long run of hen huts and pigeon cotes, where we rowdy youngsters were never welcomed, poultry eggs being so tempting. We were especially anathema on a big race day when persuasive pigeon-owners seemed hard-put-to getting the early-returning bird down into the loft, with its registration leg-ring snatched off and thrust into the all-important time clock for the ultimate perusal of awaiting officials somewhere down in Bradford. I have seen tears of enraged frustration start from hard, shrewd eyes at the antics of a bird, back home in wonderful time but perversely playing about in some nearby guttering despite frantic, nay desperate, efforts to get it safely into the cote, the valuable minutes disappearing along with the mirage of prize money. Many a grand bird has finished in the pot for its folly!

Away from this bottom, productive end, the field was a barren plateau with just one other outstanding feature: an almost flattened ruin of a brick building with a raised central platform in which were embedded several iron bars. In the earliest days of one's youth, this platform served for playing 'house'; then that gave way to playing 'forts' and 'signal boxes', so apeing elder brothers stood about two hundred yards away at the railway junction, a busy little place guarding the approaches to the bigger Exchange Station. The solitary ruin also served, when we were older, for games of 'duffings', these being games of dare in the way of difficult physical feats; and it served as a den for the ever popular game of 'relievo', though what this game of chasings and of findings owed to architecture, enough to borrow its name from the profession, I don't know.

More important, as we grew older, was a flat piece of hard clay football field, and we used our coats as goal markers. It also did as a cricket pitch, in its proper season, though mostly we used a rubber ball because the cheap composition cricket ball, all we could afford, did not last long on the ash surface. The large, rectangular stone raised as a wicket also stood for games of 'duckstone' and, again in the proper season, the pitch witnessed many exciting knocks of 'piggy'. This was a fascinating game of tipping and hitting a short, fashioned wood billet with a much longer stick, and vying with each other as to who hit the billet farthest.

But the premier favourite come autumn was a game of soccer. We had a novel approach to getting ourselves a new football, though. First of all, we had to contrive to scrape together a few shillings to buy a gross of scent cards, sold by most printers, and which smelled so exotic and had any printing you wished. Money found, scent cards procured with our name staring out so proud, we would sell these in all the nearby pubs, of which there were not a few, popping in and out of these prohibited places before anybody woke up to throwing us out; we would also go along our near streets, families, friends, near-friends, appealing devilishly to local patriotism and, lo, probably in the first evening we would sell out. The cards sold at a penny each and, a goodly profit of some eight or nine shillings made, we would all – yes, every boy Jack of us – troop down to the sports outfitters in Town Hall Square. Arrived, only a select committee would go into the shop to buy, whilst the others endeavoured to peep through the windows and glass door to witness the delightful ceremony of the ball, now ours, being blown up hard as a bomb, and followed by the near miracle of lacing up so that only a neat criss-cross showed. Then, with a last envious look in the windows at jerseys, shorts and, especially, boots so out of financial reach, we would all troop back to the brickfield, hardly able to contain our impatience to be at it, with coats hastily thrown off for goal marks, and a glorious hour or so spent thumping the very dickens out of our new ball – happy, wonderfully happy until absolute dark called a halt to all the active stuff, though we would then congregate under a street lamp and plan those so eagerly anticipated hardy annuals of soccer matches against other street teams.

But those were the elite games, when we could go abroad to other waste grounds, sometimes in parks, with proudness in every step as we took the field – in our shirtsleeves, no doubt, but with a full-sized football kicked before us and blown up afresh that very morning at the sports shop. Bob Turnbull and Dicky Bond[7] weren't in it with us lads! Leastways, they didn't enjoy their game more. Though, alas, many times before the scent cards could have lost their heavy pungency, the new ball would be burst beyond repair and we would resort to a ninepenny rubber ball which might last a couple of evenings, or one weekend, before suffering mortal hurt from a huge rent, probably caused by some player's clogs. We did try to discourage this playing in clogs, but what could one do if a lad was dying for a game and had no other footwear? We may have been rough, but we were sportsmen – and, besides, it might have been my clogs that would do it!

In those inter-street games, we had a girl play against us a time or two before being called to higher realms. Her name was Maggie Whelan, and the 'higher realm' was the Hey's Ladies football team, then famous throughout England. She was an artist with her feet and could take a bump, and give one – and she could belt a cricket ball! Another who played against us, and probably in the same Manchester Road team, was a young lad called Peter O'Dowd. Peter was a tall, black-haired boy who was just starting playing for his school team, St Joseph's. He was like a general on the field, directing and inspiring, but we little guessed that the neat (in person as in play) Peter would go on and on and finally play for England, in 1932. Afterwards, to humble eyes like ours, he became one of the landed gentry down south; stayed there, died there. Oh, they never came back home… But how I prattle on, with the whole district flattened so that nowadays

7 Rob Turnbull played for Bradford Park Avenue, Dicky Bond Played for Bradford City and England.

one would be obliged to scratch hard to say 'here's where I lived', and the old brickfield covered in, though I'm glad they still play soccer on the much larger, flatter area created.

Oddly enough, with Bradford Northern playing at Birch Lane only about half a mile from us, we of the brickfield never took to rugby league. Probably because Northern were permanently (or so it seemed) on the rocks, or because the rules were too complex; possibly because a rugby ball was much dearer; but more likely because of the fine ash on our pitch. Yet one of our boys, a natural at all ball games (and sprinting!) was encouraged to start playing for Northern, and later played for Great Britain both here and in Australia. His name was Stanley Brogden, and he was one of the finest centres in between the wars in one of the great Huddersfield teams. I wonder, did Stan spare a thought for the brickfield days when he first went out on to the Sydney Oval, Mecca for all rugby league men? And, again, that was in 1932 – surely a vintage year in the old town! Taking the oddity a little further, we didn't ride horses (which were strictly for coal, milk and wool delivery in our narrow circles), yet little Charley Brown, another of us – who also went to work half-time at the same mill as me when we were only twelve – was sent away, at no little sacrifice to his parents, to a racing stable at Middleham (I think one of the Armstrongs ran it), was apprenticed there, and eventually turned out an up-and-coming jockey on the flat in the late twenties. However, increasing weight put paid to that very successful phase of Charley's life.

On the same score, we fought. I can't recall any fighting men in our generation, though a decade before, Jerry Delaney had been one of the youngsters who would frequent the brickfield; he would, undoubtedly, have been boxing's lightweight champion of the world had he not gone to the First World War and never returned. Incidentally, he was one of a remarkable family of boys who all took up professional boxing but never attained Jerry's great promise.

Yes, we scrapped all right, and mostly in gangs, though there were some memorable single combats when a couple of us tangled horns, probably over disputed ownership of marbles ('taws', to us) or cigarette cards. But the grand affairs were when we issued a challenge to some nearby street, not with any excuse but just for the hell of it, to repair to the brickfield for a fight. Oh, don't condemn us too readily! Grown-up nations were just as trigger-happy for wars in those days – especially the power merchants with fear forever eating away at their scruples. However, half-bricks garnered from the grittiest parts of the field served us, along with brush handles stealthily lifted when parents' watch was lax. The strategists amongst us always aimed to hold the heights by the top snicket, though a sudden flanking movement down this narrow thoroughfare would worst the best-laid plans, especially if we had a chicken-heart in our midst and some irate citizen insistent on going about his business, to or from the little station, without let or hindrance. Then the floodgate was open; what might have been a glorious holding movement until bedtime was turned into a nightmare shambles of disgraceful rout with every lad for himself, and none to stop and stem the tide of battle as it lapped to the very doors of the defeated. We would be chased, aye, into our very kitchens, with mams wondering about the unusually early homecomings, as distinct from the usual nightly shoutings-in, raucous and cross, that usually preceded our going home. I can't recollect any lad getting really hurt in these mock battles, for we didn't consider a cut head, or an egg of a lump, bad hurt. Brother Bill, on two occasions, suffered grievous damage, yet recovered before we reached home… Whether it was the salutary effect of what might wait indoors at Dad's disapproving hands, or merely the therapeutic value of our loud bellockings – for we were great ones at roaring loud before we actually got hurt – or a witness to the profound truth of the old Yorkshire saying 'Where there's no sense, there's no feeling', I leave it to others to decide!

Yet we had feelings – some of us – and these of the most primeval, coming from right out of some unknown hereditary urging, as demonstrated in the brickfield, behind the ruined brick platform, when a certain nameless young lady and myself were playing 'house' by our two selves. After some little time of this seemingly harmless play of making small rooms with outlines of half-bricks, and having bits of broken pot for chattels, she brightly suggested we should play 'fathers and mothers'. I, just as brightly, fell in, though I did not then realise what this fathering-mothering business was all about. And that was the first time Eve tempted me with the apple, and this Eve was such a little girl, and I a big boy for my years, that I could smile the way she had me running off, utterly scared and bewildered. Oh, I had heard of things that went on between boys and girls; things at which I could only vaguely guess, and be horrified, at that; mysterious, whispered-of naughty rufflings that occasioned giggles and jabs in ribs when the older boys were holding forth of individual prowess. Indeed, I had made up foursomes going to Saturday afternoon pictures – paying each for ourself, of course – but I was so gallant, or numb, I never even pressed for kisses from my dames.

I suppose I was subject to overweening shyness, for I knew, then, girls liked boys to kiss them. However, until that quiet day amongst the old bricks, I never had realised the portent, the staggering import, of our differing physical makeup. I stared, like a bewitched rabbit before a snake, at the unusual sight (her being somewhat removed from my own sister) of the young lady stepping out of her navy-blue elasticated unmentionables, her eyes looking to me loaded with mischief. I was held fast when she took one of my hands, and shrank but a little as she placed it on her bared area, which was *not* her bottom. But when she started pawing me, that broke the spell. I turned swiftly and very ungallantly fled, leaving the little temptress still in her compromising state of undress and uttering loud cries of rage and vexation, threatening dire things if I told, which I never did – not until now, when I can feel fairly safe from the now surely blunted claws of this, this woman scorned.

'EE! A BIT O' NOISE IS GRAND'

It was a lady, unblessed with a large, very rowdy family, who, in my younger days, epitomised our whole outlook to noise. She was being taken to task for coming home, against medical advice, after but two days of a planned three-week stay at a seaside home, a convalescence entirely without cost, which had been designed to take her away from all the stress and noise of family and street. She pleaded, not one whit disturbed, 'Well, it wor that quiet wi' just that sea to listen to, it wor mekking me poorly... Ee, lass,' she went on before the vexed health visitor could get a word in, 'a bit o' noise is fair grand!'

And that went for most of us, I'm afraid – though I hasten to add I'm a lover of peace and quiet now, and find it most reassuring to know that lots of thinking people delve so deeply and worry into the varying problems caused by 'noises'. But they tickle me with their air of having suddenly discovered something hitherto unknown about this 'menace to some, life's blood to others' business. They have even got to measuring din in decibels, etc., and have standards of tolerance to gauge just how much of any infernal racket a human can stand. Let it be said, they have gone a long way to containing the growing nuisances attendant on new marvels of this century, which makes a refreshing change from the money-grabbing without thought that blotted the Victorians, and the could-not-care-less Edwardians, out for a good time, choose where it came from.

If there was any movement to curb, or even any awareness of, the menace of noise in the early twentieth century, it was well suppressed (excuse the unintentional pun), for nobody seemed to go out of their way to express any opinion contrary to the popular one of accepting our din as inevitable to living. Admittedly, we had not road drills or radio-transistors (that follow us to the very toilet!), sound-barrier crashings, trigger-happy cowboys on telly, motor traffic in volume, ice-cream chimes or, fitting finale – a bomb to end all bombs! But we had bones of contention, had we thought, in the clumsy grinding tramcars, the raucous honkings at every ostentatious turn of the early motor cars, high-sided empty coal carts rattling noisily across cobbles, the deafening roar inside factories and mills so that one shouted to be heard, and so on, out to the less-sustained assault on hardened ears that rose daily on our own street, a little removed from the main road.

How many decibels would Tommy Salt's donkey have rated with his long drawn-out heehawing of alarm and protest every hot Sabbath dawn? Tommy himself slept heavy and long, believing implicitly in 'six days shalt thou labour, but—'. On that seventh, he rested greatly from his hawking his namesake and scouring-stone. No doubt his poor moke shared these same sentiments, but it stood in grave peril from stifling in the near-roasting atmosphere of the small, bacon-box-made stable that had been built against Tommy Salt's toilet. There was only one thing would stay the donkey from braying, and that was the bedraggled appearance of Tommy – rough at any time, but looking particularly fearsome with his very red face, eyes odd in a terrifying squint, and matted ginger thatch flying behind him – as he noisily loosed the long-suffering ass, upbraiding it for being so obviously impatient whilst he tossed it a small feed, then shuffled back to his cellar kitchen to prepare himself a little breakfast which, being but a modest jam-and-bread affair, didn't take long.

Hours later, the Boys' Brigade would come marching along the streets to the blare of bugles and vibrant tap-tap of six kettledrums, and some thirty pillboxed heads held high and proud, all bravely trying to sow good seed on very stony ground: stony inasmuch as myself, and Bill as a cadet, were the only ones to join the noble force from our street – and that venture didn't last long, coming to grief, in the end, on the vexed question of best clothes still lying in the pawnshop on a Sunday and us having to be absent, for we couldn't turn out in our old duds.

On weekday mornings everybody, except the very young and the rather deaf, was awakened by the knocker-up, generally an elderly person who employed at least two ways of arousing sluggish customers that they might go forth, in good time, to work. Some, who slept upstairs, were awakened gently by faint scratchings from a thin wire fastened to the end of a long stick that tapped at bedroom windows. Others, who slept downstairs in shut-up beds, were roused by a hard fist thumping on the street door and a hoarse informing of 'Half-five – come on, get up!' The knocker-up I call to mind most readily was a stout middle-aged lady who, rumour had it, never went to bed proper, sitting all night in an old-fashioned rocking chair, rocking the hours away until the crack of dawn saw her issue forth, stick in hand, for *her* daily labours. For her troubles she was paid threepence a week – with 'missings', of course, from the ones who would have 'missed' if they had been the unlikely possessors of a million pounds, for to these creatures credit in any shape or form was fair game to exploit.

Depending what time of year it was, we might hear an old chap crying, 'Any nettles? Fresh nettles,' in a quavering voice that suggested he would have been better off still in his bed. He was one of the early birds on the street – together with the Co-op milk van and the cheerfully shouted news of 'Milk-kyoh-kyoh!', though the man didn't have many customers amongst us, addicted as we were to the thick, sweetened stuff in tins and commonly known as Swiss milk, and very handy for spreading on bread, as also was lard, and even sugar at a pinch, when the cupboard was distressing bare, and a penn'orth of black treacle a treat to spread on the bread of youngsters.

Coal was hawked and weighed in the streets then, with the almost daily shout of 'Coal!' and its ally 'Ovenwood!' and a chap wheeling an inverted bike around and asking for 'Scissors to grind!' And, never far away, the inevitable 'Rags! Bones! Bottles and jars!' merchants, trading balloons and other trifles for aught they could pick up. There was also the twanging, erupting tingelary, as we called the barrel-organ, and which I liked immensely with its snatches of the classics, though I did not know them as such when I first listened in my youth – I was even allowed to turn the handle for one short tune! There were tin-whistlers and one-string-fiddlers, but they hadn't the richness of the organ, and their little mite of music was lost upon the shrilling, buzzing air about them.

Late in the afternoon, after school, we young 'uns would take over. Always, we yelled and screamed at play, and the rowdiest game was one called 'piesball', rounders, and there was arguing and shouting all the time as to whether one had been given a fair swipe, or whether one had beat the hurtling ball to the 'hob', and a pandemonium when all the hobs were occupied and nobody left to bat on. Though a very close second was 'tin-can-squat', with a battered tin can kicked merrily along the cobbles every few minutes and everybody, bar the luckless one retrieving the can, shrieking and scampering away to a hiding place.

Teatime would bring a truce in the games, and we might expect a man with a milk can shouting 'old milk!' – for with refrigeration not being what it is now, it behoved any milkman to get rid of his morning's milk quick, and cheap. He would sometimes vie with a chap with a tray on his head yelling out 'Muffins and crumpets!', though he never did any good with us. They were too expensive, and we would rather wait for somebody more in our world of eats: in the early winter evenings, and at a time when green peas were a memory, a little old man would hove in sight with two large cans that looked too heavy for him, and we would rush to walk the street with him to sniff the appetising odour that thinly steamed from the lids. He would stop every few yards, fill his lungs, yell, 'Grey peys, all hot! Penny a pot!' and veritable clouds of deliciously fragrant steam would welcome the first customer as he stirred, right to the bottom (for he always kidded he had a ham shank there), then brought a piled scoop of peas to bear on the pot (biggest in the house, you could bet!) and passed over a bottle of vinegar from a pocket of his white apron. Yet, to be strictly truthful, they smelled much nicer than they actually tasted, for grey peas were no real substitute for genuine green ones and, after all, grey peas were really food for pigeons.

An election could be reckoned to produce a deal of noise, with gangs of young 'uns outdoing each other in the rendering of that old election favourite 'Vote, vote, vote for—' whoever was your man. Soon after the war ended, there was a parliamentary election pending and there was a great to-do; we never had so much attention before from sorties of well-dressed folks coming on the street to try to sway votes, but getting nothing but shouts and jeers for their troubles, and a firework thrown in among. The fever spread to school, and gangs would spend all playtime baying and in full cry, and finishing up pinning some poor little lad against the wall and having him cry their favourite. Cry he might, with great fervour, but he would finish on his backside over the knelt form of one of the gang behind him. It was heartless, sometimes cruel, for it was always the weakest to the wall, but it had to be borne without too much blubbing or worse might befall, so it behoved one to shed shyness, join a gang, and shout as lustily as any. A funny thing is, I can remember just one name in that election – a Captain Loseby[8] – and that possibly because he was a military man and we were always crying his name. Whether he won the seat or not, I have not the slightest idea.

But elections were not every day, or night; in the gloaming of most late evenings, when football was out because it came in dark soon, we lads would get together and sit on somebody's wall. We would have a rare old singsong, though we might be moved by the swift, unexpected throwing of a bucket of water from an unappreciative adult. This, mind, did not damp us down unduly, but we could never understand why grown-ups didn't care for cheering up. It just

8 Charles Loseby, the Coalition National Democratic candidate, was elected as the MP for Bradford East in 1918 and served until 1922.

never struck us we were being obnoxious, that we were creating a problem. Heck! It was being natural, this making a noise, part and parcel of our existence – honest, we wouldn't have known what to do with quiet!

Besides, after *we* had finished, there was always the noisy turnout from the pubs, with two on opposite corners, and two lots of noisy, harsh-laughing imbibers standing on the pavements for some extra half-hour before finally drifting indoors. This tardiness to go home was a fetish with the pub crowds; most times it was good-humoured but, now and again, a few hasty words would start a fight or a muck-slinging row which wouldn't cease until long after all the street was roused and looking on, from doorways and opened bedroom windows, and in all manner of undress. The end generally awaited the coming of a couple of bobbies, who would usually get things straightened out and all persuaded indoors before leaving us to our little world, now gone strangely quiet until the next morning heralded the start of the whole hotchpotch of clangour over again.

To all the foregoing could be added just one more item, and very pleasant on the ears it was, for it turned out to be something that only came once in a lifetime – in mine, anyway! This was a 'one-man-band' with a big brown bear thrown in for good weight, and a dirty old lady with a coloured shawl and a tambourine. It was even better than the rogue 'Spoons', a gentleman who came round a few times at one period: tall, bleary-eyed with drink, beating a merry rippling rat-tat with two dinner spoons. They rattled off his cheeks, elbows, knees, down his arms and legs, the while he blew lustily into a sixpenny mouth organ a bit of a jig called 'Devil Amongst The Tailors', and then cheekily trotted to every door and demanded coppers with his ragged cap pushed right forward, and not many females said him nay.

But, to return, to the odd-assorted trio: they had trailed miles that day amongst the cobbled ways of back-to-back houses, and a fair crowd of youngsters, myself amongst them, had followed, chattering, shrieking, laughing and racing around the group, for this was a treat sent on a hot afternoon in the long midsummer holidays. At long last they made our street (for I was bursting with impatience that Mam should – *must* – see them), and a concertina wheezed manfully to make itself heard above shrilling kiddies, and a big drum dully 'boom-boomed' between spasmodic clashes from a pair of cymbals. Finally, in the middle of the street, the shuffling subsided, there was a flurry of sharp booms on the drum and a yelp from the one-man band himself, and the three relaxed and turned inwards, whilst the tight mob fought noisily for good places on the inside of the small circle that quickly surrounded the performers.

Meanwhile, the bear squatted on his haunches and gazed at us with doleful air. I didn't think he looked at all frightening just as he sat; indeed, he looked as quiet as an old sheep – then. He wore a huge muzzle and a broad leather collar around his thick neck, a collar with a very long steel chain running to the hand of the grubby woman, distinctly filthy despite the impress of the flashy shawl and tambourine which, besides serving to be thumped vigorously and shook so that little bells tinkled merrily, also did for receiving the coins. She wore long dark clothes that swept the floor, and sported an incredibly dirty pinafore fronted by a generous pocket into which she popped hunks of stale bread, all begged, garnered against the bear's next feeding time.

Besides the busy job of getting round the houses cadging all she could – coins, food, clothes – with the bear trailing safely behind at the end of his long chain, she also put the poor animal through his paces, in some outlandish tongue that added to all the excitement. However, the bear's paces were very limited, consisting of a ponderous edging around the circle which did not always accord with the rhythm and melody suggested by the exertions of the music-making (crude but pleasing to us), and the beast's shortcomings brought many sharp wails of disapproval from the lady, and a more deliberate thumping of tambourine to get the sorely puzzled bear back into musical line with the busy one-man-bandsman, sweating profusely and swearing richly in unmistakeable rough oaths we all knew.

The music man was blessed with a wealth of jet-black hair, escaping in curls from under a sage-green bowler hat. He was swarthy, short, and very fat, and his ample form was girt with all manner of music-making tackle. The melody was supplied by a concertina clasped before him in podgy hands, and he had, for emphasis, a shallow drum strapped firmly on his back. Complementary to the drum, he had two drumsticks fastened to his elbows, so augmenting the gasping air from the squeezebox came the irregular boom-boom from the drum and sudden, very disconcerting, clashes from a pair of cymbals. Oh, yes! The cymbals were fixed on the bottom of the drum and, by virtue of spring and wire attached to one heel of the man's boots, he contrived to bring the brass in with shattering effect. So shattering that, every time the bear was surprised by it, he reared to his full height – some seven feet – and emitted a deep, frightening growl, which had the old woman darting to him in alarm. And it was all so mighty effective, dimmed not one whit by repetition. He must have reared a score of times, yet we kiddies aways cried out in alarm and turned, scrabbling to get away from the reach of his great paws – but, when he subsided at the old lady's insisting, there would be shamefaced guffawing and giggles of embarrassed relief, and a lot of noisy jockeying to regain our former favourable places, lost in the cowardly scamper. And, all the time, the womenfolk of the street kept to their doorways, even Mam being very careful. Mam insisted on the bear keeping a respectful distance away when the old lady approached, and quickly got rid of them with a crust of stale bread and a penny.

However, treats never last long enough. They had to visit many streets like ours to get the precious few coppers necessary to keep body and soul together and, though I trailed with them through many of these, I had to turn home, tired, happy, but still filled with their magic. I know they were scruffy, and they were perhaps cruel to the bear, but they had a magic, a magic that has persisted with me, and I dare say I would follow again, in the unlikely event of their like ever being allowed on the streets again. Well, like so many good things then, they came and they went. Where they came from nobody ever knew, or cared[9] – and where they went called for even less comment or concern; suffice they'd had their hour of jingle and jangle in our midst, and we had given them what we could as a reward for the change in our usual chord of… well, shouting and bellocking about sums it up.

9 Possibly Savoyard travelling entertainers from the Savoy region of France/Italy who travelled throughout Europe.

'THE BLOODY WAR'S OVVER!'

For some reason, now forgotten, we were off school, or I should have missed much of the high drama that November morning.

And it all came my way because of some excited words shouted by a chain-horse lad, a nodding acquaintance, employed by the old Lanky and Yorky Railway – a dwarf of a lad leading a huge Shire horse, its bright chains taut as it took the strain in front of a brother harnessed in the shafts of a long, flat dray loaded high with sheeted wool. As the lad saw my brother and me, he had shouted, 'Hey! Have you heard?'

'Heard what?' we both shouted back across the busy road.

'The bloody war's ovver! Th're giving it out i' front o' t'Tahn Hall at eleven.'

That, and nothing more, and he carried on impatiently willing his charge up the short hill, that he might be the first to speed the glad tidings about the vast, sprawling railway warehouses. We had heard rumours of no more war buzzing about the schoolyard for days past, but all was confused with nothing sure and, after so many years of this business of men going away, and coming back after a long time for a couple of weeks (the lucky ones, I mean), this strange thing called 'peace' seemed such a will-o'-the-wisp, like God in Heaven, and all that. The end of the war was something we talked of as a livener-up at times, when we tired of play, but it never came near. So, for a moment, Bill and I stood incredulous, staring after the back of the tall load, finding it hard to take in what the lad had said. Yet it was straightforward enough, no hedging 'ifs' about that 'war being ovver', and we could always go see. And because we were so young, and wanted to believe, a great joy slowly filled us as we turned to each other and chuckled in glee, and yelped 'Crikey!' repeatedly. I was eleven then, and Bill eight, and to us this meant the one important fact – Dad would be coming home. Crikey! Coming home for good after all that time. Ee, what would Mam say? Though, first, we must go down town and find out what was really happening.

As we ran down to the Town Hall, we shouted, though much out of breath, to each other. About the rationing… No more queueing… No more standing in long lines for margarine, and brown sugar, and meat; and with no guarantee of getting any, for the news spread quickly whenever a shop had any foodstuffs in, and 'first there, first served' was the order of that day. When the grocer's or butcher's shelf was bare, then it was all gone there for another week, and there was nothing more to wait for, and the devil took the hindmost in the patient, stoic queue. Oh! what a wonderful morning that seemed as we anticipated the blessings of peace and raced on, that we may have the fact vouchsafed to us.

It must have been past eleven when we got there, and the square was already filled for, besides we humans, there were some big guns around: grim, large-snouted affairs complete with camouflage nets, ammo boxes, artillery men. Let me hasten to assure that Bradford was not an armed camp, nor under martial law; it was 'Big Guns Week' in the city, one of the periodic campaigns whose objective was the bumping-up of sales for War Bonds and War Savings Certificates. A man was already speaking on a platform outside, round by the large front steps – but what he said, few heard, drowned as his voice was (in those days before microphones) by the great shouting and cheering that was being kept up all the time.

And it was all true – the fighting had stopped – and there were those of us who stood and cheered, those who danced and cheered, and some who just stood still, silent, finding it hard to believe the long nightmare of fighting was over, and simply not daring to give way to their emotions; not yet, not until they'd let it sink in, in some quiet corner. They were the ones who went home without fuss, as did Bill and I when folks started acting the goat, being joined and encouraged by others who smelled, and acted, as though the pubs had opened early.

We burst in on Mam with the good news, though by now it was all round the streets, and almost every doorstep held its clutch of gossipers. Mam was not one of these; she was sitting quiet inside the house and, though she knew, she started crying when we told our tale. Of course, weeping being what it is, we all joined in then, the whole bawling of us – Mam, me, Bill, Edie, even young Arthur (the only war baby amongst us) – and what a picture we must have looked! Then Mam stayed her tears, wiped her nose, and Bill and I followed suit on our thick jersey sleeves, thereby earning an indignant rebuke, and we were all off laughing – rich, uninhibited stuff, chiefly because Dad was coming home, and *that* any time now. So unversed were we Tempests in the ponderous ways of nations running down from war to peace that we expected ex-soldier Dad to come walking in the low doorway any, and every, hour – and, of course, we expected too much. We were unlucky, for some weeks to come.

There were lots of other folks unlucky: the fighting men who were told they were coming back to a promised land, a land fit for heroes to live in; and the dedicated ones who really believed it was a war to end all wars, a fiction freely bruited about then. They believed that out of all the evil and slaughter must surely come good – or else, why? And last, but most vocal, the bitter, vengeful souls, mostly drunk on this day of victory, who shouted that Kaiser Bill should be hanged from a lamp-post.

Instead, sick to death of the bloodbath and defeated, his lordship was quietly swept into Holland without a lot of fuss – if a royal progression of some half-dozen automobiles, sleeking to a destination up a well-kept drive into Doorn Castle, can be called 'without fuss'.

And who's to say the ex-war lord didn't come off best in his new role of retired gentleman? However, that November morn of the double-eleven (a treble with the hour!), everybody breathed happier now the war was over, except they who mourned for their lost – even though the cautious ones whispered it was but an armistice, and were promptly howled down with 'Armistice be blowed! They'll never get men to go fighting again. Get to hell with yer armistice!'

At supper time, as a special treat, Mam – all rosy and shining, as much with happiness as with the heat from an oven, freshly stoked – roasted some extra-large potatoes. They were hauled out piping hot and, as Mam juggled with them, employing her sacking apron for this hot business, she 'oohed' and 'aahed', and we laughed fit to burst. But we did the spuds justice as we ate and talked, gobbling hot potato and gabbling excitedly, and near to falling out at times, with Mam tempering our wildness as we yelped about the future in which everything was going to happen at once or, at least, tomorrow, Oh, we didn't know we were born, the way things were going to alter, and here we were celebrating. When we'd finished, there were but empty skins left, and that was our victory feasting. Yet no one in the land, that night, gave more witness of thankfulness than we did with our humble potatoes and our simple joy following the end of this evil which had dragged on for over four years, a veritable lifetime to the lad I then was.

THE THREE Rs

Reading; Riting; Rithmetic: they were the golden rule at school,[10] though they fell heavy as lead on ears not finely attuned to, nor eager for, such accomplishments. (The word 'attuned' might fit better in relation to the vexed subject of music, not to dwell on painting and drawing, which were all my detested bogeys when I was being given an elementary education to fit me for facing the adult world.) On the subject of music, according to our teacher of that time, Old Wilky: 'Never was breast more savage, nor less likely to be stirred by sweet sound, than the Bowling one'. At this illuminating shaft, we East Bowling boys were obliged to grin, though feebly, for we were never quite sure of the true line of Mr Wilkinson's sarcastic bent. Trouble was, he was too learned for us, this man from Otley, an ex-rugby stand-off; he was too clever for us by a long chalk, which article he could flick a considerable distance in speeding a sudden question to an inattentive boy.

Nevertheless, he was a good teacher, inasmuch as he got results where a less tough, less persistent man might have been excused for crying us off as a bad job. But he was well aware of his thankless task, for almost every day he asked himself loudly, with eyes bulging and face beetroot-red and frightening in very demonstrative supplication, why he should have such a select mob of blockheads visited on him. And, looking around, we were a mob: some thirty of us, with such colourful names as Dinky Barber, Fatty Smith, Res Holdsworth, Chuck Jones, and Titchy Marsden.

Our teacher was a thick-set, middle-aged man, with a marked tendency to impatience. He had an extra-strong right arm, and a short

10 Usher Street Boys' School in East Bowling.

unbending cane in a hip pocket, and he was as fast on the draw as the much-vaunted Tom Mix, king of the movie cowboys, and very generous he was with his cane. Yet he was a decent sort, as when he let us out into the playground to watch a big airship that came over the school one day. It was either the R33 or the R34, brand new and looking like a silver-grey cigar, looming very large and moving slowly across the sky. I got the impression it was almost standing still as we gazed up, fascinated, as Wilky told us how proud we should be to have witnessed such a thing, to have seen the glory of England's daring venture (zeppelins then being a naughty word!) into space with this forerunner of probable 'argosies floating in the twilit skies'. Of course, he had to ask who had written these words, and nobody knew – just as none of us guessed that this dream-ship would finish up in the Humber.[11]

Wilky got a composition lesson out of the airship incident, but that was something I could make a go of, without the inward groan that came when the pencils or paintbrushes were handed round, or the shudder when he lifted his desk lid and brought out a tuning fork, that instrument of torture travelling in the guise of a guide to true pitch. Ugh! I was all too well aware of my painful limitations in drawing and painting, though I could just get through without too many cuffs – but this shocking musical guessing business of 'ear tests' found me an absolute stumer. Things were all right for the first few minutes as we went 'dashing along with a smoothing iron' or shipped 'o-o-on board of the *Arethusa*' with gay, reckless abandon, but those carefree moments were all too short and fleeting easy, a kind of sugar coating to the bitter follow-on pill. This pill was poised before our mouths when Wilky tapped his fork and lah-lahed a few notes out of his head, then pounced on some hapless wight to interpret the phrase, and he knew where to strike for the most devastating, funny effect. Nobody chortled more at the vacuous gropings of another wretch into the deep mists of this mental musicking than myself, for

11 The R38-class airship exploded in mid-flight and crashed into the River Humber on 24th August 1921, killing 44 of its 49-strong crew.

Mr Wilkinson's humour, feeding liberally upon such cloddish fare, was very heavy and belly-laughish and, like his stick, to be heeded with a sense of appreciation. In defence of my baseness for laughing at another's downfall, I must add that I was justified by the sure knowledge everybody would enjoy a real treat when I was called upon to grasp wildly, desperately, at taunting Dohs and Mes and Sohs, all flashing around and suggesting themselves in my hot, confused brain. Nor fared I better when teacher passed from the spoken to the no less difficult semaphoring of notes with his hand and fist; for all of it, this highly technical stuff, was certainly not up my street.

However, I took rueful comfort (which didn't ease the sting of the short cane) in plenty of like company; oddly enough, all the poor painters and drawers were also the poor musicians – with Fatty, and Chuck, and most of the aforementioned sharing a common bond of dread whenever the finer arts came on the agenda.

Then, one bright day, imagine our dismay – and we were not being disloyal or disaffected – on hearing the stunning news that our class was to represent the school in a mighty choir of Bradford schoolchildren gathered to greet a royal visit to our fair city.[12] We knew, and we said as much, that we did not deserve this signal honour, and that the school head must have been barmy in picking us, though we kept that sort of talk strictly for the playground.

At the first rehearsal, Old Wilky turned it into a sorting-out practice, and he actually came amongst us whilst we still chirruped away, and put his ear to each individual's mouth. Well, that was not guaranteed to bring out the best in any boy constantly expecting a cuff about the ears, and quavering away at his worst as a consequence of this unwelcome attention. Surprisingly enough, there were no cuffs, but there was a stringent weeding – one might say, a downright pruning to the roots – and when it was all over, I was amongst a goodly company who would fare badly if called upon to sing for supper. I can't say any of us weeded-out ones were really upset, for we realised

12 King George V and Queen Mary visited Bradford in May 1918.

our dead drag on the musical quality of those who could make a pleasant sound – and besides, we chuckled, if the songbirds were to rehearse separately that, surely, meant an easing of the iron hand on us, inasmuch as we would be, more or less, left to our own devices. Or so we fondly imagined, in our youthful optimism.

However, Wilky, past master at not falling in with things desirable, thought up a devilish idea: he set up a formidable number of sums and, as none of us was an infant prodigy at that subject either, made sure we worked good and hard. Yet an imp of perverseness made us forget the urgency of work when we got together, on our own, and with Fatty's promptings – which started when he made a daring sortie to the sacred blackboard and wrote something very obscene about Mr Wilkinson that had us all laughing, so that we stuffed our mouths to muzzle our intense mirth – we soon got to pelting and strangely quiet wrestlings. And never did one hour speed so.

The Wilky brow was black and evil when he scanned the work – so few sums for so many boys – and he, following an old army practice, pulled the first three non-singers from their desks, regardless of degree of guilt, and laid about them until the short cane fair whistled through the air. Then he savagely promised much more if there was not a distinct improvement next time we were left alone. And so well did he keep his promises, there was a definite improvement, though Fatty Smith tried his damnedest to upset the apple cart – and Wilky paid us two surprise visits, just to show there was no ill feeling.

On the great day, all the school went to Lister Park in the busy tramcars but, whilst the singers were put in a special compound of honour, the rest of the school was pushed in gaps here and there along the route of the park paths. It was going to be a poor show for us, we dismally told ourselves, shoved where we were, seemingly out of the way of anything very exciting, and where we could see nothing but a couple of teachers pestering and harrying whilst we waited, very restless, for aught to start; for, as these things go, we seemed to be there hours before time.

Then, without any warning, a long procession of cars started aiming along our path, and before anything had begun to register, a marvellous car, flying the Royal Standard, was coming towards us. It came past, not six feet away, very quietly (or were we cheering so loud?) and very slowly, and we had a fine view of a grave, neat-bearded man, nodding but seldom, sat next to a fine lady who smiled faintly all the time as she graciously inclined her head.

'She's nodding to us!' cried Chuck Jones, and Fatty Smith and Res were gasping the same message ('She, she nodded – to us! Did you see?') as though I could have missed, certain as I was then that she was looking straight at *me*. How our hearts swelled, and that was our finest hour. The tribulations, slights, insults of the past few weeks were all forgotten, forgiven as we cheered and waved, same as though we were at a football match.

Then they were gone, and it was all over, and we slowly jostled our way out of the park, and we couldn't tell all the others fast enough of our great good luck.

Yes, the singers were definitely out of countenance, for they had not been within a couple of hundred yards of the royal couple, and they had seen hardly anything. And how they wailed… then changed it to scornful laughter, as though we were talking bunkum. All the same, they were eaten with envy, the way they kept harping on, with their silly sneers and catcalls, all the time we trooped across town and then on our tramcars up Wakefield Road. They never let it drop, and blood had been let on far less provocation, but we favoured boys were determined that *our* royal occasion would not be marred by vulgar brawling – no, that could wait until some playtime, perhaps on the morrow. Meantime, we had scored a bullseye, all right!

When I got home and told Mam of what we had seen, almost breathless in my hurry to tell all in one rushed sentence, she chuckled and said, 'My! You are suited, aren't you? I suppose you're that proud you won't want any tea?'

But no, I wasn't *that* proud.

CHAPTER THREE

THE BIRTHDAY GIFT

I always looked forward to my own birthdays, not because of an expectation of any gift, or even a card, for these were not fashionable locally; I always eagerly anticipated the day that meant the passing of another year because I was keen to get finished with school – or rather, to get working, for I did not really dislike school, but I did so want to get into the near-adolescent world which bore such a reckless, carefree look about it, the nearer I approached in years.

This impatiently awaited transition from wholly schoolboy to worker, even if it be only half-and-half for a start, appeared all the more desirable and tantalising whenever I listened to the older boys talking of the grown-upness of being workers, at one with youths and the girls, and free from the thraldom of schools and teachers, and all they implied. I looked after these lads with acute longing whenever they set off on a Saturday evening to squander their seemingly so easily come-by spending money, and with a vexation towards myself for being too young to join them. It irritated me to remind myself that I had spent my pittance on the pictures and a bar of toffee in the afternoon.

Sunday morning was worse, for this was the time they foregathered, prior to the usual football kick-about, and related the details of

Saturday night's adventure, embellishing all with extravagant braggadocio and gusts of laughter. First, the pictures; then an eating orgy in the pea, pie and tripe shop; and, greatly daring, an hour up at Coppy Quarry Fair to round off the night. This last essay was always regarded as a pretty cool affair, for it was a rowdy permanent funfair in a very rough district – a much tougher quarter than ours, and not to be commended to the timid or cautious, but the drawing-card, I gathered, was that there were some bold wenches on hand. These were girls of thirteen or fourteen, bobbin-liggers and doffers in the local mills, with artificially blood-red lips and saucy eyes, and a ready laugh for the coarse jokes thrown freely about. It was probably the constant reiteration of these young ladies' attractions that made time drag so very heavy.

So I approached my day of destiny, my twelfth birthday, happy in the knowledge that, inasmuch as a birthday present is something intended to bring joy, gift enough for me was the fact that, legally, I would be able to start work on that very day. No thrill from promise of bat or ball, or renewal of the boxing gloves Dad had bought us the winter before in a grand spending of his demob gratuity – none of these would compare to this eager anticipation, fermenting and hotting up as the great day got slowly nearer, and I emerged from the cocoon of scholar. Talk about a lamb going joyfully to the slaughter – I was all for it! Yet I was no phenomenon, for going 'half-time' was the ultimate amongst all our lads – we saw no further than the textile-spinning mills down Nelson Street. I can still see my dad's face, at a later date, when my brother Bill brought home a paper bearing the exciting news he had passed for a scholarship. First, Dad had a good laugh; then, contemptuously, he threw the offending sheet on the fire, asking of nobody in particular, 'How the hell do they expect us to keep him?' and 'Who the hell buys his clothes, and the other stuff, eh?' Mam, ill then, wept bitterly; yet of one thing I was glad: Bill didn't seem very upset.

However, on my day, the day of all days, as I ate my meagre breakfast, my eagerness became momentarily soured with two nagging doubts. Supposing I had not enough school attendances spread over the years? If I hadn't, they wouldn't let me go to work – it was as simple as that – and I had not been the best attender in class, not by a long way. Also, would I be able to get a job, and start, this very day? That was the most important thing. It would be no good telling me to start next week, nor even tomorrow, for that would have robbed my birthday of its very own sweet yield of happy fulfilment. It had to be today – oh, it had to be!

Mam assured me we would not fail for want of trying, for she was to go with me on this quest for the magic elixir, work. But many times, over the table, she looked worried, when she thought I was not looking; yet I was not to be gainsaid, even if I did always regard her as so very wise. True, when she looked so sad, I felt a slight twinge of conscience, for at one time she had ideas about my winning a scholarship and moving to another school, but I had let her down in the exams, some time before.

As luck would have it, the first mill we tried, I got on. We went, without any ceremony, in the mill door and were quickly brought to the attention of a gentleman known as 'the walking-boss'. He was a slight man, wearing a cap although we were indoors; he was middle-aged with an untidy moustache heavily stained with tobacco juice, and his jaws working constantly like a cow chewing the cud (he even chewed in his sleep, I was told later). As he quietly sized me up, he agreed he could do with a lad, aye – a tall lad who would do for a tube-piling job – and I eagerly nodded my head in agreement, even though I had not the slightest idea what the job was. He asked Mam, 'When's ta want him to start, Mother? Nah?' but Mam had to explain, hastily, we had not yet been to the folks at the Education Office, my being but a few hours turned twelve.

'Hmm. Haven't lost much time, eh?' the walking-boss remarked. He grinned at me and I smiled back in friendliest fashion, and Mam asked could I start when all was cleared at the Town Hall.

'Aye, lass,' Fred consented (he was 'Fred' to everybody – no 'sir' or 'mister' amongst the mill fraternity). 'He mun try to get in fur after dinner. Quarter-to-one we start, an' he mun ask fur Bert Gaunt in t'first room.'

With those fateful words clinching the matter, Mam and I were away hotfoot for town, for the precious slip of paper that would be my passport to the world of work. We were both rather overawed entering the imposing portals of our Town Hall, but were quickly shown to a little room that had to do with our special business. Here, Mam had to produce my birth certificate, and then a well-dressed man gravely looked into a large book. He seemed ages pencilling figures, and I was in an agony of doubt, for his brow seemed to get darker as he went on, and he never gave me the slightest encouragement to expect any cheering result. However, he didn't say 'nay', and at long last his pencil stopped; he closed the big book and gave an unintelligible grunt that must have meant I had the necessary attendance – but, mind, only just!

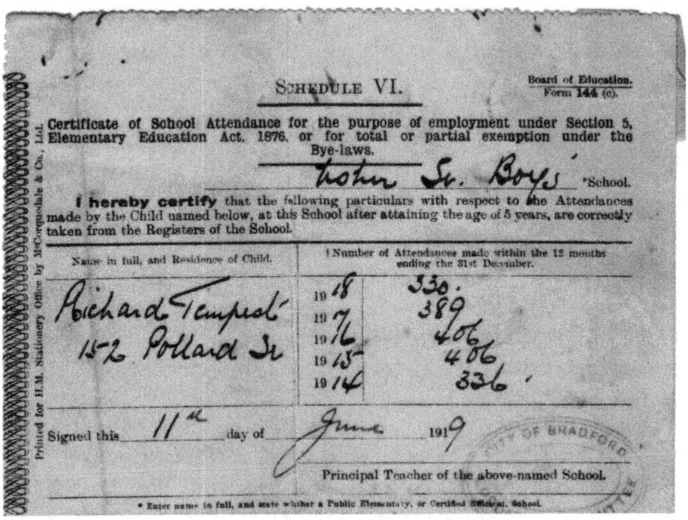
Board of Education. Form 144 (c).

SCHEDULE VI.

Certificate of School Attendance for the purpose of employment under Section 5, Elementary Education Act, 1876, or for total or partial exemption under the Bye-laws.

Foster St. Boys' *School.

I hereby certify that the following particulars with respect to the Attendances made by the Child named below, at this School after attaining the age of 5 years, are correctly taken from the Registers of the School.

Name in full, and Residence of Child.	†Number of Attendances made within the 12 months ending the 31st December.	
Richard Tempest	1918	330
152 Pollard St	1917	389
	1916	406
	1915	406
	1914	336

Signed this 11th day of June 1919

Principal Teacher of the above-named School.

* Enter name in full, and state whether a Public Elementary, or Certified Efficient, School.

Printed for H.M. Stationery Office by McCorquodale & Co., Ltd.

CITY OF BRADFORD

I could have cheered out loud as he got a small blue paper from a drawer; I knew this was the actual passport, by what I had seen of other boys'. With a flourish, the great man started copying the pencilled figures for each year onto the official form; then, after a final scrutiny and recount, he dabbed a spot of Gloy on one corner and stuck the blue paper on my birth certificate. It must have been good Gloy, for it still remains there, a constant reminder of childhood's high hopes, and a constant chastener to any boorish tendencies that might threaten my equilibrium.

That dinnertime, at home, was a travesty, for I couldn't eat in my eagerness to get into that mill, to step over the threshold into a marvellous new world, with my dearest wish almost fulfilled. I would work, and I would have real money in my pocket at weekends – one-and-sixpence per week, by way of being a small fortune to me. Little did I reck then of the small but dear privileges, now lost for ever, way back at school. No more swimming baths every other week; no more woodwork classes; no more slipping to the park, on a nice afternoon, for an hour's kick-about, for we 'half-timers' were outside the pale, with the above-mentioned little luxuries wasted on us now we had chosen the hard way and turned our back on a fuller education. Teacher, in defence, said we learned little enough without frittering still more valuable school hours away.

Nor did he speak wrong, for I would find myself falling gently asleep during some dreary afternoon lesson in the warm classroom, the droning of teacher's voice acting as a soporific, gently, so gently, bearing me away on downy clouds of lovely sleepiness, until he would cry, 'Tempest! What have I just said?' and I would start violently and stare blankly at my questioner; though, truth to tell, many times there was a blind eye turned to the tired, hooded eyes of us children of two worlds.

It would be considered hard and cruel to send any boy of twelve to work nowadays in this dear England of ours. Yet, on that glorious June birthday back in 1919, I thought Heaven had turned its especial benevolent smile upon me when I was given the privilege of doing just that!

BATTLES – WON AND LOST

Harker's Mill lay at the bottom of a long L of a mill yard. Its neighbours were a large wool warehouse, another and smaller spinning mill, part of a combing shed, and a half-submerged boiler-house that served the lot – and also lots of rats that disported in the quieter parts of the mill and along the mill dam bank, at the back, especially on fine, sunny days.

There was an engine-house to greet one on the way down the yard to Harker's, fronted by big glass doors, seeming forever open. A spotless, stationary steam engine of gleaming steel raised a proud giant connecting rod to the latecomer when it started its ponderous slow pulse to the start of another long stint of hard work. Steam hissed a fierce response, governor-balls whirled, the connecting rod fed a huge flywheel, and the flywheel doled out rotational motion to a vaster brother, girdled by a broad, sleek steel belt running away up through a high vaulted roof, away along the belt race, to set speeding a series of lesser belts that relayed power to four sprawling floors of the actual mill.

If anybody had asked me, at that time, what I most wanted to be in later life, I would have said, with no hesitation, 'An engine-tenter.' Our engine-tenter – I think his name was Albert – was a portly man, given to standing at his glass doors, painstakingly wiping podgy hands on a sweat-clout, and staring out of countenance any latecomer with a look of silent, withering disdain, as if to say 'If it wor left to me, straight back up that yard y'd go.' But it wasn't left to him, for he had enough on his plate looking after his own work, fully mindful of the envy he aroused in all us boys who would stand and stare, when the mood was on us, in the last precious minutes preceding the after-dinner start, waiting for Albert to perform his awe-inspiring ceremony of setting the mighty connecting rod in motion once more; this pent-up beast, impatient to be at it, sighing precious steam away until he was allowed his tremendously strong head. Indeed, one toyed with the idea of the engine soaring forth and landing on the far dam bank, were it not for the many nuts and bolts, big as a man's fist, marrying the engine to a massive bed of good Yorkshire hardstone.

I worked in the first room, or ground floor as it would be styled now – if a Second World War bomb on a fine September Saturday night had left the mill standing. I did not, however, stay long on the initial job of tube-piling, for this proved to be a lonesome sort of job all on one's own, half the time hidden away inside a deep wooden case, monotonously filling it with thousands of rows of cardboard tubes filled with yarn. From time to time I had pestered, and at last my overlooker, Bert – a tall, handsome man lately back from the war, and by way of being my first hero without blemish – put me on doffing, which was a job I had cast envious eyes upon from my very first day in the mill.

Doffers worked in teams of perhaps eight or ten, boys and girls working side by side, mostly half-timers, with the head doffer generally a greybeard full-timer of fifteen or sixteen. Our job was to take off ('doff') the filled bobbins, or tubes, from the spindles of the spinning frames, and to replace them with empty ones that would run about an hour before they, too, were full. We teamed an equal number down each side of a frame and, between doffings, sat and waited on a long wooden bench midway in the room of some dozen frames. We waited, ready to go into action on a plaintive cry of 'Doff here!' from a frame-minder, a spinner anxious to get her frame producing again for the sake of a few coppers' bonus. Sometimes, when chattering away or acting the goat, we might tend to ignore the first cry and have Bert, scowling black, whistling shrilly and bellowing loudly up the room, and us scurrying guiltily to the waiting, silent frame, and working faster to make up for lost time.

Now, at this time of my life, an exciting, bellicose tendency started manifesting itself in my nature. Whether this was a natural follow-up to the hours I had put in with the boxing gloves Dad had bought us – and from which he expected a second Jerry Delaney to emerge, the way he talked – I wouldn't know. He once tossed a cricket ball, a new composition one, to me whilst we were playing one day in the brickfield and, for the short weeks that corky-ball lasted, Dad talked of nothing but Wilfred Rhodes and George Hirst and the glory of my being a Yorkshireman, eligible to join such illustrious company in the county team. He talked so, when he got on, I'm afraid some of the dream-dust used to rub off on me.

However, following the gloves came the craze for brawling which was not to be curbed until I really met my match – which was not yet, awhile – and in the meantime this trend was fed by the near proximity of young, uninhibited girls and the very important factor of keeping up with one's fellows, in their sight. No cross look, no sneer nor push was allowed to go by lightly, though this went for most of us young boys, and scraps were plentiful, though not generally hurtful. Of these minor scraps I had plenty, and prospered, and got to feeling like a fighting cock. I was very touchy, to boot, and I must have been pretty insufferable, at bottom, I guess!

We were a happy crowd, howbeit, always ready for rough jokes on each other, and me thoroughly at home enjoying the first fruits of my desire to be working, out in the great, marvellous world of workaday. Also, there was a girl called Lilian. She was a good-looking lass, pleasant but reserved, rather well-spoken by our standards and a cut above the doffers – in my eyes, at least! I suppose these qualities had helped in her being promoted from doffing to a spinner, looking after three sides of spinning frames. When I got on the doffing job, I got into the pleasant habit, in any spare time, of sneaking away from the bench and down her 'gate', to help her 'piece up' the broken ends, and chattered away to her, nineteen to the dozen. She was a good listener, and I liked to hear myself talk, so we got on well, but there was a prior claimant to Lilian's first favours: Reggie, a jobber-lad and unofficial apprentice in a fair way to being an overlooker when he got older. Reggie regarded himself as Lilian's boyfriend, though she didn't say so; the trouble was, his duties did not allow him the time to spend in her gate to counter my attentions! Yet, truth to tell, he was clear favourite – that I knew by her demeanour, even though she was so nice to me. I never had a thought to dating her, for I was still rather shy of direct approaches to the opposite sex.

Reggie, however, in efforts to discourage me, started being uppish towards me, where he had formerly been friendly, and, in his position as Bert's right-hand boy, jockeyed me into the way of bits of jobs that took up what should have been my spare time between doffings. Had he not been a big lad, a little older than me, I would have rebelled then, but I bit my tongue awhile, and stood the bits of raggings the others gave me over my docile acceptance of his domineering. Then, one day, he picked a quarrel with me, down Lilian's gate, and in front of some of my pals whilst we were doffing her sides. He made a threatening move, and it acted on me same as a red rag being waved in front of a bull, and, after we had argy-bargied some minutes, we settled for a scrap the following day, straight after dinner. After dinner, because I was on afternoon work, and I would hurry from morning school, bolt my lunch, then hare off to the mill for a last, fateful twenty minutes or so. We were to fight inside, away up in the attic, in the waste yarn room, which pleased all, being well away from any fear of official interference. It seemed every lad and lass from our room, and many from others, would climb the steep stairs on the morrow to witness the scrap.

Next dinnertime, as we got sorted out in the attic that ran the whole length of the building and housed vast bins of empty wooden bobbins and yarn waste, I watched grimly whilst Reggie peeled his smock over his head; I was a wee bit apprehensive, him being thick in the shoulders and a bit of a weightlifter, and about the toughest prospect I had yet faced, on paper. In return, he scowled back at me and muttered something about my 'being flayed to start', as I took the hint, quickly peeled my smock off and stepped closer to him.

There was just Reggie and myself now in the centre of a little tight ring of encouraging boys, and giggling girls, and the usual witticisms being hurled around, and Reggie and I the only two looking any bit serious. Then, without any preamble, Reggie was at me, and I rapidly back-pedalled in some alarm against such fury. I almost broke the ring, but they pushed me back to the centre so suddenly, my fists flailing, that I caught my man one on the chest. It was then I saw a startled look in his eyes that encouraged me to greater efforts, and I went closer in, arms now going like a windmill gone haywire, fists tightly clenched – and poor Reggie, obviously, with no idea of the noble art. More by good luck than management, I slapped a full-swing haymaker plop on his nose. He staggered back, the crowd parted, and Reggie collapsed into a large bin of soft waste. I stood back and gave him a chance to get up, for we had, beforehand, invoked the unwritten 'fairs-up' clause that allowed a fallen opponent chance to regain his feet without any interference. I stood back, heart thumping hard with exertion, and the excitement and joy of doing well enhanced when I saw the claret slowly starting from his nose. I watched Reggie, in a sort of stupor, pass his hand under his nose, then blink at it in horror, and I began to realise, with a grand feeling of satisfaction, that my opponent was not going to get up. And suddenly there was cheering, laughing and joking, catcalls from the lads who had expected more, then a wholesale exodus to get downstairs, for time pressed, with the whirr of the belts, just starting moving, coming clearly upstairs to our ears. Reggie still sat there, all on his own in the waste, very disconsolate, and I felt a great compassion that expressed itself in a gruff 'Better go now, Reggie. We don't want Bert up here, looking.' Sadly, he followed me down the steep stairs, still dabbing at his bleeding nose and donning his smock at the same time, but never saying a word to me.

Needless to say, this swift success acted like drink to a weak stomach; I wallowed in an afternoon of favourable comment from my colleagues, basked in the sun of my new-found notoriety. But it was a pyrrhic victory, for a damper was cast on all this when I next ventured in Lilian's gate. She had not gone to see the fight – I would have been surprised if she had – and when I went to help her that afternoon, a trifle shyly because of the affair, she made a point of studiously avoiding me, choosing to move to the other end of the gate whenever I got near to her, and behaving very cold. I soon realised I was not welcome any more and – the boy being father to the man, inasmuch as I still quickly take a hint – accepted the shrug-off with good grace, more especially when one of the catty girl doffers deemed it her pleasure to tell me Lilian had said I was too rough and she wished I would stay away – as I did…

The sun set on my golden era of petty scraps and scrapes the day I fell foul of a boy called Herbert Butterworth. By this time I was in my second year as a half-timer, still mostly with the same set of lads and lasses, still ready to fight at the fall of a cap. Herbert had not been employed at Harker's as long as myself, which did not improve things, but he was a full-timer and worked in a little room on his own. He tended a sprinkling machine that conditioned full bobbins, for a little moisture made the yarn work better (that it also made it heavier is nobody's business!), and Herbert nursed his job and tried to keep us out as much as possible. I dare say he had been instructed by Bert to do so, but it didn't make him popular with us young lads, always seeking some place to dodge for half an hour or so of idleness. I put him down as a right nark because of this, though I had a healthy respect for a handy look he wore about his whole bearing.

At times Herbert, on business seeking skeps of bobbins, was obliged to pass us doffers as we sat awaiting the doffings, and one or two of us never lost a chance of a sly giggle at his expense after he passed. Once or twice he playfully tippled a lad in an empty skep and wheeled him away, amidst much laughter at the young 'un's discomfiture.

Then, one mad day, he picked on me. I struggled hard, and he gave up trying to get me in the skep and went on his way, growling what he would do next time. Encouraged by his failure to best me, I shouted after him, and boldly fell in with some ass's suggestion that I see him outside after work. No sooner had I said than the aforesaid ass was on his way to challenge Herbert, on my behalf.

'He's taken you on, Dick,' shouted my unwanted matchmaker enthusiastically, rushing back up the room a few minutes later. 'At the back of the Fire Station after work' – for this was well on in the afternoon. Everybody, except me, was tremendously bucked at this; myself, I would not have been upset had he preferred to ignore me and leave me an excuse to crow a while, for I was apt to do things in the heat of the moment, and rapidly cool after.

However, the die was cast and waiting on finishing time, and the open-air treat for some! We were obliged to have our fights outside at this day because the attic had got too popular and well-known, and we had been barred from going up there except strictly on business. A couple of times I had already performed, successfully, behind the nearby fire station, in a cul-de-sac leading to an old dyeworks that wore a deathlike mask of decay, with old tubs in every state of disrepair lying around, and over all the sharp, raw smell of dye. Herbert and I left work together, followed by a respectable crowd of young 'uns, and quickly made our way, never speaking, the few hundred yards to the dyeworks.

Nor did it take long to doff our coats and smocks, square up, fall to. It didn't take much longer for Herbert – stocky, strong – to rush past my flailing arms, lock his around me, and bear us both to the ground, with one very important point to be observed: I was underneath! For this was a fight with a difference, as I was quickly to learn, to my abiding sorrow, when I hopefully yelped, 'Fairs-up.'

'No fairs-up,' he grated. 'Ye never said,' he added, and lent weight to his decided advantage by pummelling merry hell out of my head.

I had, by now, wound my arms as far round vulnerable target points as ever I could, though I could not cover my ribs at the same time, to which he quickly switched and dealt them a rapid tattoo. I struggled to squirm free, but he held me fast as a thief, his legs knelt astride me as he thumped away. In vain I blustered and threatened, but he was too well placed to be impressed by empty threats, and answered with still more blows. He paused for breath and demanded, 'Give in!'; I cried 'No!' and he set about me again, strong as ever. By now, I was weakening from my desperate struggle to get free, and he was finding a way inside my arms, and I felt a stinging blow on my mouth and the salty, warm taste of fresh blood, followed by the instant numbness of swelling. Again, he paused, panted, 'Give in, yet?'; and I cried – actually cried – 'No!' for he was hurting more than my poor body now. I felt utterly ashamed at my showing, filled with helpless chagrin – but I must not give in, I vowed. I half-hoped that rescue would come at the hands of passing adults, but it never did, and I saw a myriad stars and felt sick, and that was the last straw. I moaned, and in a hoarse voice as though I found it difficult to breathe, I uttered the two words I had never spoken before: 'Let's up?'. It was all over then; Herbert was going his way home surrounded by new admirers, and a lone pal was helping me into my smock and coat and walking with me to our street end.

Mam was very upset by it all, for I could not disguise my condition as I had done with smaller hurts from other battles, and as she fettled me up, she made me promise not to fight again. Just then, I would have promised anything, for I felt terrible, physically and spiritually. When Dad came home, and after Mam had told him my misfortune, he gave a wry grin, commiserated with me, supposed – whilst Mam protested strongly – that I would be having another go at Herbert, on the principle of 'better luck next time'. But I never did have another go, not at Herbert. He always remained one up on me, for I realised I was a darned good winner, but no glutton for punishment, and that lad had firmly burst my pugilistic bubble. Never more did I emerge as knight errant, lout, petty bully, what-you-will, for I had learned an old saying, unknown to me then, that coupled discretion with valour.

'PEAS, PIES... AND POP'

The painted words that ran across three front windows of the small wooden hut were faded and almost rubbed away with constant cleanings, but one could make out they advertised 'Peas, Pies, Hot Black Puddings – and Pop'. One could also see the hut that stood next to a public urinal at the sharp point bisecting Back Lane and the main road.

Yet despite the uninviting exterior, it was cosy inside, and no time more propitious for going into the 'owd peyhoil' than on raw winter evenings, when darkness cut down all outdoor kickings-about, or frost bound the earth in its iron grip, or slush and muck from blackened snow filled the pavements – and tempting steam misted the hut windows. This was a steam generated by all sorts and conditions of things: by a crowd of young lads inside yapping away like magpies; by a black, iron set pan filled with boiled green peas and left simmering on the hob of a stove behind the counter; by another, lesser pan bubbling away and links of shiny black puddings bobbing slowly to the top in their turns; and lastly, by a heated Yorkshire-pudding tin, spread with small meat pies to add further warmth and fragrance to the general steam-up.

It was a homely interior, with a strict economy of low wooden forms and two long tables, spotlessly clean with their coverings of American-cloth, complemented with salt container, vinegar squirter, and a dash of mustard on a saucer for the black-pudding gourmet – these split down the middle, dabbed with mustard, and gobbled piping hot, with the white fat spots fair melting.

The very few times I went in before I started working, I rarely had money to satisfy the keen desire that sensitive nostrils conveyed to an ever-receptive stomach. Those times, I had gone in on the tail of a party with perhaps two spenders amongst us. On the strength of a couple of penny saucers of hot peas, the kindly lady – we called her Ma – was resigned to letting us all stay some little time, if we minded what we did. It was a frustrating time for us have-nots, gawping hungrily at the fortunate lads spooning away the savoury-smelling peas and covetous of every spooning, even though we did laugh and push their arms repeatedly in the hope of catching what dropped, earning many frowns from Ma for our behaviour. Some ill-mannered lad, no longer able to fight temptation, might drink the residue left in the dirtied saucer, whilst the refreshed one sat back and good-humouredly jeered, but not when Ma was looking, for she disapproved very strongly of this unhygienic act, calling it 'dahnright mucky' – besides being bad for trade – and would turn the lad out for the rest of the night.

The first time I ever went into the 'peyhoil', I got turned out, but for something else. We had all trooped into the hut with two penn'orth of trade and had been there some time – the only ones in, for it was a quiet night – when Ma discovered her small hand-torch was missing. It was one she used to light her home in the late evening, and she loudly wailed her loss, and got to blaming us. Vainly we denied any guilt, but that was not enough. She ordered us all out – luckily, the peas had been eaten – and also felt our pockets as we passed out, but she was unlucky. Nobody ever got to the bottom of that mystery, though it took some little time before our lot was welcome there again.

The hut opened six nights a week, with a tendency to quietness in the light weather, but picking up trade hand-over-fist when autumn drew to a close, and it stood out as an oasis of warmth and cheer, especially when most of us got working and handling eighteenpence or two bob every week in spending money. Gone were the bellyaching nights of watching others feed, of putting one's mouth forward, like a fledgling receiving sustenance, at the whim of a moneyed friend, in the hope a piled-up spoonful would reward one's servitude; we were all, or mostly all, moneyed men moving in affluential circles – or, at least, those where one carelessly ordered pie and peas as a matter of fact, every time one went in Ma's.

I remember one Christmas Eve well. We had gone in the 'peyhoil' much earlier than usual, and there was Ma waiting-on in a specially nice pinafore, her greying hair pulled back tight, her honest face shining like a red apple. I know we lads looked forward to the Eve, but I do believe she looked forward even more; she always enjoyed it. She was at her finest when she said, not very originally, 'It nobbut comes once i' t'year,' and we smiled our brightest, for she would be treating us to a free glass of pop as she said it.

Custom had it we visit Ma's twice on that night. First, for a mere saucer of peas, or a black pudding, or a pop, for this was a rendezvous. From Ma's, we all pushed off to the pictures, along the main road, past the bright shops that would stay open very late to catch the last Christmas shoppers – these generally poor housewives who, only then, had contrived to wring some money from husbands lately all too busy letting in Christmas cheer elsewhere than their humble homes. Even the trams, grinding along their important way, seemed less harsh-spoken in the mellowed air of bonhomie that affected everything, everybody – all set on being kindness itself whilst the festive season lasted.

Inside the pictures, we were the bane of the old attendant; for, the spirit of joy being in us, we were not one bit interested in the screen, and occupied ourselves throwing nutshells and orange peel around freely, and nearly stopping the show when the volume of protest grew so as to almost drown the valiant pianist – only then were we obliged to sit quiet awhile. The harassed manager, when we came out, hissed a Yuletide message to us: something to the effect of arses bring kicked if we ever showed up there again – which we did, of course, in time.

Following the pictures, it was back to Ma's, and get in where one could, for at this time the hut was fairly crowded, with everybody going the whole hog: peas, pie, black pudding, pop – the lot! And we ate, and loudly talked, and further indulged until we nearly burst, physically and emotionally, for this was the night of the year to let oneself go – as far as three or four shillings would stretch, for this was extra spending-money time, also.

There came a time, however, when all were ready to cry 'Enough', and one lad pulled out a brand new, Christmas-box, sixpenny mouth organ, and we got singing away on a medley of carols and old songs. Funnily enough, it was one of the comparatively new ones came out favourite. Its content was just pure sugar, this war song that spoke of a 'Long, Long Trail A-Winding', but it was very apt, for I never yet saw a nightingale, and I never got nearer that land of dreams that we lads sang so feelingly about – that land that one only reached at the end of a devilish long trail, to say nothing of the devious sidetracks en route. Come to think of it, it wouldn't be asking for the moon to enjoy once more another saucer of peas, with pie, and a black pudding sliced atop, next Christmas Eve – but I'm sure I would never fit in that narrow slit between table and wall again, where so many of us slim lads were wont to pack, in yester years.

THE END OF A CHAPTER

Mam had looked ill for a considerable time, worn out and nattered to rags with everything, but not willing to give them best and rest once in a while. As a matter of fact, she had been in hospital earlier in that year but – because of visiting neighbours taking desolate reports of how shabby we kids were faring; because Dad never went to see her but he was half-soaked in drink; because of my being the only one of her children allowed to visit and being able to hide little of what lay behind my woebegone face (for nothing seemed more natural than to tell Mam all, with great fun when I told things concerning Arthur's pranks; but mostly, my tales were of things going wrong or going unpaid, and I would wipe my eye and she would pat my hand and murmur, 'Never mind, love. I'll soon be home and straighten it all out. Don't you worry,' and that simple assurance would afford me great comfort until next time I sat with her, by our two selves) – because of these foregoing things, and against all advice, Mam came out of hospital, too soon.

Naturally, we young 'uns were overjoyed when she came back; we especially cleaned up, after our own scruffy fashion, against her coming, and we made such a rowdy fuss of her, clinging around her like burrs to sheep and fair hungering for her many kisses, that she finally cried out for a bit of peace, though we could see she was very happy, as were we. Also, Dad didn't seem to be upset, if any thought of her not being up to scratch bothered him, so everything seemed back to normal. But soon, very soon, the writing was on the wall – or rather, on her wan face, in her tired voice, and in the obvious efforts any small task entailed. It became obvious to us all that Mam was not well, far from it! We did try hard to help – when we didn't forget – by running errands with an air of eager willing; looking to ourselves more, which did not come too hard, for we had done so whilst she was away; and trying to be nicer to each other, but it was a losing battle for Mam, for the thankless burden was becoming increasingly too heavy for her. It soon became evident things could not go on as they were doing and, in what seemed no time at all, she was leaving us again, for another hospital[13] on the outskirts of town. It differed from the other one (St Luke's, stuck in the middle of the city) in that it was at the top of a wood, and Mam was in an ex-army-hut type of ward. It looked a comfortable place, though this judgement may have been unduly influenced by the wonderful beam on Mam's face whenever we walked into the hut and walked gingerly down the slippy ward to her side. She looked really beautiful, and more content, and reconciled to getting quite better this time, and was so plainly proud of me (in her little asides to her neighbouring bed-mates) that I fair used to blush, though it bucked me up no end, and did me a power of good. Also, she would insist that I help myself to the bits of fruit and sweets she had been given – though I always made a feeble show of declining with thanks, to be worsted by Mam's artful insistence and her play on 'Take some for the others, also.'

She still had quite a few friends, despite our vicissitudes. There was one in particular, a Mrs Illingworth, who had worked with Mam in her mill days; she lived a few streets away and she was kindness itself to us kids the few times we slipped along to visit her, at Mam's behest, in the unhappy months of that year. The trouble with us youngsters was that we were loath to go visiting anyone now – especially me, for I felt compelled to shrink from the whispering campaign that was seemingly going on all around us now, of 'Those blurry Tempest kids, brrhh!' or, worse still, 'Ee, them poor Tempests!'

There was also Aunty Fanny, my mam's sister; she helped however she could, contingent upon the demands of her own large family – but,

13 This was Bierley Hall Sanatorium

as always, Dad proved a big stumbling block to any real help, of a lasting nature, by well-meaning folks. He discouraged them, nay, insulted them – not just with his drinking, but with his growing bitter nastiness in all things, and his oft-repeated, oath-larded declarations of independence of how he'd 'show 'em all we could manage, blast 'em!' even when we were almost ragged-arsed as the weeks of Mam's absence dragged on. 'I'll not have them nosey bleeders coming in here' was his shout of defiance to the world at large, though when he was in his cups at home, only we kiddies heard it. He made a fine job, at the finish, of this business of alienating all kindly feeling towards himself, and left us starved of much we would, otherwise, have got of the milk of human kindness.

At that time I had just nicely started working full; it was a wearying time, a sad time, just when it should have been so satisfying for Mam, just when she should have started reaping the benefit of my being a full-time wage-earner. Instead, she was back in hospital, and nobody knowing when she was coming out again – for it was not going to be a week or two's job this time – and everybody evasive when one of us young 'uns asked, 'When's Mam coming home?' as we did, almost every week that God sent. Yet she *was* coming home, sooner than we really expected, and totally unsuspected one Saturday I went visiting, for she was so cheerful and with no complaint, and asking, as always, of others – still chuckling at my tales, but lying rather lower down in her large, spotlessly clean bed, much cleaner than we could now boast at home.

Sunday went by in its usual quiet, untoward way, with a friend going to see Mam instead of Dad or myself. On Monday evening, Dad had gone to his weekly show at the Palace, a third-rate theatre across town, and I was at home with the young 'uns. Suddenly, there was an unexpected knock at the door; on answering, I was unpleasantly surprised to find myself looking up to a policeman.

'Arthur Tempest live here?' he asked, rather more kindly than was usual in our neighbourhood.

‘Er, yes,’ I answered timidly, for I still feared it was some trouble Dad had got into, and nothing else occurred to me.

‘Is he in?’ he asked again. ‘Is he your dad?’

I answered a ‘no’ and a ‘yes’ and went on to explain that Dad was at the Palace, all this while watching the big man very apprehensively.

‘Can I come in?’ he went on, doing just that as I made way to let him pass. He gazed critically around the untidy kitchen, at the others who gazed back steadily at him without speaking, and at me again, before asking if I was the oldest.

‘Yes, I am,’ I admitted, fair willing him to get on and say what he’d come about, and now wondering if it might not be some complaint about the lads footballing in the street.

‘I’ve some rotten news for you, son,’ he said, very quietly, as though he didn’t want the others to hear, and I stared up at him, a sickening suspicion forming in my mind, a sudden comprehending of what was in the wind; and as a consequence, my eyes slowly welling with unstoppable tears that ran over, and down my face, though I got out a dry, croaked ‘Oh’ of having heard aright.

‘It’s about your mother. She isn’t so well.’ I could see he hated having to tell me, and he ruffled a big hand through my hair and comforted me with ‘Nay, don’t take on so… Aye, that’s better’ (this when I roughly wiped my tears away and looked up at him again). ‘It mightn’t be so bad, old lad… Anyway’ – his tone got brisker – ‘I want you to go to the Palace now, get your dad, tell him he’s to go straight to the hospital to see your mam… And now, go get t’flannel and dry your face.’

All at once I was rushing here and there, telling Bill his little jobs to do whilst I was gone, such as getting the others to bed, minding not to let them play about, and to get himself upstairs if Dad and I had not returned pretty soon; and the bobby was still with us, though he must get out again on his beat. Before he went, he stressed the urgency of my seeing Dad and taking care not to be put off by anyone, even to telling these the law had sent me, and to make sure Dad did come back with me. Anguished, I assured him I would do all that, then I was dashing away, in a panic of fear, to the Palace. I had a few frustrating moments with the old codger attendant at the bottom of the steps that led to the Palace pit, for his first reaction to my garbled, hurried request was a gruff 'Hop it! Go on, be off!' – but I stood my ground, with desperation lending eloquence to my repeated plea, plus an allusion to the law and an assurance that I would be able to lay my hands straight on Dad, without kicking up a noise. After all this, I was in, whispering hoarsely along a wooden row, impatiently urging, 'Yes, tell him – *him*, the big man with the red muffler... *Him*, that's him... Sssss, Dad!'

We both raced away to the hospital and were quickly shown into the dimly lit ward, for it was already 'lights out' in their world. This gloom heightened my fears, and I hardly dared breathe when I first looked down at Mam, with my imagination running riot, but I was relieved to see she slept. It was but a restless sleep, however, for she muttered and gave a low moan at times, and once she seemed to wake and bid a weak 'Hello!' to us, then fell asleep again whilst we sat mutely by, myself feeling utterly bereft and melancholy and recalling all the little times I had been naughty to Mam of late, and wishing I could make amends. So, occupied with our differing thoughts, Dad and I sat some half an hour before he suggested I go home and get to bed, and not to worry about things; as for himself, he didn't know when he would come home. So, with great reluctance, I went away. It was in the small hours when Dad came home, with me still awake and downstairs before he fairly got indoors. I asked him, 'How's Mam?' hoping he might give an answer that would justify my faith, poured out in tearful prayers earlier – being one of those optimists who readily fly to Him when in sore straits! But Dad could only say Mam was no different, though he had left her sleeping and, as the nurse said, 'comfortable'.

When we got up, at the first light, Dad said I must go to work whilst he went to the hospital, which I did, after extracting a promise Dad would let me know, if, if – oh, well, one didn't have to say as much in words! I had always gone to work pretty cheerful, but that morning dragged and the hours seemed intolerably long, and I heard nothing, and I began feeling better about things. The afternoon came, almost went, and my spirits were reviving quite appreciably, for I believed in miracles to help God out a little. Besides, even in the darkest hours there is a comparative light at times, and I was beginning to smile again, helped along by the contrived jokes of my workmates. Then, it happened, and slipped in so quietly, when I was least expecting it – when I was thinking I'd be home soon with perhaps some better news awaiting me there.

We had got to the last hour, turned four o'clock, when Bert came to my side, very matter-of-fact so as not to excite comment from the others, who were always on the qui vive for sensations; he sent me on some fool errand down the room, then followed me down and told me that my dad was waiting at the door, adding, 'and tek your coat, cos y'll be going home with him.' I went for my coat like somebody in a trance, feeling terribly downhearted at life's futility, and there was no need for Dad to say a word when I saw him, for he had been crying; that I could plainly see. Only too well, I knew his vigil was over and that Mam was gone from us forever. Yet I found it terribly hard to accept that incontrovertible truth during the next few, bleak days. One minute, in my very youthful mind, it wouldn't seem to be – Mam couldn't be gone – then, the next, it was all too cruelly true, with all sorts of tales being told to the young 'uns to satisfy their wide-eyed wonder at the unusual grief; though I guess the simple truth would have sufficed, had I had more oil in my lamp.

Mam lies buried in a far corner of a large cemetery in an unmarked grave[14] – I doubt if I could now find the exact spot, though we all went; by 'we' I mean the few friends and relations, and us young 'uns. Only Bill and I had much idea what was about amongst us kids. We had a nice tea at Aunty Fanny's and, afterwards, Dad went out with

14 Violetta Tempest of 152 Lower Pollard Street died on 11th October 1921 aged 42 years at Bierley Hall Sanatorium and was buried in an unmarked public grave at Bowling Cemetery in Bradford.

her husband, Uncle Jimmy, a little slaughterhouseman with a fair capacity for ale. Together, they strove to drown Dad's sorrow, as was customary in our class, in those days. It might have eased my ache if I could also have slugged back a few pints of 'mixed', but kids then were seen and not heard, and on a par with little puppies inasmuch as their joys, sorrows, loves were things of a day, and soon forgotten.

And that was all a long time ago, but whenever I think of Mam I am a child again, with my simple joys, beliefs, imaginary and real sorrows, and, always, an everlasting bittersweet regret that Mam never grew up with us young 'uns.

THE BREAK-UP (An essay into bitterness)

On the eve of my fifteenth birthday Dad promised me something. He didn't say what it was; that was to be a real surprise, he hinted. And it was – for he left us! Eight months after Mam had died, when there was Dad, myself, Bill and young Arthur at home. Edie, of the bonny face and red hair, had gone to live in another part of town, unofficially adopted by an old couple, after Dad had been made to realise she had not a chance staying with us.

Whether Dad planned to leave us, or it was a sudden impulse, I never rightly knew, though I would plump for impulse, for he did things like that. It was not the first time he had left home; he had gone off quite regularly when Mam was alive, to reappear weeks later looking very ragged and weatherbeaten, but never with any word of regret that I ever heard. On these outings, he ranged freely over the whole country, tramping and hitch-hiking (before the word was even known!) and getting himself casual work for an odd day here and there, for tomorrow was a good 'un at looking after itself, according to Dad's philosophy. Tomorrow must also have been a good 'un at looking after one's wife and kids, for we always marked time in some dwelling in the slums, fending for ourselves.

It must have been, veritably, a modern miracle of the five loaves and two small fishes how Mam fed us whilst he was away – a miracle helped by taking in other folks' washing, or dragging herself (if work was available) back into the hot hells of wool-combing sheds, to stand long days and earn a few bob, that we all might eat other things than sugar-and-bread or condensed-milk-and-bread, so often a standby when one was caught with one's financial trousers down, so to speak. Dad, true to type, always left us in that unenviable position, without any warning, and it generally happened at a weekend. It followed a set pattern of Dad ostensibly going forth to work on a Saturday morning, and when he had not come home in the late night, with all the pubs long shut, Mam would reconcile herself to the melancholy fact that her man had again left her.

There was a brutal legend amongst working-class males, supposed to be dead funny, to the effect that if one kept one's missus badly shod and full of kids, she never left home – and Dad made doubly sure Mam was well and truly nailed to her home cross of servitude. She must have had a heart like a lion; unhappily, however, she had not the physique of these animals, and gradually became but a shadow of the pleasant, buxom young lady in the scratched photo she kept in a small tin box, along with a few relics of her few years of adolescent freedom and happiness before Dad and we kiddies came into her life. And then she was gone – and we had dragged out a bleak eight months through a hard winter and icy spring, though with summer on us, the sun bade to make up for lost time.

I was still working, doffing away[15] at the mill, and my two brothers were going to school – leastways, they were said to set off in that direction. How the boys went to school was a thing I did not care to think deeply into; their toilet was pretty sketchy, I guessed, for they were left to fend for themselves after Dad and I went out to work every early morning, with Bill in full charge until we returned in the evening. I always cherished a hope they had been good lads in the daytime, and that Bill would have the kettle boiling to greet us workers at teatime. Alas, many times it was an irate neighbour who greeted me in the street, before I ever got home, with a moan of 'Ee! Your Bill has been a bad lad' or 'Little Arthur's hit our Annie with the long brush. Look!' or '… and they've both brok' me a window, the monkeys! Ooh, an' the lip off your Bill – I'll report him, I will!'.

15 *Doffing* - removal of a bolt of fabric once a specific pattern has completed it's run.

And I would stand a minute or so, commiserating with them, quietly and tiredly taking it all on the chin, being slowly borne down under it all, and far removed from the swashbuckling hothead I had fancied myself only some twelve months before.

It was one of these doorstep interceptors who told me of the lads playing truant. I was staggered to hear they had not been to school for weeks, but it seemed that day after day, with Bill leading the way and Arthur following like the faithful little lamb he was, they would walk all over town, or pull flowers in the park – which would have been another thing needing diplomatic handling had the keeper caught them. And, though I seemed pretty resilient, my heart always tending to lighten again after every reverse, I was troubled over Bill and Arthur. I began to realise my brothers were in grave danger of becoming street Arabs – indeed, we were all approaching an abyss, a plunge into something that would sweep us along with it, compulsively, for good or ill that only the future would resolve.

Yet, through it all, Dad steered an unaltered course of indifference. I would not say it was a happy course – for he was anything but that – but he kept on his own extraordinary way without any deviation because of qualms or spiritual struggles. Mostly, he left us kiddies with a free hand to do much as we pleased, except we must not get under his feet. I think the whole thing might have worked, kept us together, if he had cut down on the booze a little. During the weeknights he was tolerable, sometimes kindly, with a minimum of beer inside him, though with no women about the house, Bill and I did the chores – somewhat grubbily, but quietly accepted as our lot. Yet the absence of a load of ale did not mean that carriers of evil tidings or moans got away with their protests: he was just as ready to tell them to get to hell out of it, and spared no abuse to man or woman, so it was me who caught the backlash, homing along the street and fair game for anybody seeking to vent their spleen. It was little wonder I tried to avoid all adult salutations at the fateful teatime hour!

Dad was working at his best job, the one he liked to be at, when work was going in that direction: he was erecting scaffolding, a well-paid business where he, and we, would have thrived if only he could have 'carried corn'. If only he could have got some local woman to clean us up every week, we would have picked ourselves out of the mud of apathy and neglect in no time, for I knew we lads would do as we were told, if made to do that, and we would have responded to kindness. Instead, Dad kept to a regular squalid routine, a routine that depressed me every Saturday morning that came along. It was off to work in the morning for him, with a finishing at noon – but no homecoming, for from that time on was a drinking session until the late hours of Saturday night. When he did get home he would, invariably, be foul of temper and speech, for somebody somewhere would manage to upset him. First he would abuse the absent person in question, then the world at large; then he would have a go at me, for, in his eyes, I had one great, almost unpardonable failing: I was 'soft'. He couldn't understand or tolerate 'softness' in anybody – said I was too blurry handy with the 'waterworks' – a weakness to which I was prone, as I knew only too well, and which was not made better when he got on. As a contrast, he would stand Bill before me, for Bill was the non-crying type, and Dad would turn the knife, already scraping raw, by threatening to take Bill off with him – someday, someplace, anywhere from the blurry hole we were all now in – and the blighting prospect of five-year-old Arthur and myself being left alone would set me off again with the 'waterworks', much as I dreaded this manifestation of weakness.

I must say that Bill, at these moments, seemed quite bucked when Dad, sobering and sweeter, would start to paint a verbal picture of what lay before them. This second Eden they were to visit was a land of do-as-you-please, go-where-you-want, of irresponsibility, and not one irksome bind such as rent, insurance, clubmen (who, by the way, were getting very short shrift at Dad's hand, and, as a consequence, were muttering and sniping from all sides, no more being quietly put off by my promises of a 'little bit next week', for their big day was

Saturday, had to be, round our way, and I was the only one who ever had to confront them. One or two hit on the not-original idea of nipping in on a Monday night and, of course, they were again unlucky, with Dad at the Palace). But, to get back to this going-off of his, for it seemed definitely on the agenda: Dad would assure Bill, wide of eye and rapt with attention, of the times they would have on the road, whilst I stood by silent and desolated by it all. How I grew to dread, more and more, the horrible Saturdays with their cumulative miseries, for, with Mam gone, I was the only one who could really appreciate the depth of our distress (apart from Dad, who did not care to), and I always feared that one day, and soon, Dad would up and away again without a word or a sign of his intent. I prayed he wouldn't take Bill, for we were very close, despite not being very articulate; and probably because I wasn't asking too much, my prayer was answered – though not in exactly the way I should have wished.

My birthday was on the Sunday. On the Saturday morning, Dad and I went off to work; on the Friday evening, in a sober mood, he had promised to get me something for my birthday and I, as ever, had a simple faith he would – for if I couldn't pin my faith in him, then in whom? He did not, or would not, say what it was he had in mind, which was perhaps just as well. I was very pleased about the prospect and, of course, swanked a little at work amongst my mates, hinting at various things Dad might get me, and going home at noon with a hurried step – just in case. Though I *was* expecting a lot, for Dad never came home at Saturday dinnertime – still, I could be excused for hoping. It was late afternoon before we kids really started sweating it out, never leaving the street perchance we missed an exclusive first look at the present. We hoped he might get home now because of the special purport, but he didn't, and the others began to lose interest and strayed away to play. In the evening, and for once in a while, I did not go out blueing-in my precious spending brass, and I began to lose the fine edge of keening anticipation. I figured, with a tinge of annoyance, that he must have forgotten my gift, for he would not now be trailing anything home but his own work-stained, reeling figure, and with all his money spent. Yet we sat up very late, Bill, Arthur, and me, just on the off-chance. We played long enough with snakes and ladders, ludo, and cards, until Arthur grew very tired, would no longer play, and grew very cross; and we all got the same way at the finish. We quarrelled and all started crying, despite my desperate efforts to stem the flood – but then, Dad had never stayed out so late before, not since Mam went.

At the finish of our sob session, we stumbled up the stone stairs into our bare bedroom, lugging Arthur between us, and turned into our rough bed of tattering blankets, sheets having long gone to the winds, and lay down with the numerous other occupants that now slept there, irritating and busy late into every night. My brothers soon dropped off to sleep, but I would start at every footfall down in the street, hoping they were going to stop at our door and making ready to bound down the stairs in joyous relief. A couple of times, on hearing voices, I had tiptoed to the window, looked out, watched dim forms stand awhile under the lamp across the street, listened to a muttering of voices and ribald laughter; then they would turn to go, their footsteps dying away in the distance, and I would feel very isolated again. Once, a girl shrieked, and I started with shock, though the cry was followed by a bold feminine laugh, and a mild oath of reproof for her companion.

Many times, trains steamed noisily into nearby St Dunstan's[16], now more noticeable after the street had gone dead; but they made a welcome diversion, for my head was constantly filled with a dozen disturbing thoughts. I would not have cared if I could have really given Dad up as gone but, hope springing eternal in the young breast, I was in a torment between kidding myself he might come back any minute and asking 'But what if he doesn't? What shall I do?' – and never getting the question answered before my thoughts were away,

16 St Dunstans was a station located in the Bowling/Ripleyville area of Bradford. It closed in 1952.

on a tangent. Many times I deliberately squared up to the question, like a right man, worldly and wise, then I would panic and feel terribly inadequate and conscious I was only fourteen… No, by gum, I was fifteen now, by quite a lot of minutes!

I cried bitterly for Mam, gone beyond all this, gone beyond recall – as I realised in the midst of my tearful pleadings, pleadings so tender and intimate that their rebuttal finally cured me of any nonsense about the hereafter for, if there *was* anything in this life-after-death stuff, poor Mam would surely have heeded my heartbreaking cries to her, and manifested some sign she heard, and heeded, and helped. She would! I knew – for Mam was like that!

Then I cried in bitter hopelessness, for I realised Mam was gone as completely as the old cart-horse I had seen, some weeks before, fallen down in his cart shafts and helpless to rise, though freed from his strappings. It was in the dinnertime, on the cobbled street outside our mill, and as we mill lads, stirred to pity, gawped at the poor creature, it slowly opened its eyes and looked straight at us with a plea to help. But we could do nothing for it. There was only one chap could do aught for it now, the carter told us, for 'something' had gone, and his steed would be shot when the horseflesh man got on the spot.

It seemed terribly hard, when the knackerman did come, a farmer-looking type handling two horses pulling a long, low heavy cart; it seemed a crying shame that, without so much as a kind look at the fallen, he should shoot it, manacle its hulk with chains, then winch it up a shallow, lowered tailboard into his long cart, the dead animal's back legs dragging heavy behind. Only one hour before, this had been a noble and understanding creature, but it was now dog and cat meat; it evoked a feeling of sadness in some of us lads. This was very quickly followed by a sensation of nausea, occasioned by the shock of the pistol shot, of sudden death on a bright noon, of the pool of congealing blood staining the cobblestones – the silent, only witness of the brief tragedy, now the low cart had trundled out of sight.

So I tossed in bed and thought back to the poor horse and wished I was one with it, and dear Mam, and plucked miraculously out of this none-of-my-making mess. Then the hot proximity of my brothers, stirring and sighing every now and then in sleep as we lay in the same bed, shamed me with my cowardly thoughts and made me resolve on keeping a clear head – though, even then, I kept forgetting my fine resolve when waves of black despair shook me as the night wore on.

I won't say 'never was night so long', for blessed rays of light started filtering through the grimy bedroom window in the very early hours of Sunday and I began to feel a little better about things, a little braver, and calmer – and oh, so sleepy now!

When I awoke, it was to the braying of Tommy Salt's donkey – prisoner in his crude, home-made stable up the street – with sunbeams streaming through motes of fine dust in the thick bedroom atmosphere, and Bill squinting at me through slits of eyes and asking, very sleepily, 'Is me Dad home yet?'

'No. Not yet.'

We breakfasted frugally, mainly because Dad had always made a personal point of bringing home Sunday's breakfast and dinner. He had a capacious 'jock' (sandwich) pocket in his work coat into which he could stuff a couple of pounds of sausages, half a dozen savoury 'ducks', and a lump of steak to lend bouquet to our dinner, this foraging being undertaken at one of the many butcher's shops he would pass on the Saturday's passage between pubs. So, besides breakfasting thin, we had to improvise lunch with a hasty purchase of potatoes from a back door out of some spending money I had left, plus two penn'orth of corned beef Arthur was sent to get with a hastily scribbled note to the corner shop. This shop opened for two hours every Sunday morning, let us have tick, and was to prove a godsend in the following days of our crisis. Incidentally, we sent Arthur along with a strict injunction to keep his mouth shut, or that would have started a 'run on the bank', whilst Bill and I got our potatoes prepared for the meat tin in the big side-oven.

I still nurtured a hope Dad would come home – even made excuses for him in that he might have got sick-drunk and only now able to crawl home – or he might have got himself locked up (to which I had no answer), or, or… Oh, there could be a dozen permutations to what might have happened to him! And me with my hands tied, for one did not go round shouting the odds when a dilemma threatened, not where we lived; one played very quiet awhile, hoping for the best, for heaven knows where things might end if brought out into the light of day – probably, and worst of all, making things hot for Dad, which was a solution to be avoided at all costs. So we held back our corned beef and potato hot-up until late, until Arthur, tired of waiting, tearfully complained that he was very hungry and wanted his dinner, and Bill and I reluctantly agreed we were also that way, and fell-to on the not unsavoury dish.

By Sunday evening, almost all hope had fled – almost – for I still did nothing to make anybody the wiser of our parlous situation, and drilled the others into what to avoid discussing with the other kids, especially when they went off to school in the morning. Frankly, I didn't know what to do, being typically English inasmuch as I hoped something would turn up out of the blue to clear away our troubles. Also, I might have been accused of a sharp practice in that I gave the corner shop a real caning, 'ticking on' without any scruple, and with no knowing when they would be paid. I know they never were, and would be only too glad to make amends now, if the kind Mrs King (or her family) are still with us. However, that slightly dishonest period lasted exactly two days before a kind of economic blockade – in the guise of ever darkening looks from Mrs King, and pointed hints from neighbours – resolved the next move.

Actually, I kept the flag flying for three days in all, and what wouldn't I have given to have Dad walk in the door again, to lift the frightening, hopeless mantle of responsibility from my young, frail shoulders? Any dad, I now realised, was better than no dad at all – but he never did come, and the neighbours, bolder in his presumed absence, confronted me and demanded to know what was going on. Leastways, two of them came into the house before I came from work one evening, had a good look round, pumped the young 'uns clean, waited for me, then sailed in, primed as they now were to action. Tearfully, but with a great relief in my heart now I no longer held the horrid secret, I told them all I could.

The first job they did was to call in the 'cruelty man' (as we knew the inspector from the NSPCC), and he took Bill and Arthur away, to an orphanage, just as they were, in what they stood up in. It was a very distressing going, with a last, lusty 'turning on the waterworks' all round, for I was not to go with them. Because I was working, the 'cruelty man' decided I would be able to stand on my own feet, if one of the neighbours would be kind enough to take me in? Happily, I was taken into the home of a pal of mine along the street – a good, clean home, which I did appreciate, though my appreciating may have taken a pretty poor turn when, after some months, I hankered to go live with a workmate of mine and was allowed to do so. At that time, I bet many were afraid I was going to turn into a bit of a wanderer, same as Dad!

If there was one bright spot to follow that long, dark weekend, it was that I got to seeing my brothers quite often, whenever I passed up Park Road, which I took care to do every few days. My brothers were comfortably housed in a children's home in that road and, whenever they had finished their simple tasks following tea, they were allowed to play in a big yard at the side of the big house. At the bottom of this yard was a large gate with iron bars; it was mostly closed, but I would stand one side, Bill would fetch Arthur to stand with him at the other, and we would spend a few precious moments before some other child ran to say some official was in the offing – when, of course, I had to make myself scarce. I tell you, though the eloquence was lacking at these meetings, clandestine and hurried, the poignancy was there, the feeling of not belonging to each other now, the heartbreak of losing loved ones who still lived.

I saw Dad again after some months – and that very much on the quiet for, had he been apprehended, the authorities would, quite rightly, have sent him to jail. He was unchanged: bleary-eyed, reeking of ale, still the same old hard case who lived only for drink and an escape to the open road, and a quarrel for anyone who criticised his conduct. I never heard him, up to the moment he died – and I was there – I never heard him utter one word of contrition, nor ask forgiveness, for the long trail of misery and suffering he left behind amongst all who ever had the misfortune to bear any attachment to him. Indeed, fed by others who should have known better, he got the impression he was a hell of a fellow, more sinned against than sinning, and his frailties very human, and beer always providing a good excuse for most of the wrongs he committed.

An old gentleman, who had known both my parents and who had always listened with relish to Dad's highly coloured tales in the local taproom – tales always of wild carouses on building sites, or battles of wit somewhere along the rolling roads – once took me mildly to task for being unloving in my attitude towards Dad, a Dad who kept constantly turning up in my after life, like a horrible skeleton out of the cupboard, and completely unabashed, choose what the circumstance. This taking to task followed a long eulogy of Dad's good points, which would have sounded wonderfully impressive to a stranger. He wound up with, 'He wasn't a bad sort, yer Dad… Ye didn't unnerstand him, Dick… He was just happy-go-lucky—'

'Happy-go-lucky!' I interrupted, with a snort, my thoughts racing back over the long years to that awful June night when our family fell apart, for ever. 'Ugh! Happy-go-lucky!' I repeated, as a great anger welled inside me. It would have been a pleasure to slap the old man for the feeble ass he was, in still believing in the 'good old Arthur Tempest!' myth. Instead, I contented myself with a withering 'You! You poor simple bugger!' and turned from him in deep disgust.

DREAM OF HOME

High on a hill I saw a light that beckoned like fairy-gold;
Then found I chased the mocking sun, and he, the newborn day.
Yet, on that hill, behind that light, I saw a house – my home!
And, tremulous, crept inside the shell
where once dwelt love and grace.
But, dead ash lay in rusted grate instead of live, red coals.
The hearth was bare, its tab-rug gone, and mongrel, Benny, too.
And fled the rich warm smell of life
– decay chilled all with its stink,
And patterned with ghastly spiders' threads,
old rags masked broken panes.
I edged up stone-bound stairs, and tiptoed on creaking boards,
And woke, and groaned, eyes wet with the tears…
How sadly I dreamed of Home.

CHAPTER FOUR

A DUAL INCURSION

Coincidental with my being thrust, sans Dad, sans brothers and sister, sans home, into the big world – even though it was but the next ward of West Bowling in our city – two diametrically opposed interests entered my young life. One was gambling, of a frivolous hole-and-corner kind; the other was music, of the serious popular type.

The gambling took the form of isolated sixpenny bets on horses, and a weekly sixpence on the old-style football coupon. The first horse I ever backed was called Lighthouse. I know it didn't win, but I was delighted when I got my tanner back the next day on the score my horse had not run. I thought the bookie was no end of a good fellow – though my companions must have thought I was no end of a drip, not knowing racing rules better than that.

I also started indulging the cards – 'the devil's prayer book', as one of our older boys, with a wicked leer in his eyes, told us they were called. It comes as a startling revelation that, earlier, when we were still in our brickfield days, we never got to playing cards for money. We never did gamble in any form – but, of course, this would be due to the fact we never had any money, if one excepts the Saturday penny or so for the pictures! I will admit to our family playing cards, even though we only indulged in strictly matchstick stakes, and these on quiet weekdays when Dad, his money gone, would stay in and strive to inculcate the rudiments of cribbage into the dull craniums of Bill and myself.

My proper apprenticeship, and a real appetite for gambling, began when I started working full-time. If the weather was poor so we could not have a kick-about with a rag ball in the yard straight following dinner, we would retire to a wool warehouse across the yard (rather a nerve, for it was not even ours!) and spend some half-hour carding. It might be pontoon, or nap, or best of all, brag, with a ceiling of one ha'penny. Yet, a halfpenny limit could make for feverish brows if your whole wealth amounted to about fivepence, of which some threepence should have gone to buying a little potted meat or fish and chips for dinner to augment the bread-and-margarine sandwiches brought from home. One might go gleefully back into work some eighteenpence the richer and with evening pictures very much in mind's eye, or one might get skinned and remain very empty throughout the long afternoon, besides nursing a feeling of frustrated vexation at one's ill luck with the cards, as witness the cert winner 'one, two, three on the trot' that lost, or the nap hand that just did not make it.

Of course, when one starts flouting the common law of the land, one must not be surprised when the law starts catching up on one, though we were aware of this aspect and took care to keep out of the way. However, the best-laid plans sometimes go awry, and my first, and only, brush with the law came one fine Sunday afternoon, like the oft-phrased 'bolt from the blue'.

It was at the time I had gone to live with the second of my mill friends. I was happy, inasmuch as I got good meals and had a clean bed, and went about with a group of lads all about my own age, fifteen or so – boys who lived fairly close together in a thickly populated street, with back-to-back houses at one side and a tall spinning mill of some six floors at the other. I felt I was living life to the full, for I was freed from all responsibilities and the bittersweet worrying over my brothers (though I would rather have had them back, humble house and all!). Now, every evening was a free one – too free, really, for we were never encouraged to stay in – and Freddie, my pal, and I were out after tea, standing under the shadow of the great mill, waiting for the others and a ball game if it was light weather, or plotting some mischief to put the night in, or going to the pictures; though one could not stand a right lot of picturing, for our money wouldn't run to above twice a week, and *no* Sunday pictures in those days of rectitude in Bradford.

However, as with the brickfield in my old district, there was a vast waste ground, alongside which ran the railway from Bradford to the south, and this also provided room for our ball games and other outdoor activities, with some low hills down by the railway track that had, up to then, served as excellent cover for a quiet game of cards – though now, these very hills were to prove our undoing.

There were seven or eight of us sat in on a game of ha'penny brag at the time, sat on the dry grass in a hot sun of late afternoon. The rest of the lads, the stony-broke ones, had gone their own way to have a game of football high up the field. These boys, in themselves, would normally have provided a cover for our nefarious activity, in that any policeman approaching the ordinary way would set our friends away in flight, for the law took a dim view of most any activity we espoused. Needless to say, our pals would make a heck of a racket in going, and so alarm us. But one bobby did not approach the normal way. The first thing we knew (our friends still happily kicking their ball about) was a young bobby looming sharply into view around a small hill, not ten yards away, from the 'Achilles heel' side where the railway lines lay. This was a side we never did think trouble would come by, for we never dreamed bobbies would trespass – but this one did. He was a cunning type!

All at once, there was a confused rush – of shouting, and scrambling, and of cards and money being left to fend for themselves – and a staggering to feet and a racing away, anywhere out of the long reach of the law, as the bobby quickly came on us and frantically grabbed with both hands. I slipped on the dry grass, and my heart thumped madly as I fair felt him grab, but I squirmed, and half-sobbed, and was away running, stumbling after the others. We ran for a couple of hundred yards or so, up and along the track; then, feeling badly out of breath and hearing no immediate yelps of capture, we eased up and risked a look back. We saw we were no longer in danger of pursuit, for the policeman was holding one of our younger members, which melancholy fact comforted us none. Shakily, we regrouped and spent the next hour walking around, worrying, wondering what happened next. The blatant optimists thought there seemed a fair chance our young friend might not split on us, nobly envisaging the poor lad taking the can back for us all, but that was really too much to hope for, and opinion hardened to all names and addresses being yielded under persuasion from above. And that was the predominant reason we spent a full hour screwing up courage to go back on the street and face whatever music awaited us.

It was hot music awaited. The whole street was out, with an advance guard of youngsters crying out in front of us, and what they cried confirmed our worst fears. The beans had been spilled, with a vengeance, for our unfortunate friend had been obliged to take the bobby right back to our street, to his very home, to our homes – and that had put the cat amongst the pigeons. A bobby in the street! In our very houses! This startling news even woke men from their time-honoured after-booze naps – had everybody at their doors awaiting our homecoming, without any flags flying, but certainly with shouted threats of what lay behind these same doors when the bringers of shame got inside. I don't know whether I was fortunate or otherwise, in my peculiar domestic position, but Freddie got a whaling from one of his brothers; and a sister who worked with us in the mill, who was about eighteen and called Clara, gave me a bawling-out, and it hurt, knowing I was a party to causing the family distress. I felt they might see me as a bad influence on Freddie – though, bless him, the lad was no muggins to be led by me.

For a couple of days the atmosphere was very strained, but nothing happened, and we all began to entertain hopes the thing had blown over, with the bobby having a big, kind heart, knowing lads were lads, deciding to let it drop. But I should have known better, for I had seen – with his hot breath almost scorching me in his one-man raid – that he was young, determined, and ambitious for chance to gain a reputation. No, he hadn't gone to all that trouble to throw his cop away! One evening, when Freddie and I had gotten out following tea, a pleasant, middle-aged policeman was seen making his way to various houses on the street. He was in plain clothes, by the way, but nine times out of ten we could spot a bobby a mile away – barring our friend who proved the exception! We went very quiet, followed him with our eyes as he came out of each house after some few minutes, and sickeningly realised the hour of reckoning had come. Soon he was at our door, inside, and Freddie's mother was out, angrily calling us in to face the man.

It was too late now to be moral and weep bitter tears over our sinning; nor did we, and the pleasant old bobby, having ensured who we really were, served us with our summonses. He advised Mrs Holmes, my good landlady, to make sure we paid our own fines, with which sentiment she heartily agreed. Then he was off, on his way to some other house – for, as he so humorously put it, he was a busy man that evening. By the wailing and cries he left behind, he could be likened to the avenging angel who visited the unfortunate Egyptians in the last, terrible plague.

Within a week or so, we answered our summons to court; because of the fact we were all under the age of sixteen, we had to appear in a children's court. After a long wait in a drab passage, we were all herded in together and made to stand in a long row, facing our judges. What we had been treating so lightly, in a spirit of bravado in the passageway, began to wear a more solemn hue from the time we were ushered into the court. We were quickly, quietly, overawed in the grave atmosphere. There were many people sat looking at us, without a vestige of a smile, and this served to plunge our tottering morale down to zero. Ooh, we must have done something very wrong! Our names were asked of us by an old, very wise-looking man sat opposite us on a slightly raised dais. He peered over his glasses and did not appear very impressed when we each, in little more than whispers, answered. He turned to whisper with two colleagues – ladies both, and sat on each side of him – and altogether it began to look that ha'penny brag was a very serious matter indeed.

For a second time, I saw our old adversary of the foothills. He gave a statement, very crisp and concise, and it all sounded so damning, and visions of reformatories swam before my eyes, especially for me in my role. Then the old gentleman was asking each of us if we had any questions to ask, or anything we would like to say… and, as none of us even opened his mouth, he took it we had not. Once again he conferred with his ladies, who seemed to agree heartily with everything he was saying, or suggesting, though we could not hear one word. He turned to us again, started talking like a Dutch uncle, dwelt on the sadness of seeing us there – dwelt on the unhappy likelihood of seeing us again if we did not mend our ways. He dwelt on the perils attendant on our standing on a brink, of slipping and being in grave moral peril, and advised us to seek healthier pastimes on the Sabbath. To let this sink in, he muttered again with the ladies, and came up with their considered verdict. We were to be fined five shillings each (how I sighed with relief – the reformatory receding!), out of our own pockets, at the rate of a shilling a week. He ended it all with a tired wave of his hand to be rid of us, tiresome boys as we must have seemed, and we trooped thankfully out. Morale miraculously restored once outside the Town Hall, we had a good cackle at the old man's expense, him and his seeming old-washerwoman pratings, and all over something we accepted as our normal way of life, a normality that found such delightings in Sabbath games of football and cricket, and the odd game of cards, when finance and idle minds allowed, and for which various pastimes we were always being chased, much to our bewildered surprise.

Yet I never did fall foul of the police again – though I wouldn't say I did not play another game of ha'penny brag, or kick a ball on a Sunday. Perhaps – and subconsciously, so I was never really aware – the old man's words did register. His words and, probably, the onset around this time of a certain something that grew into a lifelong love – a blind one, for I never knew a note of music, never played anything, and… well, I suppose I just loved much that I heard for no other reason than that folks have fallen in love on slighter pretext. In fact, perhaps it would be more correct to say that the tiny seed of love had already been sown on hearing the tingelaries on the streets. Amongst the twanging, rrrp-rrrping tunes they played were a few that really soothed my savage breast, such as snatches from *Carmen*, *Poet and Peasant*, and a lovely excerpt from *Cavalleria Rusticana* – though I never know those names at the time.

It fell out, ever since I had gone to live at Freddie's, that I was going more to the pictures. We enjoyed a glut of picture palaces in West Bowling and its fringes, with the Towers Hall, Grand Cinema (a proper bughole!), the Park Road Cinema, Birch Lane – and the nicest, and most imposing of all, the Carlton Cinema. It had only been built since I went to live locally, was all plush and soft curtaining, and one thought twice about acting the goat therein, with the attendants of differing calibre to 't'chocolate bobby', a long-suffering attendant at the Grand who led a hell of a life striving to keep a semblance of order. He swore vilely, he threatened a lot, he fought a losing battle against the swarm that favoured his fleapit; most times, he gave it up as a bad job, contenting himself with a fierce buttonholing of the culprits as they emerged from the blackness after some two hours of creating a little hell of their own along the crawling wooden benches.

Yes, the Carlton was different – revolutionary, I would say. It stood on the edge of prosperous Marshfield, wore a distinct air of Marshfield's better-offness, and did not altogether enthuse over us West Bowling boys. We were allowed in, but on sufferance, just so long as we behaved like human beings – which we, being rather subdued by the wholesome atmosphere, generally did.

Its attractiveness was enhanced, for most, by an innovation only then catching on in local picture places; for at the Carlton, besides the Pathé Gazette, the comic or serial, and the main film, there was to be a musical interval of some fifteen minutes. With a preliminary flourish, this music was provided by Clement Ambler (a gentleman always dressed in evening clothes) and half a dozen strings, which spectacle had, at first, caused many titters amongst us roughnecks until the weight of public opinion behind had forced us to be quiet, to sit and listen. This interlude was always sandwiched between the comic and the main film, and it wasn't long before folks were really looking forward to these little treats – and they were certainly improving the musical education, and appreciation, of at least one youthful listener. Mr Ambler always made a point of announcing what was going to be played, so I got to know quite a few of my former nameless barrel-organ snatches, and this added a new delight to my listening.

I got to slipping along to the Carlton on my own, deriving almost as much pleasure from the music as the pictures. I grew to sense an atmosphere, a new dignity about it all, and felt just as thrilled whenever Clement Ambler and his Orchestra trooped onto the long, low staging below the silver screen as I do now, on the all too few occasions I go to St George's Hall and see Sir John Barbirolli mount the high rostrum, his eagle, pallid face betraying a slight smile of pleasure at the reception Bradford always accords him.

Generally, our cinema orchestra would treat us to some selection from a tried, loved, musical show – *Chu Chin Chow*, *Maid of the Mountains*, *The Merry Widow*, bits from Gilbert and Sullivan – or a classic, and we lapped the lot up. It was lovely sound to us, though we could put no exact label on why it pleased. It was manna to a class long starved (for this was before wireless) of any musical appreciation, and we hungered for more, once having tasted; and, being a very demonstrative lot that came from the back streets across the road to the new pictures, we always let ourselves show it. Take no notice of others saying Yorkshire folks are dour, unfeeling, inarticulate; we knew what we liked, and let them know when we liked it. More so when the fiddles, as we called them, sawed fast and furious in a thrilling finish amongst themselves, to end with a great, triumphant flourish from the maestro himself; how we, especially in the tanners, would whistle, stamp our feet, and even cheer in token of tribute to the fine people. Of course, the higher-ups in the ninepennies, and the exalteds in the shillings, were more restrained in their applauding and did not care a deal for our foot-stamping; but they couldn't have it all their own way for, after all, we had listened in silence, just as attentive as they.

We would shout for 'more!' but it had to be some special occasion for Clement to accede to the popular demand; generally, he remained adamant, not to be moved by calls. He would smile deprecatingly as though to say 'Enough is enough' – especially with the manager looking fretfully at his watch, and the main picture waiting. Mr Ambler would favour us with a last bow, nod to his fellows, and they would quickly stand, incline their heads, then leave the platform to disappear though a side door.

With something of the nature of an anticlimax, the main picture would start in a hall now pitched into gloom, and a lone pianist slipped surreptitiously into the piano stool, to provide the incidental sound to the film. You could almost bank on the *William Tell* overture for the thrilling chases, ever with us, week after week, and ever sure winners; or 'Hearts and Flowers' for the saccharine-sweet heroine who wrung our hearts by telling the sad-Sam cowboy, William S Hart, that it could never be, for she was another's, or she was dying, by inches. This seemed Hart's usual lot in the many films he made, and though he was a tremendous favourite with his hundred-per-cent-good-man roles, I marvel he never tired of the inevitable brush-offs. It would have been a real treat to us lads had he, just for once, turned and spurned the proffered little cheek of parting, and given the baby-faced pretty minx a real up-and-downer, so she wouldn't know what had hit her. We would have cheered him to a boy!

But calamity did not sit alone on his shoulders; it was staring down a raucous, mighty gun barrel at Clement Ambler and his like. The mere blast from it was going to put Clement out of business, this thing that had always seemed but a pipe dream of cinema's potential. Yet, in different parts of the world, in obscure studios, supposed crackpots were toying with – nay, getting on with – this miracle of making films that could also be heard. But when I listened to my first cinema orchestra, talkies were a long way off. I was to go out into the world and return before I heard my first one – and saw the awful black void below the silver screen, where Clement Ambler and his Orchestra had beguiled, bewitched us with the joy of sweet, wholesome music. It was a sad moment, that!

THE EARLY BIRD

I heard you when I trudged to work
As the haze of night, and dawn, made murk.
Yet what you sang for, I don't know,
For all was scoured by windswept snow –
The very branch where you trilled your air,
Stood etched in cold light, stark and bare –
Was it you sensed, this Valentine Day,
That spring was somewhere on the way?

POOR MAN'S GOLF

From a large, dimming photo on the wall, a cloth-capped man stared out across the taproom of the small inn. He was not alone, for he posed in front of a group of very evident admirers, perhaps a dozen of them, in clothes that bore the stamp of the early twenties.

The hero of the photo was in his shirtsleeves and held, in one hand, a long tapered stick – not unlike a billiards cue, except it ended in an abrupt clubbed head. Beneath the photo, and in bold lettering, ran the legend 'Willie Lamb[17]… The World Champion… 1921…' and I sat and looked at it long enough, in between drinking two pints of best bitter and having, as company, the landlord, for we were the only two in the place.

That photo set me off, harking back to another such pub, though that one had been on the edge of moors that stood high as silent sentinel over Oxenhope and Denholme, Cullingworth and Haworth. I wondered if, by any long odds, this same Willie Lamb had played in the only knur-and-spell match I ever saw? I couldn't recall faces or names at this late date, but I could remember they had played, as stated on the handbill that had lured me there, 'Twenty-Five Strikes Each – Longest Strike To Win', and I think it had been a match for 'Twenty-Five Pounds A Side', no mean money when one knew a man worked a whole week for a couple of pounds – if he was in work!

It was a raw Saturday afternoon on which we gathered at the lonely pub where, incidentally, I was served with a grin and a lemonade, and an injunction to 'behave!', because of my obvious early age. It was a

17 Willie Lamb (1885-1962) was from Northowram, the next village to Shelf, and a member of Northowram Knur Club. He worked at Dunn Ridsdale's dyeworks in Buttershaw.

farmhouse of a place, and I had gone along with many others in all manner of conveyances – pony traps, light carts, flat carts, dilapidated early Fords – though many travelled by Shanks's pony, still the favourite way of getting between places out in the country. All the 'fancy' seemed to have turned out for this match, much as though it was a prize fight of the old days – and that was not something that might not happen here, judging by the looks and speech of these lads. The little pub soon filled with these hard-bitten customers, mostly in mufflers and caps, with a couple of bowlers about, and two or three cur dogs that threatened, often, to disturb the precarious, barely held peace. It was held that the owner of a fighting dog must, of necessity, be a fighting man himself, to which belief I freely subscribed in the midst of such awesome company.

I soon gathered this match was of the needle variety, feeling having boiled up over several weeks of negotiating; and, for the most part, the men were loud and truculent of voice in discussing the pros and cons. They made a great show with their money, constantly pulling or thrusting in and out of tight pockets at the tops of their trousers, making bets or ordering, and swilling down, bellyfuls of ale before venturing to the field of battle. In the main, and as though by an unspoken consent, the two opposing camps supped in different stone-flagged rooms, though passage was quite free between the camps, and the air thick with baccy smoke, pungent ale, and the violent oaths accompanying challenges and striking of bets – with some lobbying on behalf of other knur-and-spell giants, present but not performing, and anxious to be fixed for some future match.

Incessantly, voices were raised in fierce arguments that threatened to erupt into fighting but for the landlord moving deftly around and good-naturedly warning the angry ones they had 'come to sup ale, not fight,' and seeing to it their pots were kept filled. This was a rich harvest to be quickly garnered, for he may not get such company again for months, not until another match was made for the top o' the moors. Meanwhile, the landlady had sold all the meat pies, gotten specially for this match, along with the delicious Yorkshire Relish;

indeed, with a clamorous demand still going on, she had perforce to fall back on her home-baked bread, and cheese, and pickled onions (of the sliced variety), though these soon petered out, following the pies in the great maw of hunger caused by talking, and supping, and having travelled varying distances in the keen, fresh air.

On a passage where it was comparatively quiet, and to my utter amazement, were some chaps in a world of their own. One of them had a birdcage containing a tiny canary, and another was rubbing a squeaking cork briskly along an empty beer bottle. The idea was to get the canary to sing, and the longer it trilled, the better – though they were no lovers of music. It was the old craze to bet on something, anything, and they were busy at just that, betting if it sang, or not. In the short time I stayed and listened, though the cork man rubbed till the cork was literally red-hot, besides his language, I never heard one tiny cheep from the poor bird. Later in life, seeing lights outside a London theatre proclaiming 'Canaries Sometimes Sing!', my mind flew straight back to desolate Manywell Heights, and I chuckled, 'An' sometimes they don't, an' all.'

However, the hour of the main preoccupation approaching, the principals and officials and backers, in that order, eventually made their way out of the pub, and we mortals streamed after them across a road, along a lane, then away across rough moorland before arriving at a field of poor grass. Of course, we had to pay to go in the field, where we, firstly, watched a chap hammer a gallows-stand contraption into the soft earth. This wooden affair was about three feet high and suspended a string sling into which, when the match started, would be hung a small, white ball made of pot. These balls were called knurs and were capable of being struck great distances, this being the sole objective of the exercise.

Yet, first things first, for there was still a lot of arguing between players and referee and backers, all mixed up, so that we mere onlookers wondered what was going on until, at long last, the two main men began to show a willingness to be at it. One of these was a great hulking chap, seeming musclebound, the way he moved. He doffed his coat and stood in his shirtsleeves, though he still retained a thin red scarf around his neck and knotted neatly at the side. He flexed his great arm muscles and swore a lot, made plenty of bluster, and contrasted very strongly with his opponent. This gentleman was slighter; he doffed his coat in silence and carefully removed a silver double-chain from his waistcoat – a waistcoat from whose pockets he also took two fat silver watches, handed these to the loving care of his chief henchman, ever at his side, and was handed a striking-stick in exchange. I couldn't help noticing how thick the quiet man's wrists were as he delicately balanced the stick in his hands, making certain of a grip that seemed like a clasp of steel.

Both men went through preliminary swishing and smashing of sticks and, after that, signified they were ready to start – to which we spectators uttered a barely audible, 'Thank God for that!'

There was one paramount rule to which I soon cottoned on: that whilst they may address the stringed ball a dozen times without penalty, once they touched it, even if it only fell from the string, that counted as one strike. I cannot now recall whether they took turn by turn, or so many strikes a piece; but on the ball being struck squarely from the string by the long, clubbed-end stick, the little knur soared out across the field. Its flight was followed by the keen eyes of the hitters, watched anxiously and with anguished faces by the backers – bands of gallant mates who had scraped the side stakes together in solid proof of faith in their champion. The mere laymen, same as myself, watched almost as anxiously, for by now we were partisan, and I was plumping for the little man – a fatal sentimentalism that had proved costly throughout life! To be sure, others watched just as interested as we at the top end of the field; these were men paid to mark the fall of each ball and stand by it until it was measured, or given up as a bad strike. This duty called for men with sharp eyes, and sharper tongues, to dissuade less righteous men from entertaining ideas about accidentally treading a good ball into the soft earth so that it was lost, or kicking a friend's knur a little farther along the field.

Whilst all this was going on – exciting enough in itself, I had thought – a splinter group had broken away and was engrossed in a game of pitch-and-toss, up in a corner where the wall was high, but not too high that a compatriot could not look over, and out, to the far away road, perchance the law decided to see how the knur game was faring. The village bobby got far on a cycle, even in those days.

Meanwhile, the big chap – flaysome in manner and language, as I well knew when I had the misfortune to get near his backhand (not too near, but enough to earn me a foul oath and a threat, and sufficient to quell me and make me step back a couple of paces) – was fiercer, getting more angry every strike he made. He had started well, but now the other was steadily overhauling him. The latter was striking consistently well, and getting a longer ball with every hit, whilst the big man was losing his rhythm, and temper, and getting anxious. He kept running forward following on his every strike, gesticulating fiercely and exhorting his wee ball to greater height in its swift passage through the air, and cursing at his ill success.

It was obvious to all that the big man was proving his own enemy for, in his anger, his former skill had fled – and the other's deadly quiet was now telling its tale. Vainly, Loudmouth tried to draw the quiet man to angry retort and indiscretion but, with face of stone (and it was said he was a quarryman!), this worthy kept on plopping his knurs ever further across the field.

At the finish it was a petty, purposeless demanding, on the big man's part, to have the best strikes measured with a long chain, for it was obvious to all of us, and to many of his own men, that he was yards behind. Yet when the referee, as a mere formality, declared for the quarryman, the big chap started shouting the odds about being 'twisted', whilst the other said not a word – nor need he, for a rumour, running round the field faster than sparks in dry grass, had it he and his backers had won the best part of a hundred pounds. This was quite feasible when one noted how closely his pals stuck to the winner as the match finished. Carefully, with a suspicion of a smile on his face, the quiet one replaced his watches and chain and put on his outer coat. Then, with someone tearing out the gallows as the last act, everybody made their way out of the field: the jubilant and well satisfied, the despondent and disgruntled. I said 'everybody' left the field, but that was not strictly true, for the pitch-and-toss school were still engrossed in their game when we left.

We all made our way back again to the little pub, for the afternoon had got into early evening and, arrived there, the loud-mouthed unlucky one promptly started shouting the odds again – this time of how he would drink, run, jump, throw, or bare-fist his late opponent for any 'brass' he cared to put up; he pulled a fat, rolled wad of treasury notes from his tight pocket to add weight to his words, provocative and insulting. I was slightly disappointed when the other sat and ignored the bluster, refreshing himself with a glass of ale, then looking round to his pals to signify he was ready for going. He set off in a crowd of his fellows, in a variety of vehicles that sped away along the bounding road to Denholme and I knew not whence, leaving his fallen adversary almost crying into his beer, in his thwarted chagrin…

I gazed again at the photo, and took a long drink whilst the landlord was talking away. He was telling me, 'Willie used to come in here… He was a grand old chap… I only wished I'd seen him laik, but he was afoar my time, y'knaw.'

I smiled, in a superior sort of way, for I was still toying with the idea of Willie being that quiet chap in the only match I saw.

'Was Willie a quarryman!' I asked, everything seeming to hang on a favourable reply, though I asked carelessly.

'Ee, I wouldn't rightly knaw… I had heard he worked in a dyeworks on Buttershaw way,' the landlord replied. 'Though, mind, he could have been a quarryman afoar he got an inside job in his later days… He might have been, quite easy.'

I nodded, slightly deflated, though I was still of a mind to believe Willie was a one-time quarryman and the hero of an afternoon. He could have been, so easily, I concluded in my own mind's eye.

PUDDLING AND PLAYING

After some twelve months of quiet, decent living, and having passed my sixteenth birthday, I became aware that the old bird of ill omen, thought flown far away for good, was again squatting on a shoulder, and the local word 'playing' – meaning 'not working' – about to become a regular addition to my limited vocabulary. I was still working at the mill and now exalted to a jobber-lad's position; that is, until a well-meaning neighbour, whose son worked at a colliery out Dudley Hill way, started to improve my lot. She suggested that I go along with her son (much, much older than me) and try to get a job in the pit; it would pay a lot more money, and going with her lad might just get me in.

As we went along next day to his afternoon shift, the son primed me to tell the under-manager I had worked 'down' before. There was nothing to the work, he earnestly assured me: 'You just push empty an' full tubs from the face to t'main road… There's nowt to it, kid.' And so well did he sell the idea of working down a pit that I was all for it; I got myself a job within three minutes of seeing the manager and was down the pit in another five, for I had gone geared up for just such an eventuality. Had I been anything but a gawky, impressionable lad, this eagerness to set me on should have made me smell a large rat, but I believed my new-found friend, for had he not told me there was nothing to it?

I suppose I should add: the least said, the better about my colliery experiences – short and with never a monotonous moment – for I did not set the pit on fire. However, it was soon borne on me that my mentor had done myself, and the colliers, a cruel wrong; for I was thrown in from the deep end, serving two lusty 'hewers', moving tubs in and out along a rough, narrow 'road' where most times I had to bend almost in two. And this with a lamp slung from my neck, that left most of the roof to be guessed at, to be judged by hitting of head and scraping of back and – final catastrophe – the lamp falling and going out, and me sobbing out of sheer helpless rage at my inadequacy. All this was to suffer a refinement of cruelty I would not have wished upon my worst enemy, let alone a lad from my own street.

I would also like to put on record how well the two colliers I waited upon (a nice contradiction) stuck me through a very long shift and, when we came up in the cool of a late summer evening, expressed the hope that a night's rest might, by some overnight miracle, improve my performance. They waxed a little sarcastic, as we crossed the fields to the trams, about my having told of being 'down' before; and, altogether, I began to realise I had made a first-class blunder.

Midway through the next day's shift, I was still stiff and sore, though somewhat loosened up by dint of much sweating. The manager came across me in his daily rounds, eyed my inexpert fumbling with a tub, and buttonholed me with, 'I thought you told me you'd been down before?'

'We-ell…' I began lamely, then decided on a silence and a spreading of my hands in tired resignation.

'You're a bloody fool, lad… You could have lamed yourself, besides wasting your mates' time and money, waiting on you all shift.' He didn't speak unkindly. Then he added, 'Anyway, I can't do with you here, so you must find another job when you get up.'

The next day I went humbly, cap in hand, back to the mill, but Bert's heart was hardened against me.

'No,' he told me. 'Your job's filled… No, I've nowt.'

I turned away disheartened and a little hurt, for I had always thought Bert had a soft spot for me. Yet I was a big lad now, and had fancied myself in a man's world; I should be prepared to be treated like a man.

***

As things went, from then on, I was fortunate to get even casual employment, and that of a poor kind. I worked several times with gangs of men limewashing mills and factories, and I was the one who stirred the blue in a vast tub of limewash, filled and carried the pails, brewed tea, brought fish and chips, did a dozen and one other small jobs tied up with the whitening of mills. The only trouble with that occupation: it only ran in bursts of a few days, then we went our own ways until the gaffer got another limewashing and had the grapevine summon us together again.

Twice I got jobs at petrol depots – Pratt's on the one hand, Shell on the other – painting their two-gallon tins afresh. This was a stinking job, poorly paid; and after only a few days in one, a couple of weeks in the other, I was out, and rid of the fear I might go up in spontaneous combustion if I stayed long. I might have got a job as a tram-lad, helping with parcels, but the wage was beggarly, not even sufficient to pay the very small board money asked of me. I tried hard to give Mrs Holmes something every week, but many times I failed, though she never behaved shabbily to me, for which I was always thankful.

To say I was wretched would be a gross understatement, and it was at this time that Dad again entered my life. He was in lodgings (to put a decent label on his mode of living) not far removed from where I lived and I, perforce, bumped into him at times. One day, catching me at my lowest, when there wasn't even one casual job in the bag, or the offing, he talked me into going to live with him. Though Mrs Holmes tried hard to stop me from going, I went along, jumping from the frying pan of misery – more mental than otherwise – into the fire of real physical wretchedness, and possibly worse than before.

To add to the total sum of depression, it was also winter – a bad time for 'playing', with its monotonous walking futilely after jobs that were not there, or spending an hour round town, or in the open market, generally keeping one's eyes on the situation, though what situation was pretty vague. And, of course, there were the regular attendances at the Labour Exchange – the juvenile one, in my case, not so busy as the senior one – yet not able to find work for those who did go, especially the ones like me who wanted a man's job or, at least, more brass than was the usual for lads.

It was a comfort to seek the shelter of a nearby mission hall whose people had realised the vast amount of time we 'out of works' had on our hands, and bade us spend some of it in their place. This hall was an oasis of dry warmth in grey mud – a mud of futility and drift that always threatened to engulf most of the unemployed who, without ever one word of thanks, availed themselves of the voluntary hospitality. The mission itself was there to afford Christian comfort of a nonconformist nature to its regular band of hardy worshippers; the basement room it was they put aside for us folks, and it was open every weekday afternoon. It housed a bagatelle table; there were also draughts, ring-boards, ludo sets, and old magazines, but these engendered not much faith, and very little hope, among us receivers of the mission's gracious charity. There were several texts on a distempered wall; one, I recall, ran 'Look Up!' – which command one wit, a seasoned campaigner, dismissed with, 'Ugh! An' trip ovver all them tab-ends under me feet? No ruddy fear!'

This refuge/club was looked after by an old man who, oddly enough, we lot resented as a nosey old so-and-so, though his many probings and quizzes were undoubtedly harmless. Truth to tell, past lives in our shabby district were naught to be boasted about; had the devil cast his net in that room of an afternoon he would have thrown back many a poor, small fish as already his own, docketed and tail-marked, or entered in his infernal diary as a future good prospect. There were some who thought of a better life – a few, very few, had known it – but mostly all were prepared to accept this seemingly permanent lazy life as their lot; they even argued it was up to others to improve it, for they had developed a world-owes-me-a-living complex. It was here I now lounged; it was here I heard of yet another job going. As usual it was not much, for it mixed short spells of working with long spells of 'playing', and there were so many already at the mission hall who 'played' with monotonous regularity, thumping the bagatelle balls round the small table whilst idly awaiting their tardy employers' pleasure. They were playing in every way, every day, and sometimes sorry when the call came, for they had learned to live on short commons.

***

The tip I got took me out to Low Moor Ironworks, and into the forge. It was an old business, looking very run-down, but 'Low Moor Iron' had been a byword in the nineteenth century amongst bridge and railway builders. When I first saw it, one raw November morning, the whole plant looked like a derelict lot – and small wonder, for one hot day in the summer of 1916 it was blown almost into the sky by a mystery explosion. It was a munitions factory and forge during that war, and when it went up, many brave people perished[18]. Ever after, the forge wore a desultory air, even though it did keep doing some work with tackle that looked like it might have been new in the Napoleonic Wars. Now, it is given over to something else, the old name 'Low Moor Ironworks' having gone forever.

When I got my job, it was as a 'puddler's lad', 'puddling' being the name given to the job of melting iron ore so that it could be hammered into sizeable billets, ready for waiting rolling mills. We worked in a vast open shed housing about six brick-built furnace-kilns, each manned by a team of three. First, and most important – a very despot! – was the puddler, the man responsible for the successful turning-out of the heats, as each charging of the kiln was called. Obviously, he was expert, had spent his work life on the art of bringing the raw metal to the required doughiness, then fashioning it into balls inside the furnace before having it taken to a huge steam drop-hammer. Second was his mate – in our case, a young man given to great oaths and loud talk of

18 The Low Moor Explosion was a fire and a series of explosions at a munitions factory close to the Low Moor Iron Works in August 1916, resulting in the death of 40 people and 60 seriously injured.

beer-supping and woman-wooing, though how he could manage his feats on the few shifts we worked, only he could know.

Lastly, very much at the back, was the lad: me. My job covered a lot of territory in its small, humble fulfilling, very important being the keeping-going of the fire. I also cast earthy, jagged pieces of ore into a warming side-oven, the while a heat seethed in the main furnace, a heat much like a big dumpling forming in white-hot stew until such time as the two men would prod, push, and pull the mass into about six smaller dumplings. Between times I would go down, almost under the kiln, to shake the firebars free from clinker that very quickly collected and threatened to congeal into masses of deadening slag if not attended regularly. Need I say how hellish hot it was! Down there, I also had to clear the ashes a couple of times every shift – more if my opposite number on the preceding one had dodged his work. Also, on some shifts, the puddler might call for some fireclay, and I would barrow a great dollop onto the hearth, handy so the puddler could place it (with the aid of a long rod) pat on some crumbling brick inside the white-hot hell. I can never remember the puddler's name, though his mate's was Alf. I do know he was a very crabby sort of chap, and when things got sticky, sometime in every shift, he would raise merry hell with Alf and me; and Alf, in his turn, would bawl me out with a venom that startled me at first. I, in my turn, could but play Hamlet amongst the shovels and bars, have Alf shout of my being 'a noisy twat', have me wishing the years of my coming manhood were already on me, so I might answer him back.

Yet there was one youth whom I did like. He spoke with a very pronounced Low Moor accent, ludicrous on first hearing, and he had something to cover every happening. He it was who told me, when I put my first tea-bottle atop the kiln to warm up, 'Oww… Lowssen yond cork a bit, mate, or y'll all get pissed-through when it busts.' He spoke of my gaffer as 'Allus hevving the cah-heead on,' and said Alf 'was sem as a man med o' Fuller's earth,' which pleased me immensely; I liked the work a lot better because of chaps like him.

It was satisfying work; we had some tangible end product to show at the end of each shift. It was hard, but had there been more of it, I might easily have made a puddler, some day. There was also a difficulty in getting there, mainly owing to the shifts we worked, which alternated over three different time periods. On two of the shifts, I was obliged to walk at least one way, and that for a distance of three miles. It was a custom for a puddler who would normally have finished work at six in the morning to bank the fires and leave at about five – which meant I had to walk home from that shift, for trams did not start running so early in the morning. Conversely, we were expected, when relieving that shift, to be on the job at about half-five to get cracking at once, so I must leave home at four-thirty when, again, there was no transport. Manchester Road always seemed very wide, very bare, very long when I tramped along, with a last lap enlivened by fitful flashes from the live slag heaps, as the keen morning wind coaxed hidden fires back to life; with, at the very end, the dim electric lamps that lit the shed, and the furnaces taking a brief nap between shifts. Perhaps it was a mixed blessing that we did not have to do too much of this walking, not with us working a few shifts, then hearing again the old depressing tale from the foreman: 'Sign on agen in t'morning, lads… Ah'll let you all knaw when thur is owt… T'usual, keep yer eyes on t' *Telegraph an' Argus*.'

We might play a week, maybe more, before reading the terse, stop-press message telling us to start again. Meantime, we were back at the old game. It might run to a couple of afternoon pictures whilst I had a shilling or two, but most times it meant lounging into the mission and seeing, always seeing, the same faces again… the same faces you bumped into all over town… and most certainly in the public library where one dropped in for an hour to look at the morning papers. Funny thing about the library was, the librarian always cut the racing page out, for it was considered to breed idleness, nay criminality, for folks to be interested in the sport of kings – as though a threepenny accumulator was going to make or break, or drive a chap to crime.

One bright playing day, and maybe because we could smell spring, even in Manchester Road, a pal and I set out for Ilkley Moors, bussing there to walk back to Shipley Glen. We set off as we were, without any raincoats, for these were refinements of dress, by our standards. We were still on top of the moors, three miles short of our first objective, Shipley Glen, when drizzling rain and a mist caught up with us. For a long time we pushed on in a bleak world of outcropping rock and soggy bogs, peopled only by inquisitive sheep and us two very wet youths. Afterwards, in the dry of the mission, we could chuckle over this – especially when, to paraphrase the old Yorkshire song, we discovered we had been 'on Ilkley Moor baht coits' – though we didn't laugh then!

It was incidents like that which made life tolerable until one got back to the balm of work. I was always happy to be treading the puddler's hearth again; to be tossing the rough lumps into the side-oven with youthful celerity; to be down below, shaking the bars with renewed vigour. I felt a grown man when we were all about our jobs again, the while the metal was softening and being fashioned into the smaller balls, and I took surreptitious swigs at my warming tea. I would, in my few spare moments, also watch my mates at work; they would spend the best part of an hour pushing, pulling, kneading the slowly yielding mass with a battery of bars and prods, and all done through a little hole about four inches square. As the time approached to take the balls (the dumplings) out, I would come into the picture. I steadied a wheeled cradle whilst the two men, with the aid of tong-shaped irons, quickly and neatly extricated a ball from the inferno when I, with one hand, swiftly pulled on a chain to lift the furnace front door.

With all speed the white-hot dumpling was plopped carefully on my cradle; meanwhile, having dropped the door again and with a quickening sense of urgency hot at my backside, I sped away with my glowing load to the nearest drop-hammer. The man behind the hammer seemed a giant in his ragged, spark-burned shirt, leather apron, goggles, and with a huge tin shoe fastened on the foot that advanced nearest the cooling billet dumped from my cradle. He held a forked bar, much as though he was going to toss hay, whilst another being, in the shadows, eased the steam hammer up and down its guideways, as though sizing up the job. Then the serious business began: the hammer would pin the billet with a jarring thud, then start to pummel; sparks would explode and fly, the jarring shake the earth, but they did not stop the giant in apron contemptuously tossing the metal this way and that until it lay conquered, pulverised into a rough rectangle. Then, and only then, the hammer would slow down to a full stop, and comparative peace.

At this stage there was a youth, much to be envied, stood behind the hammer, on the alert to take the billet away. He picked it up with a pair of grips suspended from an overhead rail, and hurried it round to a rolling mill at the edge of the shed. Here, two men pulled it to and fro through diminishing rollers until the metal fairly screamed and squirmed, and snaked out into an ever-lengthening, ever-thinning strip. It wriggled plenty but never got out of the grip of the two men, who finally pulled it free of the rollers and left it to cool its ardour under the open sky.

From beginning to end, the whole business of puddling took hold of me. It fascinated, it was a chorus, mostly of discord, of jangle, of violence – Bang! Crash! Thud, thud, thud! – from everywhere in the shed, every few moments. And the constant hissing of steam escaping from leaky valves on the steam hammers; the sharp, angry shriek of almost red-hot bars thrown into cold water; the rough oaths, the smutty jokes shouted from hearth to hearth, the harsh coughs, the rawking to spit. It was also a portrait of many colours, more so during the night shifts. There were the dull glows from strips cooling by the rolling mill; the white, shimmering heat from balls going to the hammers, the ensuing showers of sparks, the white curls of steam, the dim lights high up in the tin roof. Each hearth had its glimmer of light, with the sudden glowing and glare as furnace doors were sharply lifted to take the balls out, or load for another heat. Outside, in the long winter nights, stygian dark settled over the railway lines and the rusty trucks that brought life, and work, in the shape of ore, coal, coke, and fireclay to the monsters that ate fire. Many times, during the winter I was there, snow, soft and noiseless and very wet, insinuated itself under the edge of the shed, to live but a few seconds on this all too warm, welcoming hearth.

The men were a hard lot – a race apart from my former workmates, excepting my suffering mates I left in the pit. They were grim, not given to laughing easily, and men one wouldn't want to have bother with. They were not necessarily big men, but they were wiry, with arms of steel and the eyes of hawks as they peered through their peephole, judging to a nicety just how the pot was boiling. Mostly, they were spare men, all avoirdupois burned off in this continual struggle of pushing, and riving, and lifting those heavy balls from the fire. Obviously, they were rough of tongue, and rather lopsided in the bestowing of their affections, with pigeons and hen-runs first and their womenfolk a poor second when families were once started. They kept the women on pretty short shrift, as though the economic situation did not allow for anything soppy to titillate the female fancy. Primary consideration must be the worker, and the man had to have his bacca and his beer, choose what else went short – and most women accepted this with resignation, more so when the man worked in heavy industry. He was a hard man, the puddler, even to himself in physical things, as when he suffered any burn he would thrust the throbbing limb close to the terrific heat of the furnace wall, until he could hardly bear more, until he was satisfied the burn was drawn out; only then would he stand back with a wry grimace, a spit, and an oath.

They took their pleasures sadly, and had an earthy sense of humour. One spoke freely of a lady he called 'Ahr Paulina' – his wife, a lady who had got him to sign the pledge of temperance but, he chuckled, 'Ah got that wick i' bed wi' her, she begged me to start drinking agen… She did, an' all!' They talked of another puddler, before my time, who walked most every day he played around a local reservoir, in the hope of recovering some poor bloated body drifted to the steep, paved side. Ironically, he found his final rest after being washed to the same steep, paved side – which fate did not seem half so funny to me as it did to the chaps who retold the story so often – it was always good for a laugh.

Yet all this was not solving my economic problems, arisen every time I played; I was still living in Dad's lodge, still very much a duck out of water there, still happy to be at work away from it all. And that was just it: I wanted to be away from it all – oh, miles away! Yet I was frustrated at every turn. For months past I had longed to be a soldier; the posters that beckoned 'Join the Army and See the World' had twice drawn me to recruiting offices in Leeds and Bradford, and each time they had turned me down because they suspected my youth and asked to see my birth certificate.

Then, one April morning – and what better time of the year to start life anew? – I set off on another hopeful trudge on Shanks's pony, this time to Halifax Barracks. Ever an optimist, I was spurred on by the old adage 'third time lucky', and warmed with ill-concealed joy when the recruiting sergeant (bless his red sash!) turned a Nelson eye to my youthful, downy cheeks. At parting, he pressed my palm with a few small silver coins and sped me on my way to the threshold of a new life, namely the barracks at fair Pontefract.

So I exchanged a hearth for a world; apathy for hope; and, lastly, plodding instead of playing – plodding along as a happy, keen infantry soldier, responding sharply to a drill-sergeant's shrill of 'Look up, Tempest… You'll find no tab-ends here… Look up!' and muttering through my pursed lips, 'Hmm… I've heard that somewhere else – afoar!'

CHAPTER FIVE

PILGRIMAGE TO HAWORTH

It's a long time since I first went to Haworth, way back in the autumn of 1924; and it was not to pay homage to the famous sisters, for my literary likings had not then aimed higher than Nat Gould, Sexton Blake, or a good Buffalo Bill, all to be had in popular limp-backed fourpennies. Nevertheless, it *was* a lady I sought, for I had gone to pay courtship to a sweet lass of seventeen who came from nearby Stanbury, a neighbouring village standing somewhat in the shadow of more glamourised Haworth.

Cupid had winged me two weeks before, when I was on a weekend leave from my recruits' training at Pontefract; and, of all places, he had winged me on a roundabout in a fair in Bradford. As we whirled round, my eyes had been attracted to a gaily laughing girl, so fresh, so genuinely happy, oohing and aahing with another girl astride two bright-coloured animals cavorting up and down in their circuits. Then our eyes had met across the noisy, garish roundabout; the thing had eventually stopped, and I had managed to step into a strategic position to meet her full-face. She didn't spurn me, and we talked inconsequentially, and I was then allowed to walk with them partway home to her friend's, with whom she was staying the night. I had gotten her address, had exchanged a couple of letters and, as a result of that roundabout ride and the wangling of another weekend leave, here was I hurrying from a fussy little train on Haworth station and there was she, smiling so demurely from a bridge beyond the station.

It seemed the world, and Haworth stood still whilst we clasped hands on the narrow planked bridge over the railway lines, with the sun, hot and friendly, beaming his approval that Saturday afternoon. We stood there smiling, but saying precious little until I broke the blissful fragment of time held still with 'Hey! Are you hungry?' and she replied, 'Ee, yes… And I know a nice shop up the High Street,' and we were galvanised back into ordinary life, hungry young animals that we were.

We chattered and chuckled all the way up a rough hillside, where now stands the park, then along up the main street, and then into one of the cafés – which is still there, and graced with the very unoriginal name Brontë Café. I grandly ordered a knife-and-fork tea, for we wanted none of your mucking about with fancy knife and squashy cream cakes, but a slap-up do of eggs and chips and lashings of bread and best butter, with buns and a pot, twice filled, to follow.

This was a feast for the gods, with me looking into the clear, merry eyes of a goddess, no less – that is, in between the more earthy sessions of attending to my own inner needs, and marking the undoubted fact, not to be blinded by the dust of enchantment, that my lady was a good trencherwoman, comparing favourably with my not inconsiderable intake, for which I liked her all the more.

We sat awhile, eating finished, drinking our tea and talking of our families – leastways, she did, for I didn't want to spoil things by spilling out my woeful history, not yet awhile. And then we got on deciding what to do, where to go next, and she thought it would round things off to see the first-turn pictures across the bottom of the village, with which suggestion I readily fell in. It was a silent, of course, and the main picture starred Mary Pickford, the world's sweetheart, and that was right up our street with its old theme of Mary, a poor little orphan

Annie, ending up happy ever after. When we blinked our way out, after some two hours of hand-holding, it was to learn that Cinderella, in the comely shape of my companion, must fly back now along the rolling road through Haworth, for young 'uns were not encouraged to keep late hours. Also, it was my clear duty to see she did get homing, and this liaison unsuspected, for casual boyfriends were not taken into the bosom of a family on the strength of a fortnight's acquaintance; and love, especially young love, was very much frowned upon. Her parents would probably have thrown a fit had they known their daughter was 'seeing' a young man, and a soldier to boot, picked up on a roundabout in Bradford. My! That girl would have had to do some staying-in as a mark of penance, had they found out.

However, we breasted that first hill again, were attracted into a gaily lit fish and chip shop, and suppered off papers of the hot, appetising fare whilst walking, seemingly on air, through darkened Haworth. Then we were racing along the switchback road to her village, with the world again at our feet and the evening a black velvet cloak around us, conspiratorial, hinting, though time was running out fast against us. Then we had reached a deadline, under a lamp out on the bare, deserted road, and my girl was insisting we *must* part, for fear we bumped into folks who would know her and might carry fearful tales to her home on the morrow. Here it was we were to make our farewells... and – plucking up courage, for I was fundamentally shy – I kissed her like a real man, and ever so gently, considering the clumsy lad I was. And she responded! Yes, she kissed me back... Shyly, I admit, but nonetheless willing and deliberate, and I was absolutely bewitched. It was all so boy-and-girl innocent, as though the Lord Himself was with us on that lonely road, that wonder night. Then she moved and whispered, 'Goodnight!' and we were hurrying apart – or rather, she was hurrying away and I stood gazing after her figure disappearing into the dark; stood until all that remained was the noise of her shoes pattering along the hard road. And, somehow, it all seemed so significant – for I was never to kiss her again, because that was the last time I saw her.

It was a long, hot dashing-back to Haworth station, but I could have saved myself the trouble, for I cooled my heels the best part of one hour waiting on the small platform for a train that would take me to Keighley, and then another change before I got back to Bradford – and that was the beginning of the end to a romance that never really got started. It must have been that time-killing getting back to Bradford, and the sobering reflection of those Brontë hills, so hardily reached, plus a little jiggery-pokery on my part that came to her notice. Howbeit, after three or four letters during which the temperature of our passion dropped rapidly, we ceased writing, and that was the end of the affair, short, sweet, and lovely.

Since then, I have been on pilgrimage to Haworth many times to pay homage to the sisters but, of course, with never the same wand-of-youth spirit as on the day I went courting there. Sometimes, when memories crowd, I wonder whether my fair lady, who may now be a gracious granny, ever does recall that Saturday afternoon idyll of so long ago – when two artless seventeen-year-olds clasped hands in joyous greeting on that wooden bridge, whilst the world and Haworth stood still?

TALKING THEATRE

The first time we marched through town, catching a glimpse of a battlemented fairy castle perched on top of a densely wooded hillside, our reactions were along the lines of 'Hell! Have we to march up there? Christ!'. But it was a good billet, and Dover a good garrison town. The folks were good to us squaddies, the pubs were homely, there was a grand music hall, and there were many good-looking girls about. It was an epoch-making couple of years I spent there: Gertrude Ederle[19], watched through glasses from our eyrie on the cliffs, a small speck inching her way to England to be the first girl to swim the Channel; and the General Strike of 1926, with our platoon on duty on the breakwater. What I should have done with my seventy rounds of live ammo, had the idle miners from nearby Betteshangar turned nasty, is anybody's guess. Then, it didn't bide thinking!

The music hall, the Hippodrome, was on a short back street that paralleled the seafront. It was here I saw that grand mystery thriller *The Ghost Train.* It was here, also, I took a quick glance at a paper a pal of mine had brought into the first house. It was the gee-gees I was really after, but my attention was drawn to a headline stating that a lone American had flown across the Atlantic; it had been flown before, but never solo, nor in such a small plane. The year was 1927, and the man's name was Charles Lindbergh. That certainly created a sensation, and brought to mind that it was in a meadow backing Dover Castle where Bleriot, an intrepid French flyer, crash-landed his frail craft after his historic flight, so long before, across the formidable English Channel. This spot is now marked by a concreted outline of

19 Gertrude Ederle became the first woman to swim across the English Channel on 6th August 1926.

a very small plane, with a tablet to record the details, and wandering sheep to quietly nibble and crop the grass close around this pastoral, mostly forgotten, setting.

With us soldiery in the Dover garrison, the Hippodrome was a weekly must; that, and eggs and chips (or char-and-wads at the Soldiers' Home if things were a bit nipped, financially), plus a few gills to follow the first-turn Hippodrome. Then, quite happy, we'd tackle the steep hill back to the castle that perched so picturesque atop the cliffs.

The theatre catered for two different kinds of entertainment. First, and favourites, were the variety turns: the comedians, the acrobats, conjurers, the speciality wallahs, all of whom were the life, the meat-filling, of the live theatre. Here, I saw a hero of my first films: one Pimple, a comedian of high standing on the first silents. He was appearing with a band who were cashing in on his former greatness, but he was not the same Pimple at all. I fair ached for him as he strove to get laughs with his comic band, failing lamentably – and that was the end for poor Pimple, for he never made that comeback and dropped right out of the picture, as it were. Second, there were the revues, hodge-podges of noise and song and dancing all rolled into one, with bags of 'leg and tit' from the half-dozen bonny lasses of the chorus – whom, at that day, I'd have given a week's pay to date, for they looked so desirable from where I sat at the back of the hall.

I nearly did date one of these young ladies once, one grand summer's afternoon, when our platoon was on an official bathing parade on Dover's pebbly beach. When we got down there, we were delighted to see, on the shingle adjoining our strip of beach – strictly 'for troops only' – a group of young females, laughing and shouting, and whom we readily recognised as forming the chorus from the current show at the Hippodrome. So four or five of us, happily including the corporal in charge, quickly got to work making the girls' acquaintance. I made a beeline for a tall, leggy girl who had taken my eye on the Monday night as she went through her stage paces with flashing eyes, and smile to match, and a figure that was oh, so divine in an abbreviated series of costumes. But disenchantment followed quickly when I was privileged a closer, more personal view. She had a hard Cockney twang I had already encountered on the steps of the Union Jack Club, in London's Waterloo Road, and an even harder pair of eyes that surveyed me with a cool, mercenary evaluation and finally, guessing rightly at my financial low waters, found me short change. Also, she looked much older face to face, and it took weeks of succeeding waves of chorus girls to wash out that latter, unfavourable impression.

There were a couple of leave visits to the London Coliseum; once, Anna Pavlova graced the vast stage with a young man called Anton Dolin, and she also danced by herself in 'The Dying Swan'. I wish I had been older, for I think it would have meant more to me later; I was only nineteen then, and ballet something to be sniggered at amongst us troops, yet I sensed it was great – and I did see Pavlova dance. And there was GH Elliott, 'The Chocolate Coloured Coon',[20] the debonair joy of everybody, whom I was to see again a full thirty years later at Halifax's Palace, though this time he had a young lady on with him, on whom he leaned when he had finished. I saw Layton and Johnstone, Debroy Somers and His Band, and a good-looking girl called Aileen Stanley, 'America's Gramophone Queen', though I never heard of her again. And *The Desert Song* at Drury Lane on my last leave before India, with Edith Day and Harry Welchman and the rousing songs of the legionaries and the riffs to send me on my long voyage. These I heard again and again on many a long, dusty mile of North-West Frontier Road and plain; these, and Harry Lauder's immortal 'Keep Right On to the End of the Road', did wonders to many a weary, sweaty-arsed infantryman after a long day on the march or in the field. Gosh! – that stirring music when the band tagged on the front, making warriors of weary soldiers during that last terrible hour back into camp. It was especially magic stuff to ears like mine, with a little personal remembrance to back it up.

20 GH Elliott was a Lancastrian music-hall singer and dancer who performed in brown-face make-up. At the time, this was seen as a respectable form of entertainment, though it later came to be regarded as unacceptable.

Many years later, there was the Crazy Gang at the Palladium, and the terrific fuss they made of a guester called Harry Champion, an old-time Cockney comedian. That was it, I said to myself: 'They'd laugh at aught down here… Him and his "Any Old Iron"… Ugh!' – and I wasn't by myself, as I found out a couple of evenings later at Hyde Park Corner, where a fierce, hungry-looking Scot with fire (and class hate) in his belly was declaiming, 'Some of ye gyuid folks wad reyther go wi'oot a meal to see a show or a Royal procession.' But I wasn't with him all the way, for a little glitter was always impressive to me. I was a glutton for it, if the truth was known! – that and the rags-to-riches so tied up with showbusiness. And it is with a glow I say that I saw Morecambe and Wise as young lads appearing as solo turns in a show Brian Michie, late of the BBC, was taking around the provinces. It was called 'Youth Takes A Bow' and was on at Bradford's Alhambra in the early days of the last war. They were both brought onto the stage by Michie, who told us, in so many words, 'These two, they're only boys. Well, they've begged me to let them have five minutes in a double comedy act they've been cooking up off-stage. So, with your kind indulgence, ladies and gentlemen, I introduce for the first time anywhere: Morecambe and Wise!' There was also a good-looking girl, Celia Lipton, on the same bill. She was the daughter of dapper Sidney Lipton, famed dance-band leader, but I believe she married well and dropped out of showbusiness.

Lastly, to an incident that happened to a certain Church Ladies' Guild, not ten miles from Halifax. They had arranged an evening's outing in Leeds, which was to consist of a good meal and a theatre after. Well, whether the title sounded highfalutin, something better-off, or whether they left it all to the secretary is not clear; what is clear is that they found themselves shocked to their righteous cores when the full import of the Greek comedy *Lysistrata*[21] was borne home to them but, like true British matrons, allowed not a muscle to slip

21 Aristophanes' comedy *Lysistrata* concerns a group of women who withhold sex from their husbands in an attempt to persuade them to end the Peloponnesian War.

conveying their mixed emotions. It afforded them a huge laugh in the coach later, though there was a tacit understanding not to noise it abroad.

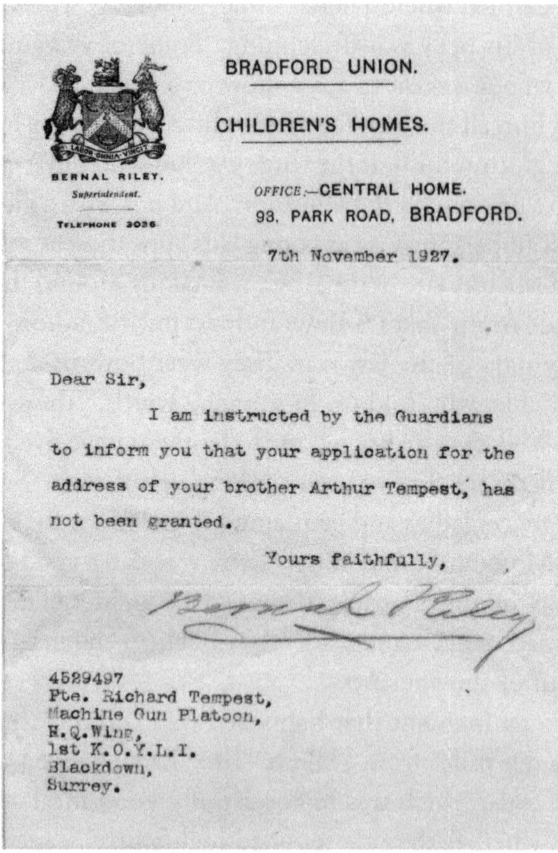

LABOR OMNIA VINCIT

BERNAL RILEY.
Superintendent.

TELEPHONE 2036

BRADFORD UNION.

CHILDREN'S HOMES.

OFFICE:—CENTRAL HOME.
93, PARK ROAD, BRADFORD.

7th November 1927.

Dear Sir,

I am instructed by the Guardians to inform you that your application for the address of your brother Arthur Tempest, has not been granted.

Yours faithfully,

Bernal Riley

4529497
Pte. Richard Tempest,
Machine Gun Platoon,
H.Q.Wing,
1st K.O.Y.L.I.
Blackdown,
Surrey.

BLESS 'EM ALL!

It was January '28 when I put my name forward for service in India, outraging – significantly, as it turned out – an unwritten army law that said 'never volunteer for anything'. At once, I wrote to the children's home people in Bradford, pleading that, in view of the fact I was going abroad for at least three years, they let me have the address of my younger brother Arthur, now gone from our ken some considerable time.

For two years or more, whilst I soldiered in the south of England, my other brother, Bill, had been working and had eventually been 'boarded out' from the home where he and Arthur had gone in the first place. At one time Arthur had been removed to another home, though still in Bradford, then suddenly he was moved again right out of it, and we lost sight of him. No amount of grapevining yielded any information – not even from a certain Mrs Knowles, matron at the original home, who had known Dad as a child. She would not (or could not) say where Arthur was, not even to Bill, for whom she had a high regard; and so the matter rested, with Arthur given up for lost for the time being. Then, when I got drafted, I thought that was the ripe moment to ask officially about my brother – surely they would heed my plea? But they did not; about a week after my application, I got a reply telling me the committee could not let me know where he was, and with no reason given.

When my embarkation leave came along, I spent a fortnight in Bradford trying to get to know something of Arthur, but I was hitting my head against a brick wall. I even paid a personal visit to the home, but I got exactly nowhere and, finally disheartened, I bade my adieus of Bill – now out of work, just to make matters more dismal. He had lately returned from London after a fruitless stay – a sojourn taken under Dad's wing (the one he had always promised Bill). But the lad's prospects, or education, had not been improved during the few weeks he had spent in the Borough and hanging around Billingsgate early every morning to earn a few coppers portering goods up that world-famous narrow, steep thoroughfare; and Bill had come back to Bradford slightly disillusioned. I said goodbye to Edie, now a bonny redhead and happily working with a friend, though little did I guess I was seeing her for the last time. I also had a week in London, staying at the Union Jack Club over Waterloo Bridge – that is, until my funds ran out, when I went back to barracks at Blackdown (which could more appropriately have been called Bleaktown), and awaited, impatiently, the call to India, and my first peep at the wonderful world beyond England.

The call came in early March, and the big troopship was three weeks and two days sailing from drab Southampton to noisy Karachi, by way of the Suez Canal. Then it was another couple of days across the country by slow-moving train to Peshawar on the North-West Frontier. I liked the place at once, and could truthfully say it almost broke my heart when I left it the way I did.

To say I loved every minute in India would be an exaggeration, for we soldiers always moaned about what we had left back in dear old Blighty – though my moans were somewhat muted compared to those of my comrades. Yet we felt it was our privilege to moan, and took full advantage of this safety valve. But it was a full life, where no man need ever die of boredom. There were alarums and scares in this savage world of ours where we attended Divine Service with rifle and bayonet, ten rounds of live ammo in our leather pouches, and the rifle fitted discreetly into a bracket on the pew fronting, next to a prayer book. No one could be quite sure of the sleeping beast in this corner of empire. These sleeping beasts took the shape of illiterate hill tribesmen who could not read our 'Keep Off The Grass' notices; who had an unhealthy disregard for the sanctity of property; who sporadically woke to life, at their own convenience – certainly not ours – and came scrounging in no mean fashion. They would sidle down, in the dark, right up to the five-foot-thick snarl of barbed wire, which shut tight like a trap every dusk, and they would sit and hope to creep under it when one of our numerous 'wire patrols' had just passed.

These chaps we termed 'loosewallahs', individuals who would try to get into barrack rooms in the dead of night, stripped of all clothing and covered in grease, and hoping to pinch firearms. They were very brave, fanatical men, for an alarm meant death, and they had to get past soldiers sleeping across every open doorway in hot weather, with rifles locked in racks, and Lewis guns, and ammo boxes slept on in the centre of each room. And yet these ruffians did get away with it at times, with our lads none the wiser until they woke to the grey of a day that meant severe punishment for their laxity, choose how they pleaded.

The first thing I remember seeing of Peshawar was from the train, and was a vast earthworks fort, Bala Hissar, that stood between, and frowned upon, the native city and the European cantonment. This awesome battlement was manned by us infantry in fortnightly spells of duty, and there I went, several times. It was there I was introduced to Edgar Wallace's literature, and there I spent many happy, carefree hours with a pal, drop-kicking a rugby ball in a clearing outside our barrack block. I spent many less strenuous ones in the MI room, along with the medical orderly and a few chosen cronies, helping lower the contents of a pail of beer – this kept topped up with a couple of bread rolls thrown into the precious liquid – playing cards, or enjoying a musical soirée. This was provided by a gramophone that was probably the daddy of all portables, which was lent us by a Lieutenant Rowlandson, who had lately joined us from the UK for twelve months' preliminary training before joining his permanent regiment, one of the Native Frontier Force. He had a grand selection of records, though favourite with me was one of the music from the then current Drury Lane production

Show Boat; I especially liked the side where the sonorous voice of Paul Robeson sang the haunting 'Ole Man River'. These were grand sessions that made the fortnight's compulsory isolation less tedious; these, and the hours laid sprawled atop the highest emplacement, looking down and contemplating the hodge-podge of Peshawar City that lay at our feet, marvelling on this weird and wonderful sprawl that was our part of the guardianship of India.

The city had a mutty wall around it, and scores of mosques, minarets and towers standing out of a hopeless jumble of mutty, lath and wood, looking as though some giant had thrown them from the top of the fort at intervals in the city's progressions. There were so many signs of the city's religious beliefs because Peshawar housed some 800,000 souls, of all kinds and conditions, a seething cauldron of conflicting creeds and passions – Hindu and Muslim, Sikh and Parsee, Jat and Buddhist, hillsman and town beggar, dacoit and loosewallah[22] – with so many professing neither tribute nor loyalty to any, and Pakistan still a name to be conjured up by a jubilant minority. Peshawar: journey's end for nomads and caravans from Afghanistan, Samarkand, Tibet, sometimes from China, all resting a while under the great shadow of the fort; camels, humans, goods all slumped down together in one happy stinking heap in an enclosed stockade. Peshawar: gateway to the glamorised interior of Mother India, guardian against covetous eyes looking down from the far north, from away across the Hindukush Range, beyond half-civilised counties where near-anarchy and communism jostled along a common border, and kept an uneasy peace.

In the streets of the bazaars, the noisy crowds jammed almost to suffocation: the rich and poor, the holy and not-so, the trim gharrie[23] and the water buffalo heatedly disputing each other's right of way, and the native policeman trying to straighten things out in his own gently persuasive manner that might mean a bleeding head for some hapless slow-off-the-mark. There was also the Pathan down from the

22 Dacoit: a bandit; Loosewallah: an intruder.

23 A small carriage.

barren hills, wandering about the city like a proverbial country boy, bemused by much he saw; but this country boy would be tall, spare, his eyes hawk-keen, and always carrying his settler of all arguments, a rifle, carelessly slung over a shoulder. He was a man of few words, a lonely man, left very much to himself, for he was not to be trifled with. Quickly he would get himself provisioned and set off back to his mountain village with his donkey, and Lord knows what impending mischief thought up in his city stay. This mischief generally waited upon the hottest time of the year, our detachments strung out in the hill stations, malaria and other plagues starting up their annual torment and we military men at our lowest humour point as a consequence, and maybe prepared to let our bête noir get away with a little, if he would but let us alone.

There were times, however, when charming words of warning through our agents, and even money, did not count, and then the air force would be called upon to blast at hundreds of rocky caves, with the inmates going ever deeper, and the infantry being brought in to winkle them out, though this generally ended in chases from one hilltop to the next, with them apeing mountain goats whilst we ponderously toiled after them in vain, in an unfunny travesty of the old English game known as 'Can't Catch Me'.

There was another occasion, in this game of power politics, when we had King, or ex-King[24], Amanullah of Afghanistan in our midst at Pesh; this whilst he changed his linen in flight from his barbaric throne. He was evacuated through the kind office of our air force squadron, and it was a business that took several trips, on several days – for he had a very large entourage, with more than his fair share of women. This bore particularly hard on us rank and file, for a puritan spirit up on the Frontier denied us the pleasure of a brothel, as enjoyed by our comrades elsewhere, and the sight of so many women for one man didn't seem at all justice. We made vile cracks about it – unprintable ones, I'm afraid, though one went 'Wharralotowives… Wharraman!'.

24 King Amanullah went into exile in October 1929

Much more to our liking in this game of showing the flag were the ceremonial parades for the whole military district. I think we had two of these per year – for the king's birthday, and on New Year's Day – held on the huge airfield, across from our barracks. Everyone was on the job for these parades, excepting the planes; even the District Commissioner turned up in his morning suit, and his aides and graces behind him, dressed like the Ace, King, Queen, Jack in all their trappings. Apart from the ubiquitous infantry, there were armoured cars, artillery in all forms, and the Indian cavalry, all going past the bigpots in review order, but with a grand finale reserved exclusively for the horsemen with their lances and pennants. These people, having trotted past in the review, would form afresh at the far end of the field, start off at a canter, then break into a full-blooded charge with a noise and a dust, like a mighty storm, right across the front of us lesser mortals lined up as mere spectators. It was wild and thrilling, though distinctly chilling as we infantrymen recalled that cavalry's main role in war was – had been – to rout us foot soldiers from the field and reduce us to rubble. Yet we recovered morale with the knowledge they could be and had been stopped, as we remembered the glorious Battle of Minden in 1759 when our regiment, along with others, had rolled back charge after charge of French cavalry and put them to hopeless rout on one never-to-be-forgotten first of August.

It was a double pleasure to recall these feats at these parades, for it always stood out a mile how drab we English county regiments were compared with our comrades-in-arms, in dress and gimmicks. Even the Welsh, junior as they were always regarded in our hierarchy, had distinctive black neckbands hanging from their coats, and fierce goats to head them on posh parades. As we Yorkies so feelingly put it: 'It's a flaming good job we have a blurry cricket team'. Yet, undoubtedly, the cavalry took the palm, looking as if they had just stepped out of a picture book, with their British officers really taking the bun, looking as if they had stepped straight out of Technicolor, if one could anticipate the future.

One year we had a Gurkha infantry battalion parade with us, and I never saw a better drilled lot. They also had a bagpipe band, kilts and all – and all slightly bizarre, but very inspiring, with the pipes wailing their wild war airs whilst the lines of stocky, slightly bow-legged men marched with a cocky swing and heads thrown far back in great pride. It was all so impressive to us, but the important point was that it must impress the native populace, lining the road off the parade ground in their thousands and thinking… we knew not what.

While he was on main guard duty fronting the barracks, part of a sentry's duties was to keep his eyes strictly to his front, well opened in the direction of Jamrud Fort, which lay some nine miles along a flat road that led to the foot of the Khyber Pass. If anything boiled up out in the wilds, we in Peshawar would be warned by Verey light alarm rockets, in a combination of colours now forgotten. It behoved a sentry to never forget Jamrud, even though the planes in the field opposite drew one's attention, and had one wondering what business they were about that day. The planes permanently based in Peshawar were small ones, single-prop biplanes used mainly for army co-operation work, though they could carry bombs, albeit very small ones. Now and again, there was also a subtle by-play between working party and sentry, especially if this party was a Sikh one, for they seemed to hate our guts, at the bottom of them. These bearded boys were past masters at the art of a quick snigger from their rear ranks as they passed the lone sentry, and him standing smartly to attention, as was his job. Most times, uncomplaining, he would manage to reply in like fashion, so honours were pretty even in this 'ribbing' game – but the Sikhs always took it out of our ribs when they played us at hockey, for they were world-beaters.

In passing, I would like to mention that India was a great place for sport among the servicemen. A chap who had any inclination to ball games could play something different almost every evening whilst the light held – soccer, cricket, volleyball, tennis, rugger (which I dearly loved to play), the lot – not forgetting the aforementioned hockey, so fast and furious as distinct from the girls' high school game I had always regarded it as at home. I had seen a player's shin opened to the bone with a bit of careless stick play, the way we played. Despite slight buffetings, there was a fine concept of comradeship out there, so far away from the ordinaries of life, with outbursts of feeling freely dissipated on fields of play, though most of us went over the top at one time or another, and like the poor Negro soul in 'Ole Man River', landed in jail – the service one, that is!

I met that unenviable fate the second summer out whilst I was up in the hills, and whilst I was on, of all things, a cadre for selected personnel. Unmindful of the honour thrust on me, I started acting the giddy goat after a few drinks. Anyway, I landed up in 'clink' and got myself ten days' CB for my little bit of fun – and was promptly kicked off the cadre. With this, I earned the unmasked hostility of the officer running the course, a Lieutenant Livosk, who called me all sorts of a washout, in rougher language, and made my life merry hell whenever he saw me, the rest of that stay up in the hills. I was glad of one thing: he was not one of our officers, though he was a brilliant soldier, and got to the top, I bet.

However, in spite of my military backslidings, I like to think that on a hillside at Cherat there is tangible evidence of some pioneering months worked there. I refer to the making, laying, hewing of a carway, a track that one of our officers might take his newly acquired car along, up to his bungalow where, before, only foot or ass had trod. It was Jock Middleton, one of our old sweats with the MM, who got the job, and I was to be his mate for the rest of that glorious stay in the hills. Three months in all it proved to be, lopping down small trees, tearing up their roots, heaving chunks of rock out of our way, and spending quite a bit of time in the canteen 'char-and-wadding', for the work was strenuous, our brows ever wet, our throats ever dry. Jock and I were quite proud when we'd finished the job and the little car gasped its way up the crazy path for the first time – and we had a feeling akin to what the engineers who fashioned the M1 must have felt like when their task was finished. We felt at one with our predecessors up there, fifty years before, who had carved regimental crests on a great rock that frowned down on the main road, amongst them being our own modest French-horn cap badge. I wonder if the powers that be in present-day Pakistan have seen fit to leave the carvings untouched, as a memorial to warriors who paused, made their mark, then passed on their way into history?

Richard (left) North West Frontier, India 1929

In those days, before speeded-up communications, it took the English mail three weeks to get to us (though, unofficially, we got football results the day after, through the kind office of the air force wireless!); likewise the popular English Sunday papers – and they always came on a Sabbath. They were usually there straight following church parade, before we had our dinner, and the lucky ones spent the afternoon reading and cud-chewing the precious morsels from home, at times putting the luckless ones in the picture with little cameos – funny, or whimsical, or downright sad. Most times the folks at home were hard up, but the epistles were magic inasmuch as they came from home, however humble, or wretched these might prove to be. Every week or two I got a letter from Bill, which might include a few lines from Edie; at times, a word or two from Dad – for all the family, excluding myself and Arthur, seemed to be orbiting around the Manchester Road area again.

One week I got a short note from Bill telling me about Edie being taken ill. It was flu, and it must have been an epidemic, the way the papers talked of it. I wrote back sympathising with Edie and telling her she would most likely be better the next letter I got, though I naturally worried a little about her.

The next Sunday morning, my platoon had to go up the Khyber Pass on a bit of business that took us right up, past the old battlefield of Ali Masjid, up the railhead at Landi Kotal, and right out to the border with Afghanistan. It was all very interesting, for it was country dotted with odd villages and their tall lookout towers, and mostly arid waste either side of the pass. We took time for a drink with our compatriots in Landi Kotal on the way back, had photos taken with arms wound around each other's necks, then set off home to Pesh. If I have not done this visit to the Pass full honours, it is because I was preoccupied with the thought of a letter that I wanted waiting for me in barracks, a letter that would tell me all was now well with Edie, so I was rather impatient of our tardy track homewards.

It was sometime after tea when we got back, and I hurried along the verandah and into the high barrack-room – and interrupted the room orderly having a rare old stare at me.

'What's up?' I asked, rather crossly.

'Er, nowt,' he answered, and I rudely snapped, 'Couldn't be much less,' and went to my bed.

I picked up the Sunday paper from where the orderly had dropped it earlier in the day and saw that, whether by accident or design, it covered a letter laid on the dhurrie.[25] Dully, I took in its dumb

25 An Indian cotton mat.

message, for it had a black band around the edge of the envelope. I opened it; I can't express how I now felt, except to know it was a mere formality now, this opening. However, as I pulled out the couple of sheets of paper, a long mauve ribbon dropped on the bed. I picked it up and read, through blurred eyes, the short obituary of Edith Tempest, aged sixteen, beloved daughter of Arthur and Violetta Tempest, and there followed a short appropriate verse, in the trend then fashionable. Edie had died[26] some weeks before, and I sat myself on my iron bedstead feeling very much alone in the world; though, later, at canteen time, one of my pals, a Geordie, came to my bed and exhorted, 'Away, man! Get some wallop in you – why, it'll do you the worrld o' good.' And that is what I did: get good and drunk.

Edith Tempest 1913-1929

***

26 Edith Tempest died on 28th February 1929 aged 16 years old. She was described as a doffer of 14 Granton Street and was buried in an unmarked public grave at Bowling Cemetery in Bradford.

There had been, all the time I was in India, a prickling thorn of Indian nationalism tormenting the august Imperial body, with Mahatma Gandhi leading and inspiring in every new move to harass and embarrass us British. On and off, throughout the rest of India, the troublesome National Congress had kept our resources stretched to the full to contain them; but up on the Frontier, we had got off pretty light, if one excepted our usual, expected quota of the local trouble peculiar to Pesh. Then, in '30, in a new all-out drive by Gandhi and his disciples, nationalist trouble started fermenting in Peshawar City itself. It started off as a little something that boiled over on the occasion of two Congress bigpots getting themselves arrested for seditious activities, and us not being able to keep it as dark as we should have liked, for these gentlemen had got themselves apprehended for the sole purpose of stirring it up.

In no time at all, the polyglot crowd got to know, got all het-up, tried to free the leaders, failed, and started rioting. The military were summoned after the first clash, and they sent along a couple of armoured cars to cow the mob. But unfortunately the mob were not daunted, for they set fire to one of the cars, and killed a despatch rider bringing up the rear – and the fat was truly in the fire along the Frontier. There was no stopping the mob now for, having tasted blood, they were not to be reined in and took the law into their own hands. Of course, the infantry was called out – though, unfortunately again, some of these lads were natives to the province and could not be persuaded to fire on their own folks (not an unnatural reaction), and that made things very sticky for the can holders whilst the telegraph wires fair hummed hot between Pesh and down-country. Happily for us, our battalion was able to push another company into the city and, temporarily, maintained the status quo whilst plan and policy were being resolved on a higher plane. Then our people moved with lightning speed, for the disaffected battalion was moved on the same evening, entrained right off the Frontier, the while the cantonment bristled with machine guns 'at the ready' – just in case! A battalion of Johnny Gurkhas replaced the reluctant ones, with more British troops coming up as fast as they could be moved, for there was more in this than met the layman's eye, according to dark rumours muttered around the wet canteen: 'Gandhi himself,' somebody grunted, which was enough to flatten the brew in everybody's glass.

In such a setting there were crises galore, with the hillbillies exacting every possible ounce of advantage. It was rumoured, one hot trying day, that ten – or was it fifteen? – thousand wild men were coming down to sack Pesh. And that same day we saw the unusual sight (for us!) of about thirty planes, of all sizes, wheeling about the sky for a long time, as though giving a demonstration – as, no doubt, they were! Anyway, we never saw the ten thousand warriors, though various smaller bands did attack that summer. They almost got into a sprawling railway depot for a rare old looting one time, but were beaten off; an armoured train service started running after that, for these lads had a disconcerting habit of straddling the lines out in the country and outshooting aught that passed, though they were never strong enough to cut us off. There were pitched battles all over the plains surrounding the city, and the garrison swelled to a small army corps during that summer, in a white-hot heat of hellish sunshine, with no relaxing for the troops up the hills this season. It went on, desultorily, into the next year, and all this was happening so far away from Westminster that it took our government three further long years, when it was dead and buried as regards the rank and file, before they reluctantly agreed NWF '30–'31 was a full-blown military campaign and the soldiery – sorry, *services* – worthy of a silver gong apiece.

In the midst of all that, I went and did an incredible thing – I started coughing blood! And all so unexpected: one minute I was happy and gay (actually I had helped despatch a venomous snake that had got under some sacks in a small storeroom at the end of the block), and the next, I was coughing away, irritated by a hellish tickle, and staring at the blood on my hankie, on my fingers, on the verandah, and asking, 'Ooh, hell! Why doesn't it stop?'

There was enough of it to warrant the medical orderly bluntly exclaiming, 'That's f—ed it! Blighty for you, mate... You lucky bastard!' and straight away sending me along the Mall with all speed in a gharry, to the fine Military Hospital, a place I had already a nodding acquaintance with on account of touches of prickly heat and mild malaria. There, lying still with plenty of time on my hands, it occurred to me why it had all happened: the snake excitement and the shindig round about us had, undoubtedly, topped up a malignant 'something' that had plagued me some months before. I recalled how I had been ill for weeks, had lost a considerable amount of weight, had 'walked about same as a ghost' as my mates had it, but foolishly had not reported sick, and now I was paying the price – a terrific one, as I was to find out.

I was in Cherat, a summer camp in the foothills of the North-West Frontier of India, when I made my first indirect, long-distance contact with the shattering new miracle of talking, singing, musical films. Cherat was a hill station serving the garrisons of Peshawar and Nowshera, and I was in hospital at the time, with a pretty good idea my army days were numbered, and so hoping I would be going back to Blighty in the near future. It was in one of the hospital wards that I got to know Danny Quinn. Danny was in the Border Regiment and suffering from a rib infection, suspected to be out of the same stable as my complaint. The hospital people had put Danny and myself together, though all on our own, in a former barrack-room that held twenty. This room – or rather building – was built on a little hill upon a hill, which partly explained why we were left so much to our own devices, and only visited four times a day by a native boy with our meals, an orderly when he was obliged, and an assistant surgeon (an old-soldier Englishman in charge of the tiny hospital) on his daily round that we may assure him we were all right, comfortable, and wanted for nothing – except a bit of companionship!

We were comfortable all right, but fed up to the teeth with loneliness and boredom, and the enforced idleness, for we were at a restless stage of convalescing, with not a thing to do, and long hours to kill before taking to our hot, starch-stiff beds in the early evenings. Below us, on the steep hillside away from the hospital, and always hidden from view in a near-forest of deciduous trees, was a small settlement, probably housing the hospital boys and their families. Early every morning, and at intervals during the day, some anonymous chappie with a very musical voice would call the faithful to prayer and – an unofficial reveille – us two lonely Englishmen to the fact another long, probably incident-free day was at hand. We would wait eagerly on every little diversion: somebody from the Soldiers' Home, though they were just a little too given to asking questions instead of soothing souls; or the assistant surgeon, for from him came all vital news, such as going down to Pesh for a medical board, or an unofficial letting-out into the nearby bazaar for a couple of hours, or the time I got the tidings I was to go home to England, or the question of changing diets. At one time I was on chicken every day, and I got heartily sick of this small bird, and humbly asked that I be downgraded to what was called 'ordinary diet'. I was granted this small favour, and probably somebody else surprisedly found themselves on the chicken diet, until they would cry 'Enough!' at the monotony of it, in time.

We read all we could lay our hands on, including a big pile of film reviews, which were just then making a big shout about a young German girl, Marlene Dietrich, who had 'arrived' in a picture called *The Blue Angel*[27] and was exciting unholy desires amongst all male filmgoers. We talked a lot about Blighty and our prospect of getting back there before Christmas, though I panicked a bit when Danny went in late September, and I was still there, with but an enigmatic smile from the assistant surgeon in answer to my anguished cry of 'What about me?'. We talked of our unambitious little hopes, in the boiling-pot of uncertainty at that time, then always drifted out to a more pleasant subject – girls. Girlfriends past, present (Danny had a nurse interested in him, somewhere in England, though I was

27 Released in 1930.

fancy-free) and future – especially future, when we would again see real English girls, as distinct from the distant, frigid females who must never, never speak to the soldiery they passed every day of their lives out in this powerhouse of imperialism. That would be the day! – when we spoke to a girl again, held her hand, made love to her (and how unreal *that* seemed, at this long distance). Illness and wisdom faded into the drab background when romance of an exotic, erotic, nature was in the mind and our waxing-eloquent talk. Sex (mild or piping hot) explored for that day, we would then get on about boxing, with Gene Tunney[28] retired; and football, with Arsenal tops; and cricket, with Yorkshire just coming after a couple of seasons in the wilderness. But, temporarily more important, the menace of a young Australian cricketer who was creating havoc amongst English bowlers and rewriting the record books, back home in this summer of 1930. His name was Bradman, and he had already gone to Leeds (of all places!) to slam the MCC bowling to the tune of 300-odd runs[29]; we ruefully supposed nobody would ever beat that.

When we tired of yapping, or of looking at each other (as we did quite often), we would go sit on the steps of the verandah and stare into the distance for long enough, for we had a marvellous view. Far out we would gaze, beyond the buzz and yatter from the little settlement that snuggled below us; far out beyond the lesser foothills that rose in front and that we felt we could have touched, given longer arms; and farther out still to the plains, to a dark smudge we knew to be Peshawar, where our battalions lay, uneasy and alert, for they were just then up to the neck in Gandhi trouble, and hordes of hill tribesmen harassing and raiding whilst, they fondly hoped, their iron was hot.

We would start talking again and Danny, with my encouraging, would start reminiscing about the England he had left so lately and,

28 John Joseph ('Gene') Tunney was an American boxer who held the world heavyweight title from 1926 until his retirement in 1928.

29 Don Bradman, then aged 21, scored 309 not out on the opening day of the Ashes Test at Headingley.

very important, he would get on about the 'talkies', for he had actually heard them before coming out here in the last trooping season. I would hang on every word, open-mouthed, as he led me through the magic French windows of my imagination to this new wonder he had left behind him in Blighty. It all sounded so fantastic but it was all so true, for had not Danny seen and heard? – and Danny was very truthful, graphic, articulate. With no encouragement at all from me, he would burst into popular songs of the films, start babbling about a certain 'Sonny Boy' and, after some little time, he even had me joining in, and we would go on until some dullard from the hospital compound below would shout that it was high time we tiptoed to *bed*, in lieu of those bloody tulips we kept yawping about. But Danny had his own favourite song. It was infectious, and smittled[30] me with its fitting into our mood when we were prone to give way to a dollop of self-pity about our frustrated plight, dumped up here almost on top of the world: a sparsely populated world, given over to sudden storms of red sand, sighted from afar off on the plains and very rapidly swirling up to our hill and blotting out the very daylight for the few minutes it took in passing, and all being so awesome. Oft-times, torrents of lashing rain hammered on the thin roof in a violent frenzy of short duration, though these angry manifestations of Nature disturbed were always succeeded by a brilliant sun – a sun that was cruel, pitiless, indiscriminate, and that made the theme of our adopted song all the more welcome.

It was a little thing that went 'I'm singin' in the rain, just singin' in the rain... What a glorious feeling, I'm happy again' and it was sung, Danny assured me, by a talkie-film star with the sophisticated name of 'Ukulele Ike'.[31] Many times I have heard it sung, I'm afraid, with the implication that it came out but yesterday, with never any reference to its origins way back; yet every time I hear it, my mind conjures up afresh that long, dreary hospital ward; the two lonely beds, severe and

30 Infected.

31 Cliff Edwards, an American musician and actor, who had a number one hit with the song in 1929.

painfully white; the dusty verandah; the long view, the storm clouds approaching; and my comrade and me shouting to the echoing hills how we were 'laughing at clouds... Singin', just singin' in the rain', and the ward-boy hurrying up the hill with another meal, giving us a meaningful look that surely said 'Deolali Tap!'[32]

Danny left me after some couple of months, and I was sad at his going; he wasn't in my regiment, and I might never see him again – though I did, for a few brief moments, in another hospital ward at Netley, when I had got back to England. We promised to write each other, but never did, and I wonder if he stills sings as chirpy in his native Cumberland. I bet it isn't our old favourite! And whatever became of old Ukulele Ike? He doesn't seem to be around any more, nor does anybody ever mention him, the jolly troubadour whose real name else was Cliff Edwards... Probably because nobody ever remembers, quite as vividly, his rendering of 'Singin' in the Rain' as passed on to me at second hand.

Whilst I was never critically ill, I could not resist myself the luxury of a little self-pity in hoping I would be spared until I saw dear old Blighty again, for it was agreed by all, and myself reconciled to the dismal fact, that my army days were over. When the troopship got me back to dear old England, it was to the depressing fug of Southampton Water in early December, passing about ten rusting ships, liners, tramps, swinging on long lines and nobody wanting anything to do with them, and the lone man on board watching us pass with never a word or a wave, for he was the death-watchman come aboard. It was very deflating, for the old country hadn't changed a bit, now I came to think of it – the muck and the squalor and the bleakness were still about, and some dozen unemployed dockers watching the few who serviced our ship, with eyes from which no rough banter could hide the wistfulness. Yes, these, and other things, took the cream off my homecoming, though I had got my wish.

I spent a few weeks in Netley Hospital whilst they went through

32 Or 'doolally tap', meaning 'camp fever' – a kind of madness associated with waiting.

the empty business of boarding me and formally declaring I was 'unfit for further service' and all that bullmuck, then they kitted me out as a civvy and sent me north, back to my native city, and a long spell of sanatoria in the hope that one day I might be made fit again. All in all, it wasn't a very encouraging era to get fit in, for now our American cousins had caught the infectious disease of 'a slump', and were quite bewildered by it all until Franklin Roosevelt whipped them into shape with his revolutionary ordinances. This was also the time of the talkies – so what more characteristic than that the Yankees should make capital out of their troubles with an excellent new ballad that cried 'Brother, can you spare a dime?'. Was it any wonder my rehabilitation was to take years more?

THE FIRST LAMB

It so happened that, when I arrived at the sanatorium up in the Dales, I landed in an absolutely new world. It was rather ironical, this involuntary finding of a brand new world on Bradford's doorstep after I had gone seven thousand miles to another, and one in which I had come off second-best.

In this new world – in which there were men, women, and children in separate places – we sick people had our own cubicles, or shared with one other, on landings and verandahs where we slept and lived and, gradually, got better (the lucky ones) in God's good time in an atmosphere unlike anything I had known before. We lived almost on top of a long slope that rose, steadily, from the benevolent waters of the River Wharfe. It could have been described as a bleak hillside had it not been for the scores of young trees that had grown up with, and around, the sani. From open doorways, shut at one's own peril – unless to halt a blinding snowstorm such as fell one howling weekend in February '33 – we had uninterrupted views across a wide valley, wooded in the bottoms, across to echoing rocky hillsides and hidden roads and lanes, one leading to lost village Thorpe, others on to the moorlands that stretched to Bolton Abbey. If one stepped out onto the well-kept lawns, to the left one would see the mighty crags of Simon's Seat frowning down on little Appletreewick and genteel Burnsall, which village always reminded me of a deserted hamlet, so quiet did it seem when we ever passed through on a half-day out.

And that was another thing – the wonderful freedom we had, a kind of bonus earned for getting better. We were kept in bed only so long as was absolutely necessary, then were started on a graduated scale of getting up, increasing until one was up all day. Then one started doing little jobs of light work designed to keep one's mind, and hands, and time busy so that, if he kept his medical sheet looking healthy (which I did not, being back to bed many times), a chap might ultimately, and to the envy of his less fortunate fellows, get pottering about the extensive gardens for two or three hours a day, though never forgetting the rest periods, compulsory for all. Then, one happy monthly-exam morning, this same chap might be deemed fit to go back to ordinary workaday life – though many times, going back to Bradford and its industrial atmosphere undid the healing months (sometimes years) of gracious living on the hillside in the Dales. It was always a rather melancholy, sobering occasion when we welcomed back somebody who had left us and was now back again – a disillusioned body, sometimes bitter and not knowing who, or what, to blame for his backening, yet, after the initial sorting-out whilst lying in bed, reconciled to starting all over again, reckoning the time when he would be up and about again.

Richard outside Hebden Post Office 1935

As one climbed the ladder of progressing good health, one was given permission to go out of the grounds for a couple of half-days per week. He might go down to Grassington village to do bits of shopping, come back along the riverside, walk on the left bank and take in the peace of clear water rippling over pebbles; see the strands where sand martins were ever in and out of earthy nests in the bankside, or catch a rare glimpse of a kingfisher dipping to the water; or, standing still, see a water rat swim silently under the lee of a bank to one of many holes. Or sprawl on the grassy side to contemplate a quiet pool away from the swirl of the main channel, and relax in the still blessedness, and get to quietly thanking God for His favours, though not with closed eyes, or muttering lips, or clasping of hands; and, some distance away, an angler plays for a fish, and cares not if it takes him all day.

It was a wonderful world to me, for I had never seen the English countryside, in its fulness, before. I had never seen a horse-drawn cutter draw its first swathe down the wall side of a meadow before, had never smelled the sweet cleanness of the laid grasses, had never seen hay gotten. Nor had I seen a calf born – not before a distress call bellow one day, heard through a drystone wall the other side of which some few lately-of-bed patients were sat killing time, and which pain-filled cry had us all peering over and beholding a cow delivering her calf, all wet and shiny. And yet within a few minutes, this same calf was rearing up and collapsing in turn, much like a music-hall drunk, in its efforts to draw sustenance from the patiently awaiting mother. I was amazed by this, and by a lot more, for within a quarter of an hour the all-legs calf was behaving as though it had been on this earth quite some time. It was so hard for a townie to assimilate that the little 'un was only minutes old, even having seen it all.

By dint of loafing around – all other jobs done as one progressed – and encroaching, unofficially, on adjoining fields, one got to know the neighbouring farmers (grand chaps, all!) and, in course of time, I was privileged to make a friend of one Tom Longthorne and his wife, Annie. Tom was a hill farmer whose chief source of income, though he had a few milk beasts for butter, was a flock of sheep he brought up on the steep hillside of his farm, away to the north side of the sani, where the land dropped sharply away into a narrow ghyll with a fast-running stream in its bottoms. It was limestone country, with outcroppings of rock in most of the fields that stood ready to revert to moorland at the least sign of human neglect; and, altogether, it was not a land flowing with milk and honey – not for the farmer, anyway. Yet Tom was a happy man; I never heard him grumble though, truth to tell, I never heard him swank about his 'brass', either. To me he was a typical Dalesman with his rich, strong twang so vastly different from my rough, flat Bradford dialect – he was a native, bred and born, and weathered and stocky – and hard as hell, to boot.

Richard Tempest and Edna Dodds (bottom right)
Tom Longthorne (bare headed holding rake)

At special times, and most times because of a situation I will not dwell upon now, I would have a cup of tea and a buttered scone, or a teacake, in the farmhouse, and have a bit of a chatter with Annie, for she knew Bradford well, having relatives there whom she had been in the habit of visiting regularly when she was younger, and before she wed Tom. She had not a lot of time after, being kept busy one way and another, as only a farmer's wife can be, with also the running of a rambling old farmhouse. It was bare and beetling, and built into the hillside, and glorying in the name of Pickering End. Yet every stick of old-fashioned furniture therein (antimacassars, Victorian pictures), and the rather heavy air (peaty-smelling at all seasons, for Tom cut this dust-laden fuel out of the bleak moors behind, out where the old lead-mine workings stood, long since abandoned) – everything of Pickering End shouted 'home' to me, who had not enjoyed a great deal of that in the past.

Whenever I saw Tom in his fields, he would halt his work, stare very keenly at me with deep-set blue eyes, salute with 'Aught fresh, Dick?' and give a broad grin which, at first, I found a bit disconcerting, as though he already knew all I had fresh. I would mumble some pleasantry, Tom would chuckle, probably exclaim, 'This weean't buy Babby a new hat,' – though, bless 'em, they didn't have one – then get on with his work. Yet he did pause once, just once, and this after I had met him along the bottoms and had started towards home with him, the time we came upon the sheep.

It was on the short-cropped hillside where we came upon them, after a long toil of a pull which had the effect of making our pause to look all the more welcome. There they stood, just a little away from the main flock – the guilty and the innocent – hand in glove, in a way of speaking. She, the guilty one, old enough to know better (as we humans have it) but who, nevertheless, had played away with an amorous ram, on the loose – and this some weeks before officialdom (in the shape of Tom) had intended she should – and thus the resulting bundle at her side, her lamb, and the first of the season at Pickering End.

They made a grand picture, this drab, rather stupid-looking sheep, dirty and matted, with the small snowball at her side, a bundle that was ever on the qui vive, with all-curious eyes and trembling tail, and ready to dart away at any given second. This very young lady (for Tom insisted she was, and he should know) had come into her bleak world of limestone drywalls and sparse grasses some thirty hours before in a sharp flurry of stinging snowflakes, and Tom had found them in the long field early yesterday morning, on his way down to milk in the barn at the bottoms. He guessed the lamb had only then been born for, as he came on them, the ewe was licking her lamb clean and dry, and Tom had wisely left the couple to their ablutions, happy in the omen of this surprise, straightforward delivery.

Tom now whistled – a low, lilting sort of whistle which, at first, only had the effect of making the whole flock lift up their stolid heads and stare towards us in dumb inquiry; but, as the notes persisted and Tom's sheepcur poised to slope off in action, they gradually started in other directions, but not the mother and the babe!

'Dahn!' growled Tom of his dog, and down sank the bitch at his heels whilst the two odd-ones-out came almost up to us, with the young 'un indulging all the tricks of her slight repertoire. She would burst forward in front of Mother, then make a sudden stop and throw her head down; she would leap with all feet in the air, for all the world like a little wild horse leaping for the sheer ecstasy of living, or maybe for the sheer hell of it all. And every leap brought a response from somewhere inside me, for I was not Tom, I no farmer on his matter-of-fact routine bent. To me, these unexpected leaps no one could anticipate spoke of joy, of a great happiness; they even autosuggested promise, of new hope, for what was beginning to look like a rather gloomy personal future. These infant antics stirred spiritual emotions that always dwell inside our dark prison of a body and, yet, remain vague and undefinable – and, in some poor fish, are probably never brought to the surface. To some, only the things that cost 'brass' or are shouted from the housetops count to stir emotions;

they never find anything for themselves – but perhaps I was lucky?

Above, all this while, I was aware of patchy clouds drifting across the sky, of glimpses of blue beyond, of the sun glinting brightly through at times; of, far below, beyond a rutted car track, vast patches of deep-brown bracken and rock rioting in a confused mass through which burbled a stream, over pebbles and sandbars, to join a big brother, the Wharfe, by the footbridge and the stepping stones beyond Hebden.

And now our lamb stood irresolute, with a glance at us, a brisk run and leap, then another puzzled, speculative look – and then it was she cottoned on to what really bothered her. Of course! It was hunger! Plain, keening, bellyaching for food… Straight into Mother she piled, yanking and pulling away, stretching a dug like so much rubber, without any regard for the old lady's comfort. But Mum was not standing for it, not in any sense as, without a glance or even a shrugging-off of her offspring, she set off down the hillside. They finally faded out of sight, the mother making for a windbreak of fallen stones, the lamb in hot pursuit, yet still finding time to indulge her Chaplinesque antics.

'Come on, lad.' Tom's voice broke into my reverie. 'Tha'll stann all day… Let's goa see if Annie has t'kettle on.'

He led the rest of the way up the hill, through the low door, into the dark, warm, cosy interior of Annie's kitchen; and the big kettle sat atop of the peat lumps in the fireplace, and Annie sat smiling, awaiting us.

THE CYCLE

(Time on our hands, to fool and fashion as we may!
Who knows what die he'll cast on this fateful day?)

DAWN

Aye, it was grand to be out this morning,
When the young birds raised their song o' dawning,
As the sun rose slow, like a ball, up the hill,
And the farm dog sped at the whistle's shrill –
Aye! It was wondrous, abroad this morning.

NOON

The heat of sun, the smell of hay,
The quiet lull of middle day;
When even dogs lie still, and pant,
And nothing stirs but a busy ant.

SUNSET

Cottage, and barn, and the old pigsty
Etched black against the western sky;
The sun, with flaming gesture grand,
Salutes, then sinks below the land.

NOCTURNE

Candles are snuffed, and night begins
Casting its black cloak over our sins;
And into restful sleep we glide,
So deep, complete – as though we died!

CHAPTER SIX

YOUTH'S A STUFF...

It was about this time Arthur came back into our lives again – this after some years with him gone and never coming back. There had been one unsuccessful advert put in a national Sunday paper, then I decided to put one in the Bradford evening paper, and this met with an immediate response. Yes, somebody had seen Arthur: a young boy who had lately come back from a training ship, the *Exmouth*, a ship where selected boys from orphanages all over the country were sent. Arthur had been one of these – though he might not now be there, the lad informed, for senior boys were sent out to the mercantile and navy on reaching a certain age, and Arthur was all of sixteen, maybe seventeen.

After a fair amount of correspondence, Arthur was, at last, traced to Southampton, where he was working as a 'bugle-and-bridge boy' on the transatlantic liners and, when ashore, was living in the local Toc H boys' hostel.[33] He sounded very happy through his letters; I was not able to see him, as I was then fixed. He was managing to look after himself all right, even though a seemingly permanent depression held sway, and working shipboard and walking the streets of drab

33 Arthur's first voyage was on 8th June 1932, as a 'deck boy bugler' sailing from Southampton to New York on the RMS *Olympic*, sister ship to the *Titanic*.

Southampton rated a fifty–fifty chance. This was the age when the phrase 'a bobby's job' really meant security and permanence, along with the postman's and the railwayman's lot – maybe with miserable pittance in actual wages, but with jobs coveted by all us working-class, for these chaps were anchored in deep, still water, far away from the treacherous quicksands of pernicious unemployment.

It was because of this hopeless economic state of no work – or a job of two pounds per week being a standard yardstick used by lots of exploiting employers – that my other brother, Bill, had gone back to London again: back to the usual round of jobs that drew the workless from the provinces as barmen, navvies, snack-bar attendants, porters, and all the rough stuff that smart Cockney boys would not look at. Bill was also lodging on a day-to-day basis in a seen-better-days large house out Camden Town way, with his landlady (whom I was to see quite soon), a pleasant blonde woman of about thirty, with a husband temporarily removed to one of HM's Prisons for, as Bill so nicely put it, he was a convicted 'tealeaf'. But beggars could never be choosers and, Bill never professing to being fussy, he was happy to be there, having known much worse places in the capital city – which was a useful attitude in those days, those times.

To return to Arthur, at first his letters were merry and bright – inconsequential scribblings of a lad happy at his work – but, as more good boats joined the ones I had seen so long before rusting in the idleness out in Southampton Water, his shipboard spells got shorter, the idle spells got longer, and his spirits sank very low, with his letters now fewer and rather gloomy. I worried, though I felt rather out of touch and helpless, until I hit on what I thought was a bright idea – why not get Arthur to London, to Bill, under his wing? I wrote Bill, though I did notice he was cautious in his telling of how jobs were rather scarce in London just then, but I replied with a lot of optimistic claptrap and, at last, Bill agreed to try it – I suppose not to hurt my feelings. So, like thousands of other boys before and since, Arthur took the high road to London, probably slightly amused with my fond joking there might still be a small nugget of gold waiting to be picked up on the streets of the fair city. And, good deed done, I sat back in the shelter of the Dales, congratulating myself that all would now be well.

It was not a success. After about a month during which both lived off Bill's slender wages, the breadwinner himself fell out of work following a disagreement he had with a very hard taskmaster, the melancholy facts of which Arthur duly acquainted me with. Needless to say, I got to worrying again about Arthur, for a youngster could be on his beam-ends months (strange as that may sound to present-day youth) and I did not want the lad again eating his heart out down there. I didn't really worry about Bill, for he was used to fending for himself, but with Arthur I felt different. Somehow he was still the baby of the family, choose how rough we might seem, and something had to be done, and quick.

After some little hesitation, I went to see 'Doctor Bill', our nickname for the wiry little Scots doctor-boss at the sanatorium. He was very helpful. He sat me comfortably in his study and we talked a long time, and the outcome of it all: I would be allowed to go to London on three days' leave – to see what could be done, to get Arthur to come back to Bradford with me, back to where he really belonged and, maybe, there the luck would change and he would find a job. I knew I could get him fixed up for digs with a lady who was very kind to me at this time and, on the face, he would be quite at home there. I lingered on at the finish of our talk, and the doctor, canny Scot, guessed my further trouble. Money? Yes, I answered him; I wanted some badly, though I had a Post Office savings account, given time to draw on it. Without a murmur, he advanced me a fiver on the strength, and I went back to my bunk all geared up for the morrow's long journey south, and with Doctor Bill's parting warning: 'Don't get too involved, mind… Y're still a sick man.'

I minded his warning when I reached London but, though it was wintry and cold, I lay awake long and sweated profusely in the small room where we all three kipped down at Bill's place. I was mighty thankful when the dawn came casting its cold light through a high window on a scene so different from the challenging one I had left on the Yorkshire hillside so few hours before. I found myself feeling actually homesick for that small, open-air cubicle up north – that, and a little something else!

Bill's landlady provided us with a good breakfast; we had a serious pow-wow in the small bedroom, then decided Arthur and I would catch the afternoon train to Bradford – though first we must go see a fellow townie of ours in a certain large pub where he was resident as one of the many barmen. Pom, our friend, was very busy and never spoke to us above half a dozen words at a time, so occupied was he pulling foaming pints for thirsty Cockneys, and tossing the pence, shillings, pound notes into a very large tray that served as a depository where the ever-watching landlord could more easily see what happened to the cash – which was as well, I supposed, in this less trusting world removed from the Dales. We had a couple of quick shandies apiece, then bade goodbye to Pom and were away to the station with all of us feeling things were going the right way, though we had no concrete evidence for uplift. I can well remember Bill, in his usual careless way, and with no more than a couple of bob in his pockets, buying a shilling glossy magazine, a near-smutty affair, from the station paper stand, then tossing it into the carriage for Arthur and me to read on the way up; and me grumbling, good-naturedly, 'He's no bloody idea, hasn't Bill.'

That night I spent in Bradford with Arthur, then late next day I was off back to Grassington, leaving my brother in the care of May Brown, a grand woman who never did anything but kindly for all us lads. Arthur was to stay indefinitely at her house, his digs money being met by Bill and myself until such time as he found himself a job – oh, anywhere! – as I so easily said: in a textile mill, or a wool warehouse, or outdoors, or… or… Oh, anywhere! After all, it was said God looked after the smallest sparrow, and our Arthur was a strong, likely lad, only wanting a weather eye keeping on him; yes, I guessed he would bed in – somewhere. Even May Brown thought he stood a fair chance of finding a job so, with her smiling reassurance, I left Arthur in Bradford and got the bus back to Grassington.

Grassington "Sani" patients, Richard (left) with spade.

It was such a relief to get back to the Dales, away from the knockings of the big, rough outer world with its grim realism and gospel of the devil taking the last man. As Doctor Bill had said, I was not yet out of the woods of doubtful health and an inherited burden of great weariness under pressure. I was glad to get back into my little cocoon where one's chief worry was for oneself. I suppose it was escapism, a shrinking from responsibilities, though I must admit there was also another, very compelling reason made me glad to see Grassington again, in the attractive shape of a young lady.

Edna[34] was a winsome girl of twenty, a laundress at the hospital, for whom I had, for some time past, formed an attachment that found mutual response. It had been arranged, through the good office of conspirators in the know, that my fair lady would be waiting my return and would walk back with me, along the mile or so that lay between sanatorium and village. As I got off the bus in the darkened, almost deserted village square, I was immediately welcomed by Edna as though I was some wanderer returning from a long sojourn abroad. It was all so warming on this cold night, and it felt good to be with Edna again, an Edna so obviously overjoyed to see me again, as I her. We set off, hand in hand, along the narrow, twisting Hebden Road that was hedged, variously, with broken stretchers of limestone drywalling and stunted thorns; and, as we walked, all the weariness accumulated over the past three days dropped from my shoulders. Edna's presence cast a worry-killing spell over the problem of Arthur that still lingered faintly, and we got on to other things, as we invariably did, for we never tired of bringing those things up – you know, of the magic of being in love with each other, and of being young and resilient, so we could face up to the mundane, lesser things that plagued one or other of us, so we could jointly make less of them, for a two-man load sits lighter then a single one.

We would get to talking of a daffy, wishful-thinking afterwards – and how rainbow's-endish then seemed my future for, at rock bottom, there was never any end to a succession of ups and downs. One time I would be up and full of the joys of spring and eager to be at aught; the next, I would be back in bed with weeks of 'absolute rest' stretching out before me, all because of some darned leak – or was it more? – that never would set about healing completely. It was all so demoralising

34 Edna Dodds born Sacriston, County Durham 1912

but, one redeeming feature, I was a chap who soon bucked up with a very small token of encouragement, such as my girl smiling from afar as she walked abroad, for the main driveway was in view of my doorway; or, more wonderful, a hurried few words and a touch of hands as she came along the verandah on some cooked-up errand to the ward-room. If my pulse beat a little faster after her surprise incursion, nobody got alarmed about it, not that once in a while.

That was a nice thing – none of the nurses went out of her way to be nasty or obstructive, or ever read the Riot Act, for which I was always duly grateful. Even Doctor Bill did not deign to notice, and I can now relate of these things happy in the sure knowledge of nobody being hurt by my prattlings; for, apart from many demises, surely time heals all, forgives all with an imaginary statute of limitations? I can tell of our hole-and-corner meetings, along the riverside, or up Hebden Ghyll, or in some quiet tea shop. And there was an old water-powered mill, down by a wide bend of the Wharfe, alongside some stepping stones that led to Linton churchyard and its village, and by this mill was a cottage where a Mrs West made grand teas. When we were walking that way, Edna and I would call in for tea and a good old yatter over the past week's happenings, though we had probably seen each other every day, but only on discreet nodding terms. How precious fleeting were all those clandestine meetings!

Other times, we might sit high on the moors above the hospital, over the hill, out of sight, and oft-times beside a rough track that led away out to the abandoned lead-mine workings of Yarborough, with nothing but a few screaming peewits, or maybe a sheep, or a farmer passing us with a brief nod of head and all-seeing eyes. Up there was a no-man's-land of humps and hollows, rank grass, bogs and fat reeds, bracken and rocks, broken-down walls, but we were as happy as two little kiddies away from it all – *it* being everything divorced from our world of whimsy and make-believe; *it* being the depressing fact that my affairs got to the low pitch (after the time of this tale) where I never had any money. But perhaps that is not strictly true: I had an allowance of ten shillings per month for stamps, etc., granted me from my sick pay (the remainder being put away until the day I left hospital). If I ever wanted any new shoes, or a shirt, or (once) a new suit, I was obliged to write asking for an advance, and giving my reason, to the Health people, and then send them the receipt I got for my purchases. This was a period when I, unashamedly, looked as eagerly forward to Edna's monthly pay day as she did. That day would mean lashings of chocolate bars, or a really nice tea, and I took all without so much as a blush. Admittedly, the first time or two I baulked a little, but Edna soon had me acting more in accord with my impecunious position, had me swallowing the built-up, foolish pride I affected, had me accepting it all as the done thing. She made it seem natural that we were mucking-in chums as we talked of all our beautiful thoughts, of being married, of Baby Temps; and sometimes it almost made us cry.

Such was again the trend of our talking as we walked back that night, as we reckoned we could afford to, indulging our fantasies to the full, for they cost nothing; and to be rational and look things square in the face meant we would chuck each other – or rather, Edna would chuck me, with the joy and richness fled for ever. It was all plumb barmy, I used to tell myself in the privacy of my own thoughts, but I was very reluctant to be cast in the heroic mould of renunciation – not if Edna never gave the hint. I wanted what I could have now. Besides, how was renunciation of my right to be loved, and to love – how would it ever make either of us happy, having regard to the fact we were in love? Anyway, we always told each other it was all pretend – with me sometimes making Edna almost cry when I would cruelly tease that if she got another boy I would drop out. Fate had seemed to land a dice of misfortune against us two ever realising the simple, natural fulfilments of courtship into marriage, yet we never moaned unduly; rather, we thanked our lucky stars for being able to see each other, to talk, and walk, and laugh in each other's sight. It was very rare we did not sort differences out in the last few quiet minutes of holding hands, before going our separate ways back to our little rooms.

So we stood that night at the sani gates (somewhat daring, though all was quiet), stood until the bewitching hour of ten approached and Edna had to hurry up the drive to forestall locking-out. After a discreet hanging-about for another few minutes, I also made my way to the men's block, fairly bursting with happiness and knowing I could face the doctor in the morning with a tale of a task, if not quite done, at least well started, in my eyes.

But, as always, I was playing my wildly optimistic bent too far and, as things can go in everyday, kick-in-the-pants life, this went. It went the wrong way with Arthur, in every sense a fish out of water, washed up in unreceptive Bradford with its mills and tall chimneys, and its warehouses and cranes, and back-to-back crowded streets, but with never a smell or a hint of the sea, or a river, or even a canal now that gloomy-looking ribbon of foul water was filled in with earth, and with certainly no jobs for bright young lads lately returned from ploughing the deep Atlantic furrows. After some disappointing weeks trailing the streets of his native city, Arthur came, disheartened and depressed, to see me at the sani. He told me of his desire to get back to Southampton and, though I argued the wisdom of his going, he stuck to his guns. He did not like Bradford, he had never been happy in his short spell as a landlubber, which now stood out a mile to me, and so I gave in. 'Well, Ah'm sorry, Arthur… Ah thought it was for the best… Anyway, Ah can let you have a couple o' quid to get back to Southampton… And, well, the best of luck, lad.' With which he left me a sadder man, for it all sounded so weak and lame and as though I was letting him go without a fight. But that was it – he went, and I was sick to death at his going, feeling very bitter with failure. We were at the very beginnings again – he was lost, then he was found, and now he was lost again, probably for ever, for I couldn't guess what he might decide on, in the future. Yet I need not have taken on so, for he was shipborne inside a week, and always got a boat after, this seeming to prove there was a law of compensation lurking round somewhere, after all.

Arthur standing on front of launch.
Ship, *Empress of Australia*, West Indies cruise, 1936

***

It worked for me also, this unpredictable law, in a real fairy-tale ending, though it was to be a long time after the foregoing, when my dearest had left the Dales to seek her better fortune in faraway Croydon. Alas, it had proved that whilst everybody at the sani looked upon our affair with a benevolent eye, it had stopped any promotion for her and so, with my blessing, she had gone to a better job elsewhere. But Edna did not forsake or forget me. She still came to see me in our loved countryside, every holiday when this was permissible, even to the neglect of her own family – for a whole magical week or ten days, in the summer, when she stayed with friends, the Longthornes, or two precious days at Christmas (yes, a mere two days from far-off Croydon), when we would live afresh our wonderful little saga; though partings were hellish hard, especially when she would say, at the Christmas farewell, 'Ugh! That's that… See you then sometime next summer.' It seemed such a long, cruel time to be apart, even though three letters a week broke down the loneliness of separation somewhat.

Edna had probably been gone some two years, and me still up there, one of the oldest inhabitants, with so many friends gone home or fallen by the wayside, when one day, out of the dark cloud of enforced hospitalising, there appeared a small silver lining. At first it was a shot in the dark, having to do with a pension the army had not seen fit to give me on leaving the service but, through the initiative of good friends and also the doctor, this pension became a distinct possibility. There followed long, chafing months of seeming nothing doing but, gradually, progress was made, the silver lining grew bigger, and one bright post-time I found myself suddenly a man of substance, staring delightedly at a cheque for some three-hundred-odd pounds sterling and the news of the granting of a full disability pension. Of course, all the place was agog with the good news, for I was never one at keeping glad tidings to myself. Doctor Bill sent for me, congratulated me on now being a bloated moneyman, gave me the morning off to get myself on nodding terms with the Midland Bank branch in the village, then got down to asking what I really intended doing in my new role. Oh, I just didn't know, not just yet, I told him; it was all so confusing. He pressed further: what did I intend doing about a certain young lady in Croydon? When I recovered my happily surprised breath I told him I intended wedding her, if I could get his blessing about leaving the sani. He smiled enigmatically; said he would see about it; advised me to get to know Edna's answer, for he even named her now; then turned me out of the duty room with a shrewd Scot's smile of approval. I was in a state of mixed emotions the next few days, for Edna's reply had been a definite 'yes'; my whole world was about to undergo a vast transformation, and I was a little sad at leaving everybody of the past four years or so, at leaving the sani, that quiet, blessed haven that had seen so many of my ups and downs, my joys and disappointments, and had at long length restored me to a goodly measure of health. It was rather fitting it should now be the setting for the one triumphant hour that must come, surely, once in everyone's lifetime.

As good fairy tales end, Edna and I got married (though more of that later), and were so eager we did it by special licence with, in quixotic fashion, hardly a stick of furniture in our little cottage, such was our hurry to capitalise before we woke up and found we were dreaming it all, atop of the moors. If there was one small fly in the ointment, it was the fact that neither Bill nor Arthur were there to see us wed. Bill had dropped out of it, for I had not heard from him in a long time even though I had written a couple of times to his last known address. We had been married some weeks before we got a bright and breezy letter from Bill, readdressed from the sani, writing as though he had but wrote last week. He *was* surprised when he knew I was out, was wed, in a cottage of our own, and made a special point of coming to see us – and bringing his girl along. It must have been an infectious atmosphere, for Bill got himself married to Claire shortly afterwards, which wasn't a bad thing, the way we had knocked about.

And Arthur? He stayed a seaman, and he also came to see us between his many voyages. Sometimes he would stay a week or more, but he was always glad to be getting back to sea again for, as he laughingly said, he was not built for the quiet life ashore. The last time we had him stay was in the summer of 1942; we received two letters from him whilst he was away, the last one whilst he was serving as bosun on a cargo boat, the *Harmala*. She was in convoy in the North Atlantic one Sunday night when a torpedo hit her, and she never had a chance. There were some survivors, as a subsequent note from one of his officers told us, but Arthur was not one of them… So he got his wish – the sea…[35] It was his only love, and he's there forever now, a small part of a vast canvas of salt water, and big ships, and hosts of shipmates – and if these few words can serve as any sort of epitaph, it's the least I could do.

I'm sorry to end on a gloomy note, but that is how stark life can be; you take what comes your way, good or ill. I nearly said 'You take your pick', but quite a lot of folks never get a pick. It behoves one to affect rose-tinted spectacles most of the time and, if you're young and get somebody else along with you in the same frame of mind, then you should make a go of it. Come to think – it was marvellous being young. The only trouble was, it did not last long enough.

35 Arthur Tempest was lost at sea on 7th February 1943 in the North Atlantic aged 26 years.

J. & C. HARRISON LTD

MANAGERS OF

NATIONAL STEAMSHIP CO LTD
GOWLAND STEAMSHIP CO LTD

DIRECTORS:
JOHN HARRISON.
F.J. HARRISON.
A. TUSKETINE.

TELEGRAMS: HARCALO, FEN, LONDON.
CABLES: HARCALO, LONDON.
TELEPHONE: ROYAL Nº 3120

MARLON HOUSE,
71-74, MARK LANE,
LONDON, E.C. 3.

AND AT 13, JAMES STREET, CARDIFF.

IN YOUR REPLY PLEASE QUOTE REF. CR/R.

30th January, 1947.

Mr. Richard Tempest,
11, Pepper Hill,
Shelf, Nr. Halifax,
YORKS.

Dear Sir,

s.s. "HARMALA".

We are in receipt of your letter of the 25th instant with reference to the loss of your brother, Mr. A. Tempest, on the 7th February 1943.

According to a report given us by the Chief Officer, who was one of the 13 survivors, the vessel was torpedoed in the North Atlantic at approximately 30° West at 3.15 a.m. She sank in three minutes but the survivors got away in the port lifeboat and were picked up some time later by a Corvette. This Corvette dropped a Carley float at the time of the sinking, but there was a gale blowing at the time and no other survivors were seen when daylight came.

We are sorry we cannot say to what medals your brother would have been entitled, but if you communicate with the Superintendent of the Mercantile Marine Office at the nearest port, giving him your brother's wartime record, the Superintendent will be able to advise you.

Yours faithfully,
for J. & C. HARRISON LIMITED.

A QUIET 'DO'

It was a hectic month when I got my windfall. Within a week or so, we were celebrating the Silver Jubilee of King George, on a day made to order as regards weather. That day, we went the whole hog at the hospital, with a slap-up lunch, an imported band on the lawn in the marvellously hot afternoon, a tea-buns-races for the young patients, and a smoked salmon tea for us adults. We surely lived it up that day, and it seemed everything was looking up in this new, grand atmosphere of good fortune and happy augury. That same morning I spent down in the village, taking snaps of the High Street en fête, with every house and shop making its own brave show of flags and bunting, and the pubs all open early and bright. I still had that same camera – still serviceable – a box type that Edna bought me the first Christmas we ever knew each other.

Grassington High Street, 6th May 1935

I had not a care in the world the last three weeks I was at Grassington, for all I wished seemed to be coming my way – and about time, too, I told myself. But I was also growing increasingly impatient to be out trying my luck in the world again, fortified as I now was from a material point of view and waiting, daily, for Doctor Bill to say the magic words that would set me off down the drive to Bradford.

At last they came. I was to go home on a Friday which, when it dawned, was unusually cold; quite out of the blue, snow started falling, and this in mid-May! There was a boisterous leave-taking of laughter and chaff as I climbed into the ponderous old ambulance that was to take us to Bradford – for there were, also, three or four others going on a weekend's home leave. Yet, once away down the drive, I felt an awful sense of melancholy at leaving less fortunate friends, some of whom would never recover, and would certainly never know the same amazing good luck I had. I felt humbled in comparing our lots but, gradually, as distance lent disenchantment, I shrugged it off by telling myself that was the way of things: some were lucky, some were not; and, after all, I had dwelt a darned long time in the shadows before I was favoured by Dame Fortune. And, more urgent, it was still snowing, a regular blizzard swirling as we took turns peeking through a narrow slit of transparency high up in the van side.

It snowed all the way home and went on into the afternoon; so much so that the following day's cricket programme, of which I had promised myself an afternoon's watching, was called off, an unprecedented thing that has never happened since in the Bradford League. Added to all this, Edna was working her notice out at Croydon, prior to coming north to join me in Bradford, and I had in mind a cottage out on a hill beyond Bradford. Truly, it was a month of moment to me!

When I first saw our cottage, it was on a pleasant Saturday afternoon. I had walked up a steep lane, made quite pastoral by virtue of the fact of hawthorn blossoms clouding three or four stunted thorns that dug in tenaciously to the lane side, leaning over from the bite of the blustering west wind that was, year in, year out, such a menace to their very existence. Then, around a bend, I had come in sight of a row of cottages, and my companion had said, 'These are 'em,' and I had realised one of these could be mine. None of them looked up to much, I told myself – but what did that matter? I hadn't come up here to view a palace, and Edna wouldn't be expecting one when she came. All we asked was a place of our own, out of the smoke and grime of the city, and here it was. Yet I oft-times wondered, afterwards, what part the scattered show of May blossom played in clinching the issue that afternoon?

It was my intention, in the interval of my arrival in Bradford and Edna's coming, to go up to the cottage daily and fettle it out against the day we would go up as man and wife. But gradually, I became aware that things disturbing, unpleasant, were beginning to manifest themselves. Reactions were setting in arising from my being transplanted out of the clear, thin air of the Dales into the thick of the city's industrial atmosphere, though I had been aware of this danger through the past experiences of other chaps who had gone home from Grassington before me. Now, I found myself unable to sleep; going off my food, which was most unusual; found I was developing that old horror feeling of helpless lassitude. I felt I couldn't get enough air into my lungs – oh, I could feel myself sinking into a dreadful state, and was terribly disheartened, more so because of the tremendous fillip my morale had enjoyed so recently. It made matters worse with Edna still being down south, blissfully thinking all was now well with me, for I dare not even hint of any backenings to distress her afresh.

Then, one morning, the whole thing boiled over. I had got up and must have looked as I felt – low and thoroughly miserable – and was playing about with my breakfast so that May Brown, with whom I was staying until the cottage was ready, asked, 'Why aren't you eating?'

'I dunno,' I mumbled. 'Probably cos… Oh, I dunno…' I rambled away, peevishly. I wanted to be left alone, to stew in my own bile, extremely bitter as that was. I didn't want to hear the I-told-you-sos I feared were coming.

'Go see your doctor for a tonic,' May tried, sympathetically.

'Ugh! I'm sick o' seeing doctors,' I beefed, now feeling very sorry for myself. 'What good have they done me?' I asked in base ingratitude. 'Four years I've had, doctored to death. Oh, hell!' I almost choked as I concluded with, 'It's all been a waste of time,' and turned from May to hide my shame, for I knew I was going to make an exhibition. I was utterly defeated, desolated, for I hadn't even had the satisfaction of seeing Edna, of sharing with her what should have been my one glorious hour of joy and happiness, which now seemed to be fading fast. My eyes dimmed with tears at the wretched, returned hopelessness of everything, now made cruelly worse for my having touched the cup of joy-over-sorrow to my lips, only to have it slowly pulled away. Already, in my heart, I conceded a victory to malign fate – I hadn't even the will, or the guts, to want to go into the fight again. I was beaten to a frazzle as I stood with my head bowed.

'Look, love!' May was talking to me again, having given me a few minutes to regain my composure. 'It isn't doing for you here, that I can see… Trouble is, it's going to be weeks before you can go in your own house… Eee, I wish…' Her face wore a worried look as she lapsed into a helpless silence.

We surveyed each other for a few moments in glum stalemate, then a slow smile started playing on her chubby face. She chuckled, and I asked, 'What's the joke?'

She answered, 'Hey, why not go up now?'

'You mean – Pepper Hill – just now?' I queried, looking very puzzled.

'Yes, now. Straight away!' Then she hastened to assure me. 'Oh, I don't want to get shut of you so bad, but why not try it? You stand to lose naught by trying, do you?'

'No, I don't,' I agreed, my face lighting up at the very simple truth of May's suggestion, my former defeatism now spurred to positive action. 'Aye, I'll go now. I can easy get a bed sent from the furniture shop, can't I?'

'Course!' encouraged May. 'And I'll fix you up with your bedding, and Wilf'll[36] give you a hand when he gets home.'

When I took up residence, straight away as suggested, our cottage had not one stick of furniture until the furniture people brought a bed up for me that Saturday afternoon. I might mention they brought it up under protest after I put the screw on with mild threats of taking my furniture order elsewhere, for I had already been to them regarding setting up house when the cottage was ready. Of course, I did not get the bed I asked for, and had a bit of a barney with the driver, who went away promising the world on Monday; though we still have the same bed, for I did not make a case of it, being thankful for small mercies that day.

It might provoke a smile when I state how I started picking up instantly – yes, instantly. With my large carrier bag of provisions, long nights of refreshing sleep, and solid eating stimulated by the good air, I was again looking presentable when Edna, not a moment too soon, finished her notice and came to Bradford. It had been intended that she would stay with friends to cover a necessary residential period before marriage in church, but all that now went by the board, for Edna took a dim view of my being in the cottage on my own, playing up as though I might be marooned on some Arctic waste. The outcome was, we went on a Monday morning to a registrar's office in Bradford, to make arrangements to marry by special licence.

'How soon can we get married?' we asked a very pleasant gentleman.

He told us, 'Wednesday.'

Wednesday, at the earliest, because of the necessity of one full day elapsing, when our names would be displayed on a board at the back of the office door so that any may see and protest against our wedding, if any such protesting could be justified. We came away with an appointment made for nine-fifteen on the Wednesday, and then spent the rest of the day making hurried preparations – though there were not *so* many, come to think of it, not from my point of view.

36 May's husband.

It was a very simple ceremony with but four of us present. Edna remarked on the lack of pomp and emotional buildup, and I assured her, 'Well, it's for keeps, missus, just the same as if we'd been wed in St Paul's.' After that, we had a quiet meal in town, then set off for the day by our two selves, having promised to see our best man and his wife at the Alhambra Theatre in the evening, for my friend was a market gardener in his own right (and still is) and had to get back to more pressing business.

My bride and I had no clear idea where we were going to spend our day and, eventually, found ourselves at Temple Newsam, a vast hall and estate which I understood had, at one time, belonged to the Irwin family but had now passed into the hands of the Leeds Corporation. It was a gracious place, filled with lovely things and commanding fine views, but I'm afraid I was too preoccupied, and failed to appreciate all as I might have done at any other time. We did joke in drawing a comparison between the little dwelling awaiting us and this magnificent house, though we were not at all envious. And it was such a lovely day, without a flaw in a cloudless sky, and we sat a couple of hours in the grounds, serenely happy in just being together again – only now it was for ever, as we delightedly kept rediscovering every few minutes through the happy afternoon, until we found we must be away, if we were to eat and get to the Alhambra as arranged.

It was a grand bill that night, topped by Layton and Johnstone, and Teddy Brown, a huge American who could make a xylophone talk. It was a wonderful night's entertainment by top-line stars whose names, alas, mean nothing now in this new world of theatre values. It was a wonderful, starlit night after as we went along to supper with our friends, before making our way homewards for the very first time.

It caught us going up the hill. A violent, howling storm of rain that caught us without raincoats or any other conventional weather garments as we struggled the last half-mile, with no shelter on this hillside, and got drenched to the skin before we reached our cottage. Edna was near tears when we let ourselves in, for the old place looked so bare and inhospitable; we hadn't even a table, for I had lived from the tops of upturned drawers for the time I had already been there. No, there was nothing romantic about our crossing our hearth for the first time, for the immediate thing was to make a fire. However, we soon had a great blaze roaring up the chimney of the old-style oven-and-boiler fireplace, and we got a pot of something hot and sat stripped of our wet things, and Edna grew more cheerful then. So we came home on our wedding night, to a place of our very own, to a place we had often drawn fancy mental pictures about, to a place that had seemed so far out of reach only months before. Edna quoted 'Be it ever so humble…' and we kissed on that sentiment with thankful hearts. As I led upstairs over the bare stone steps, feeling very much the man of the house, I envied nobody, and Edna – well, she looked radiant!

In the large barn-like bedroom, the sole article of furniture, the three-quarter bed, stood to welcome us and looked very small in the emptiness. Long shadows flickered from the feeble light of a candle (the electric not having yet been reconnected) and played ghosts on the walls and ceiling of the sombre chamber. Edna shuddered and took my hand, and I took her to look out of the small back window, the rain having now ceased. We looked up and saw myriads of stars twinkling in a black firmament, all so peaceful and clean-washed after the tempest we had suffered on the way up. And, again, we felt so happy in the knowledge we really wanted for nothing, stood together at the window. At last I yawned, muttered, 'By, I'm sleepy… Anyway, we'll not be getting up soon in the morning, dear, that's for certain… An' I'll tell you what, I'll bring you a cup o' tea up, eh?'

In the morning, we promised ourselves sleepily as we lay in bed, we would begin the inspiring, yet rather daunting, task of putting our house in order, of moulding this shell to our own fashion. Tomorrow, we would set about doing things we were sure nobody had ever done before, for no one else had ever quite been through the same mill as us… But that was tomorrow.

Edna Tempest, possibly on her wedding day

HOUSE ON A HILL

It did not take us long to discover there were to be many tomorrows of starting to do things, and so many of our tasks of love to be left unfinished until yet another morrow, in this exasperatingly nonconformist cottage of ours that always seemed to mutely beseech to be left well alone.

I have said there was not one stick of furniture there when we went in, but I was mistaken – there was a lumbering shut-up bed pushed away in a recess upstairs, and an old iron mangle that must have been poured into an almost inaccessible place under some stone steps, so snugly did it fit. I soon moved this with a borrowed maul hammer, and Edna said the old bed might serve as a wardrobe for the time being, though we did not have it in service very long, Edna having quickly seen a bedroom suite that took her fancy.

The first thing that excited our visionary emotions was the electricity, and though this ran but to three sixty-watt lamps, we saw cookers, radio, electric irons, a clock, and a host of other small things coming along in the wake of progress. Optimistically, we talked of the minor miracles we could perform in this one-up-one-downer of ours, in between deciding whose turn it was to bring yet another pail of drinking water from a pump in a field, down the lane and not yet revealed in its worst light in this high summer of our honeymooning. But, after a lot of talking and theorising in our small castle, when we got down to the practical side of things it began to dawn on us we had set ourselves some job. There were no two walls alike – concave, convex, one side lower than the other, these walls were a ghastly joke on the ancient builder's part. Nor did any two windows measure the same, though they appeared the same size looked at casually. No two lines ran parallel. And nothing ever repeated itself. The uneven stone floor – the cure for which was to have been a simple task of lifting a flagstone here and a corner there, and slapping trowels of cement under – was not playing fair at all. Most of these great slabs were hollowed with long and hard wear, and, having stared some time at them without effecting any other remedy, we reluctantly compromised with a great square of coconut matting and no lifting nor no show of cement. If one touched wood, it crumbled – not exactly to ashes, just to a fine dry dust that conjured up a nightmare of tumbled rafters. A nail driven heartily into any wall was sufficient to bring down a shower of plaster, and left a rugged scar right down to a bleached face of massive sandstone blocks. Ordinary plugging of these walls was out, for the simple reason that it was the hardest thing in the world to find a nick, for one could never make an inspired guess where lines or divisions lay. How I could have used a nick-diviner, had such a magician existed!

At weekends this first summer, especially if the weather was fine, we got plenty of friends along, and also the downright curious, just to see how we were making out. They would puff hard, rendered at once critical-minded because of this puffing up the Hill; have a grumble, a cup of good tea and a rest; then walk around with a devil sat on the end of their tongues, and always they would touch something that would drop BANG! Of course, their visits gave birth to such classics as 'Eee! Have you to fetch your own water?' – this after they had exhausted our pail of that valuable commodity. They would sniff disdainfully and cry, 'Ugh! I wouldn't live here rent-free – straight, I wouldn't.' Or ask maliciously (for Edna had not yet admitted to being in love with the place), 'Whatever did you let him drag you up here for, lass?' And, after an extra spot of noseying around consequent on relieving bladders distended with too much tea-bibbing, 'Ah! Pole-squatters, eh?'

We got ourselves a dog after a few revealing weeks on the

Hill – though, at the time, we were not particularly fond of animals. Benny, for such was the name promptly given him, came after we discovered that what appeared to be a pack of stray dogs was, in fact, our neighbour's pets given a very free rein, with almost every house contributing its quota. They overran the Croft, as everybody called our row of cottages with the patch of wasteland in front; they especially favoured our pocket-handkerchief bit of garden to frolic in, and made out a good case for squatter's rights, so long had they apparently played there unhindered. They leaped walls and gates like hunters and – the crowning indignity – barked furiously at us on our own midden. Nowhere, nothing, was sacred to them. They were a vexing problem, for we did not want to fall out with our new neighbours over their dogs – but we found that whilst they never bothered about restraining their canines, they were very proprietorial in defending alleged rights and wrongs. So we patted, coaxed, shooed, edged away, got in crafty backheels when we hoped nobody looked, but it was all so annoyingly futile, with the dogs still very attached to our property.

It seemed the answer to a prayer when I got chance to buy a puppy, from our best man's father – or rather, he knew a man who knew a man, etc. Our dog was some three months old, smooth-haired, the colour of chocolate, a downright mongrel with large, pathetic eyes that smote one's heart straight away, these and his cowering before us at the first meeting. We paid three half-crowns for Benny, and it was two days before he summoned enough courage to look us in the face. Poor little fellow! He was pathetic, but he soon showed his keep, and proved to be a worthy answer to our former problem. Very soon he outdid most of his pals in being a regular fellow and relieving his high spirits, and our pent-up feelings, on neighbouring scrubs of garden, and thus the status quo was restored.

Benny was with us thirteen years, an out-and-out old scrounger who gave his heart to anybody for a bone; Benny who, because of his scraps, scrapes, outrageous affairs with the feminine gender, oft-times lay heavy on my conscience; Benny, so popular with kiddies for a long way round. It was with very heavy hearts that, at last, we had him put to sleep when he was almost blind, dragging himself about with much effort, no longer cocking his ear to outside interests. I swore never to have another dog – nor did we, not for a very long time.

Arthur (on leave from the Merchant Navy),
Edna and Benny

Meantime, we were pressing on with the many chores, and one of the most exacting was the time we undertook to scrape the downstairs beams and baulks of many old layers of wallpaper, for that old paper seemed very loath to part. It took gallons of hot water and hours of scraping before we made any impression, and the exposed surface lapped up quarts of paint, for all the world like a pot-bellied pup sopping up his water. Because of all this, we gave due thanks that nobody had ever thought of papering, likewise, upstairs. Up there, we surmised it would be a simple matter of shearing level the lumpy, limewashed walls with a big scraper, but our guess proved utterly wrong: the walls almost disintegrated in lumps of old plaster at our feet every time we made a speculative jab – and yet, three days later, under large buckets of foamy pink distemper, you could hardly tell where was plaster and where was not.

It was quite some time after this essay into the decorating game that I ever dared to paper my first ceiling, following closely on my watching a professional fix a ceiling in a couple of hours, and that with consummate ease. It was all so easy, I told myself, now I knew the tricks of the trade, and I talked Edna into us having a go.

There was quite a palaver fixing the stands, just so I could stand without strain and be able to move with safety and freedom, for one had to be slick – that, I had noted. Having got this far, and Edna having wetted the first long strip (the longer the better, I supposed, for the secret seemed to lie in the folding), I mounted with the sheet held high. (I might remark here, at this stage, I did not consider Edna had made the paste quite thick enough, but this was no time for splitting hairs). Having stuck the pasted, free end to the virgin roof, I moved with speed and grace to smooth more onto the limed surface. To my dismay, I found I was not moving fast enough; the supposedly stuck paper was moving after me, noiselessly, deliberately, spreading its cold soppy length along my back, into the nape of my neck, and arresting its further fall by staying put upon my outraged head. I blared off a bit, which was excusable, and gave out distress signals, but Edna had hurried downstairs to attend a knock at the door. Even when she did return, she surveyed the hapless mess with a titter at my plight; then stoutly maintained, when I got awkward, that I was no fit person to handmaiden upon, with my infuriating habit of blaming the tools, or blasting any hapless helper, or bewailing the very fact of living here, in this last place that God made – as I was so guilty of stating, at times.

But we were going places, as we told ourselves after every small success that first few months, though some of these were very dubious compromises with the old house. Yet a cooker (or, more correctly, a small griller), a wash boiler, and a clock spoke in eloquent silence of our faith in electricity; and, with the house filling up steady with furniture, the long days of that summer gave way to mellow autumn. In the November, the little chapel blew down[37], a disquieting portent of the weather, though they had it up again, stronger than ever, within the next twelve months. Christmas, however, found us two well entrenched and Fortune kind, except that (just a wee moan) there was no sign of the Baby Temp who had figured so much in our dreamings. Perhaps we were being a little too impatient, though we were also not wholly unaware that wisdom would have said 'nay' to such a fulfilment yet awhile… It was a vexed question!

Chapel wreck coutesey of Pepper Hill Unitarian Chapel.

37 Pepper Hill Unitarian Chapel, on Cross Lane in Shelf, blew down in November 1935.

The start of the heavy snows came on a black day in our first February, just when we were beginning to think we had got winter well licked. The snow was there at dawn, coming down silent and steady, and it was still falling, like most unwelcome manna, when all the electric lights on the Hill flickered a couple of times before leaving us flat on our bottoms without a glimmer in the late afternoon. We were plunged straight back into the Ice Age – though, luckily, we had candles, and a blackened old kettle, and a heavy frying pan which Edna, with more oil in her lamp than me, had insisted on keeping in the house, just in case, despite my scoffing at her seeming hoarding of rubbish. And right well they served while the electric equipment, whited ghosts of futility, mocked us as Edna crouched like a Pendle Witch over the old fireplace, hissing feminine imprecations onto the hot hearth, which mild cussing did not help the boiling of spuds or the frying of vicious, spitting sausages. Incidentally, this was the forerunner of many such breakdowns over many winters (through one cause and another, and not forgetting the infamous power cuts), and it could happen again this winter, despite what we folks have done about harnessing this, that and t'other.

I almost forgot to mention the one outstanding building project that first summer: a glass porch, not a very ambitious affair, that I put before the front door to baffle the east wind, which I was assured would plague us later. My porch was a success, allowing a few drops of water, now and again, as discount; but it was to be the next year before I put a window in the back wall of our kitchen, that there might be light from two windows. After it was finished, and not one minute before, a helpful neighbour told me I should have first submitted a plan to the local council and awaited their approval. He reckoned, just to rub it in further, that if they saw it they would have me take out my window and wall up again – that is, if they wanted to be awkward, mind! He said this so complacently I could have spat at him, and for months afterwards I cringed whenever I saw a council employee walking along the lane, and once dreamed of Edna, of all persons, walling me in where a big hole gaped, and not minding where she jabbed with large trowel. It might have been more beneficial if the council had found out, had made me wall up again, for this misfortune of mine faced 270° west and I had built it flush with the outer wall, with no protecting overhang to take off a little of the weather, always wet and windy from that quarter. Consequently, whenever a fresh gale blew from the savage west, which was often, I winced to a succession of loud plops as the driving rain probed, found, dropped into dishes placed, hopefully strategically, on the window bottom. A building friend of mine, with a slightly disdainful shaking of head at the amateurishness of it all, assured me that all this leaking was due to capillary action and that, short of taking the window out, I would never cure it – nor did I, not for long years when, I guess, I finally tired it out.

It was staggering what other weaknesses a good, roaring downpour of rain would unearth. One morning, after one such shocker of a night, I went outside to find a fallpipe spouting like a stricken whale; and, in my stupid, perverse way which I glibly put down to a fine spirit of independence, I decided to tackle the job myself. It was made no easier by the fact of the broken pipe being some eight feet from the ground, just too high to tackle from terra firma and necessitating using a pair of steps. It was a hard enough struggle getting the new section of pipe braced to fasten, but that was the easiest task, as I soon discovered when I tried the treble task of placing a wooden bobbin behind a retaining lug on the pipe, keeping the pipe in position, and driving home a fixing pin (even optimistically trying to push it a little way with my hand), somewhat like a balance act. I rang the changes several times in now desperate efforts, for I hated being beaten, but only succeeded in working myself into a cold rage. It got so bad Edna fearfully put her head round the door, prevailed upon me to cunningly sit it out until the milkman would appear. Edna couldn't help me, not just then, not in her delicate state of health; she would have cut no figure at all perched on those steps at that particular time, so tied up with our coming firstborn – dear Baby Temp.

I sat it out and simmered down, and we had that pipe fixed in no time when the milkman came along. I had looked in mute appeal; he had responded and, at the finish, had dismissed my thanks with 'Doan't mention it – it's naught… Good job you didn't try fixing it thisen.' He caught me grinning and added, 'Well, thur's some fowk 'at wod – y'knaw, them's queer, as likes to feel independent.'

Short by just two days of two years, Baby Temp came, after a long summer's night of tea-drinking, pacing the bedroom floor, swearing to be away for the midwife the very next time Edna winced, or stifled a groan. However, Edna was adamant there was to be no going for Nurse Brook until *she* gave the word – and that would not be yet awhile. She wasn't having the poor nurse trailing out here until she was absolutely sure her time was at hand. There were to be no false alarms for Edna, though this hanging-on did not exactly allay the disquiet I felt, being the only person there with my wife – brrh – me with a baby on my hands!

The warm night slowly passed to dawn, with Edna now looking horribly bloated and me still threatening that the very next muff from her would send me away on my long-delayed plan of 'Operation Baby Temp', yet Edna held me in check to exasperation point. Then, suddenly – following an alarming manifestation which she admitted signified baby was now definitely on the way, without any more doubting – I rushed from the bedroom and was away like a racing greyhound from its trap. I ran to a neighbour's, roused her to go and stay with Edna, then I was off farther afield to wake a friend who was to transport me to the midwife and bring her back – and she lived some two miles away. It seemed an eternity before he came to his window in reply to my thrown pebbles, irritatingly long before he sparked life into his old Morris, woefully slow as we chugged away for nurse.

Nurse Brook, bless her, was soon roused, with her reiteration that she always slept light. She wasted no further words or time, and we were back on the Hill some half an hour after quitting Edna, with me fearful, every minute we were away, of getting back and finding Baby

Temp already in this world and Edna chiding me for my tardiness. But things were still very much 'as you were', with Edna peering over the banister as we opened the stairs door, and Nurse bundling her straight to her bed when she got upstairs. With my profuse thanks following her, the neighbour started down the stairs to get her husband up and fed before he went to work (a point we had nearly overlooked), and the midwife banished me to the downstairs region at the same time. I was to occupy my time boiling water, making a pot of tea, standing ready for any summons; and later, disposing of some very ghastly things.

It must have been some twenty minutes after Nurse arrived before anything of incident happened, as far as I could judge from straining my ears. Then everything seemed to happen at once... Suddenly, Edna was shouting, crying out in alarm; Nurse Brook was shouting something. I was on my feet like a flash, trying to sort out a garble of words that kept repeating 'Benny' and invoking me to hurry! Hurry!! God! I cannot tell what I really thought had happened – something dreadful – as I bounded upstairs and, first, caught a fleeting glimpse of Edna knelt, naked, on the bed, of a little body beneath her, of the nurse occupied with Edna, and them both still crying about Benny. On their prompting, I took a quick look under the bed and found poor old Benny cowering, seemingly frightened to death with the cries, of knowing he was dead in the wrong, choose what it was. With a wrathful curse, I reached right under the bed and dragged Benny forth and, pulling and pushing, got him downstairs with me – a dog in deep disgrace, and Nurse insistent I keep a better eye on him whilst events of great significance were about.

Whilst I was furious with Benny, and evinced a show of wrath, I was really elated, for now I knew I was a father, though I had not been told, and it seemed an age before Nurse Brook's voice was calling out, bidding me to go see my baby. My baby? Our baby! Baby Temp!

When I got upstairs, leaving Benny with an affectionate pat – by way of a change, that morning – the nurse was stood by the bed, beaming very broadly; Edna was laid quietly at full stretch and smiling weakly from a very white face; and, laid on the bed at Edna's feet, wrapped like a cocoon in a strip of clean, old blanketing lay the crinkliest, brownest little morsel of humanity I had ever seen. I don't know why – but at that moment I felt a great clod, useless, under the feet. My voice croaked in crude jest, 'Joe Louis!' and the midwife cut in with, 'Nay, it's a girl… a bonny little lass,' and Edna warned, 'That'll do, Dad.' Whilst I still gaped with tongue tied and lip atremble, Nurse Brook invited me to 'pick her up, Mr Tempest', and when I hesitated which way to hold, scoffed, 'Go on, she won't bite you.'

Our baby got the most natural name in the world for her – June[38] – and was baptised at the little Unitarian chapel that stands, a monument to the tenacity of great followers, at the top of the Hill. But June came into a world becoming increasingly dark, a world where violence and the big battalions were altering maps every few months, a world dominated by Hitler, Mussolini, Japanese warlords and Spanish generals, whilst others tried to stay them with a show of papers.

However, Edna and I were preoccupied with our own little problems. We realised the big bedroom would break down into two smaller ones, to solve *our* living space problem, though it took quite some time before I got right down to it. By dint of good advance planning, plenty of sound advice, and knowing just what I wanted, I was able to get my extra bedroom up before Hitler made hay of 1939's summer. We were very proud of it when it was finished, with double Essex board for the partition, plenty of paint, and both rooms nicely papered. It was a far remove from the night when Edna and I had gone up those bare stone steps (now laid with a warm strip of carpet) and gazed in the barn-like room that summer's night. But all was not honey yet… One night, during a blustering southwest gale, a manhole in an upstairs ceiling flapped loose and banged noisily and alarmingly for long enough, until I rose in desperation and tore it from its moorings, with my old cry 'Tomorrow, I fix!' to quiet Edna's muffled protest at my drastic act.

38 June Amelia Tempest was baptised at Pepper Hill Unitarian Chapel on 25th July 1937. Richard was described as a shopkeeper in the Baptism Register.

We slept again, granted amidst plenty of howling from the wind, but with no more startling bangs, and I felt my summary action justified.

Downstairs, we did not appear to move very fast, with the old fireplace still silently rebuking us with its bulk. First, we had to get a proper electric cooker put in; then we decided it was time we had a new fireplace on the job – a nice, front-room tiled affair. But it caused some muck, with all the rubble and bits of old oven strewing the garden for days, and the putting-in of scores of bricks to plug a gaping hole in the chimney breast which, had next door not stood where it did, threatened to have our cottage toppling off balance for the few hours of the transition. During that spell we could so easily have passed upstairs through the gap that yawned that day. Perchance it be thought that I put the fireplace in (perish the thought!), it was the work of a professional – and a very good job, at that.

But I almost forgot to mention the most exciting event that happened to us: the coming of water. Water! Water to be had by turning the tap, instead of a foray outside, choose what the weather. Water by the pot, the pan, the tub, full to the top and all lovely clean liquid. The first house to get water on the Hill put up a Union Jack to mark the occasion; we had to wait, quite a while, because of a tiring dispute that dragged on, a dispute regarding the whys and wherefores consequent on our pipe going through somebody else's land. It's an awesome thing to see what bitterness a bite of land can generate when fed carefully.

There was another thing put an entirely different complexion on living here: the coming of Walt Hill's farm tractor. This vehicle, with its contempt of snowdrifts, banished the old dread of the lanes filling up with snow following a night of fall and wind. Never again would we have to chop our way through walls of hardened snow whilst awaiting the council making their slow progress to us – after all, they couldn't be everywhere! Nor would we need to issue forth, shapeless, great balls of clothes and heavy boots, men and women alike without outward distinction, to contact tradesmen waiting some hundreds of yards away at the main road. No more humping of potatoes, bread, even small quantities of coal (as the 1947 blizzard); Walt Hill could be said to have shown the way to beat winter and made but a fireside tale of our former exploits, though we still had our electric supply leave us in the dark without a moment's warning.

And naught, short of erasing our hamlet, would ever kill the odd equation that two and two do not necessarily make four, not in our houses. It was, is, always so easy to be a bit over, or a trifle under; and, after all, what is a mere fraction between friends? We oft-times joked about the old masons who ran up these houses 150 years ago. They must never have employed any medium of measure beyond their span of hand and their two eyes, and must constantly have had a large jug of ale at hand to blear those same eyes – else why all the odd angles, and bumps, and eccentric depressions, and a general following of the Earth's contours instead of the horizontal?

Edna and I quickly developed a grand philosophy of leaving well alone where possible, and God seemed to side with us by smiling benevolently upon us and ours. An old gypsy woman, round hawking pegs at our door in the early days of our marriage, told Edna that she would never want – though she did temporise by saying the lass would never have a lot – and she wasn't far out, as things have gone. Many times we have been short of money, but there has always been a next meal in front of us. We are still up the Hill, and our cottage stands mostly immodern, for I never seemed to catch up to that elusive 'tomorrow'. Down the lane the gaunt thorns still retain their grim purchase, and the May blossom is still heavy with promise in its season – but, unfortunately, my wife and I have not also found the secret of renewing our faded blossoms every year. We no longer come up the Hill with the hurried, impatient steps we took the night of the terrible storm – indeed, we bypass it and go the long way around – the days of hurry now having passed.

TUPPENCE HA'PENNY A TUB

When I went navvying, for the first and last time, jobs were as scarce to get as butter in Germany, where Marshal Göring was firmly plumping for guns, and his countrymen backing him up with an enthusiasm that frightened. It was 1938, and my new job eventually took me to a delph[39] of a small brickyard, a delph set in a hillside steadily disappearing before a manual assault on its shaly earth, ideal to fashion and bake into building bricks.

11 Pepper Hill as a shop

I had not done any manual work since I had left the sanatorium. We had tried to get a small shop going in our cottage but, after some eighteen months, had given it up as a failure because, whilst our little store was handy to nip to for a packet of cigs for Dad when he was caught without, or a couple of bob's worth of 'tick' for some, we were

39 A pit or trench. This particular one was on Brighouse Road in Queensbury.

never in the running for the regular orders, long delivered by such as the Co-op, John S Driver, or Gallons's vans. There were a few of our neighbours who tried darned hard to help us, but they were not sufficient to warrant going on after we had given it a fair trial. I even went down to London to stay with Bill and Claire for a couple of weeks, in the hope of getting a job there, and having Edna and the bairn come down, for good. But employment was equally scarce down there, or one was fobbed off with, 'Oh, yes, we want somebody, though really only a youth… Sweeping-up, and all that… Wages? Oh, about thirty bob a week.' I came back north a sadder and wiser man, leaving Bill and Claire and their baby girl Patsy (two weeks older than June) in their couple of rooms – with Bill, incidentally, himself only home one night a week, away the rest of the time on his resident-barman job.

That was the dreary outlook one sunny April morning when our butcher hailed me from his delivery cart with, 'Hello! How's things going?'

On me facetiously answering, 'Still so-so, how else?' he replied, 'Now then, steady! I heard about a job this morning. Anyway, I was asked if I wanted it.' I knew things were not going so well with him either, carting his sausages and pies, and tripe and potted meat, and small cuts and joints, round to us rustics out in the wilds. 'Aye, they assed me, but I thought o' you' – I was getting interested as he went on – 'up at the brickyard. A navvying job.' He seemed to be having second thoughts about telling me, the way dubiety spread on his face; he shook his head, muttered, 'But, I dunno, it mightn't do for you,' then lapsed into silence. We looked enigmatically at each other a long time before he finally shrugged his shoulders and summed it up with, 'Well, it's up to you – if y're interested?'

I *was* interested. I had to be in any job, good or bad, for the impression soon got abroad that a chap was a slacker if he appeared diffident or questioned the proffered job's potential or suitability. People soon got it round one was a loafer – I had heard it myself on my strictly rationed visits to the local pub – and once that label stuck, it never rubbed right off again. But Milton was moving off. 'Course I'm interested, Milton,' I hastily shouted. 'I'll get me up now before they set somebody else on.'

'Gradely, lad! And mention I've sent you!' Milton shouted back over his shoulder, already clucking his nag on to another of his isolated customers.

The foreman wasn't very impressed when we met. 'Can you use a shovel?' asked that gentleman after I had found him in the dusty, busy brickyard and minded to mention that Milton had sent me.

'I can that!' I lied stoutly.

'Y' can start now,' he told me, starting to move off at the same time, to take me to the delph. I demurred, for I was in some decent clothes and my best shoes; asked if I could start after dinner, when I had changed? He tardily gave way, though he uttered some scathing remarks about blokes seeking navvying jobs in their best clobber. I hastened home, hoping I had not made a bad impression, little knowing then that first impressions counted for little in the world of the brickyard. But I did feel I would need an understanding foreman to tide me over the first few days.

Afterwards, I thanked my lucky stars for that shortened breaking-in day. It did give me the chance to get a second winding between days, for I do not honestly think I would have gone out for an afternoon session had I started before lunch that first day. It was hard, exhausting rush stuff all the time, hard on stamina, harder still on morale – in more ways than one, as I quickly discovered. And it soon dawned on me that the foreman, in his brief look at me, had forgotten another vital question. He might also have asked about my handling of a pick, for this useful instrument was also a *must* to riving a living out of that hillside.

A navvy's job was to dig out the shale, always sensibly called 'muck', and fill tipper tubs that each held about three or four hundredweight. The full tubs were then hauled up a long incline on the end of a wire cable, away up into the brickmaking yard where the muck was tipped into huge roller-crushers, then taken up again into large storage hoppers. That first afternoon was not very old before I began to dread hearing the rattle from afar, the increasing roar that meant more empty tubs were streaking down the haulage-way, and me with my tub naught near filled, though my new colleagues were most times stood awaiting, their filled tubs drawn out of the holes. I longed for the winding gear to break down so I might catch up, for I had already heard the others grumbling about the many times this could happen in a day's work, but it did not break down that afternoon; my fervent wishes went unfulfilled.

My mates were six in number: younger than me, tougher, weatherworn, and with muscles like whipcord. They did not, and I put this mildly, enthuse over my coming into their midst. It seemed I was a stand-in for a pal of theirs who was in hospital and had been there for about a fortnight when I went down to keep his job warm. The others had been quite happy to manage short-handed, filling the absent man's tubs between them and sharing the extra money. But this streamlining of labour was not altogether to the foreman's liking; he wanted all the tubs he could get in the shortest possible time, for it was now spring, with the building trade waking from its long winter hibernation, and wagons queueing for still more bricks. So it came about that I was thrown into the breech, an innocent abroad, a much-harried pawn in this game of playing off each other. Of course, the foreman won, for I stayed ten months, and the chap whose shoes (or rather tubs) I filled died in the early summer, whilst still in hospital.

Each of us worked in a clearing, simply styled a 'hole'; generally two men side by side, though each filled his own tub and took it out himself. We worked all day with pick and shovel, forever filling tub after tub, ad nauseam – just that, nothing else. Pick! Pick! Pick! If the going was rough, to be followed by a sliding of the heavy shovel forward into the loosened muck, then up and over into the tub. Pick! Pick! Pick! Slide shovel forward, up, over! Slide shovel forward, up, over! So went the deadly fatiguing, monotonous drill hour after hour, each shovelful adding but a mite to a chap's earnings. I must add here (in fairness to the man who did a spot of shot-firing) that we could put the pick to one side for long periods and enjoy comparatively easy going if he brought down plenty of muck with a well-placed shot – though not with a lot of grass sod, or slabs of stone, for these did not make bricks, or brass for us delvers. If it was not a good shot, and muck at a premium, then we were unlucky, for we would not – could not – get another shot put in until we had cleared all the bottoms out, which might last a day.

We were paid by the tub. Tuppence ha'penny a tub. Tuppence ha'penny, for ten minutes of the hardest physical work I had ever performed. Needless to say, it was poor pay. If we did have a good day, from seven in the morning until five in the afternoon, filling steadily and with no stops, we would make about ten shillings. We did not need a mathematician down there to tell us, when we sent the forty-eighth set up, that we had earned ten bob, or a 'thin un' as we called a ten-shilling note. Ten bob was a target we always had before our eyes, but lots of days we fell short, many times far short. Bad weather was the worst enemy and a hazard we had no control over, and bad filling from the holes, and breakdowns, and a dozen and one other things. The haulage rope might snarl, the rails buckle, the brickmaking plant wink up with the giant muck hoppers choked full, and we navvies sat waiting idly by our shovels, without so much as a 'by your leave!' or a 'sorry' from above, killing precious filling time until the brick presses started doing their stuff again. At these times we would drop ourselves on some dry heap and hurl imprecations aloft – though, at first, I hurled mine with tongue very much in cheek, for I couldn't have it both ways.

The most devastating factor to me was that the slowest filler made the pace, for everybody's tub had, perforce, to go up together, six or seven tubs forming a fresh haul when they were all filled and ready at the rope. The poor beginner, especially if he was new to the game, would sweat blood in his frantic efforts to keep up, with the others waiting about in no happy mood. This unenviable bringing up the rear happened to me most every time that first afternoon, and I grew sickened, physically and mentally. I would have given a lot for a steady drizzling of rain to drive us into the hut, for a 'rained off' respite, but it was not to be, and it was to be much later before I enjoyed the normal respite afforded by waiting for somebody else.

Even the lesser task of bringing the filled tubs to the haulage rope was fraught with hazards. There were no such things as split points in the rails that led to the holes; there were three or four short sets of straight rails running from the holes, half-circling a large steel plate dropped at the end of the haulage main rails. Having brought a full tub to the plate, I was set the delicate task of twisting this on the said plate to line the tub wheels with the main haulage rails, then pushing it forward to run sweetly to the rope along these rails. This was a manoeuvre that called for speed, dexterity, confidence and, of course, strength, for it was a hell of a grind trying to turn a full tub on its own axis. To be successful without courting a hernia, I found I had to approach the plate fast, hence the need for supreme confidence (or a spilled tub); give the tub a violent twist as it rolled across the unrailed area, thus the need for dexterity and strength at this point of no return; and, all being well, it would go along without further effort to join its mates at the rope end. Many a time my tub never found the rails beyond the point of no return, and I would have a back-breaking session trying to lift a full tub back on the rails, with the boys sprawling on the bank, cynical and hard-boiled to hell. They would let me struggle so long, then one of them would jump in and darned near throw the tub back onto the elusive rails. Yet, through keeping my eyes very wide open, I quickly found that shoulders and back well down to lift were the big secret of dealing with ditched tubs.

Just once that afternoon I was lucky enough to get my tub to the rope whilst they still heatedly talked rugby league – of Harry Beverley[40] having recently joined Halifax, of his merits and demerits – and I

40 b. 1907; loose forward who played for Yorkshire, England and Great Britain.

knew it would last a while longer, though I hesitated, and one of them suggested, 'Get thi bacca, mate.'

'I don't smoke,' I said naively (as it turned out), instead of sitting and saying naught.

'It's a blanking good job you don't, cock,' he retorted, and left it at that.

I asked, 'Why?' and everybody roared with laughter – everybody but me. I couldn't see anything funny, or faintly subtle in the remark, but I compromised with a weary grin. I had to grin and take things, for I was in no shape to do otherwise.

That first evening, I limped home like a wounded animal slinking back to its lair, and I couldn't tackle the huge, hot tea Edna had prepared, for I was too exhausted. She was distressed, but not more then I was, for I had always been a good eater and now even this blessing was being denied me. Edna begged me not to go down to the delph again, but I quickly excused my deplorable condition to not being toughened up enough, not yet. I would be, I assured her, given a day or two's steady breaking-in. Even as I said this, I wasn't convincing myself – I hadn't a clue, and the job, viewed from a distance of some hours, still looked pretty bleak and hopeless, and myself now given over to going on until I dropped – a man couldn't do more, surely!

However, the scene not altogether set in the heroics, I went to bed at about nine o clock, fortified by a cup of cocoa – thick, very sweet, very hot – which Edna told me was a sure inducer to sleep. But there was no deep, satisfying slumber. I was awake, hour after hour, filling those vast tubs in that hellhole on the hillside. It was a fixation I couldn't shake off until the early hours of the morning; then I started sweating profusely, and that was one thing I had learned to dread over the past years, and a thing I had thought myself rid of long ago. It was all so reminiscent of my past illness, and so enervating – and I couldn't do a thing about it. I would push the bedclothes away from my body for coolness, but I was still on fire; or gently awaking in an ooze of sweat that sapped strength and knocked hell out of morale.

I had this demoralising performance every night for the first week or so – though, fortunately, I began to pick up on my eating. I had to, or I would have cracked up completely.

Needless to say, I was very depressed. Inner pep talks seeming pretty inadequate, Edna entreated, 'Chuck it up, Dick... You can't go on like you are doing... Y're going to be poorly again.' When I said I could not chuck up for I would have neither job or dole if I walked out, she shouted in anger, 'Y'll kill your bloody self then, for the sake of a stinking job like that, eh?'

I turned my face from her, or I might have given in, admitted defeat.

She wept in almost hopeless despair and tackled me afresh with, 'Don't go on... Please! Oh, please!' though I still remained silent. Then she urged, 'We'll manage, somehow. There's surely bits of other jobs you – we – can do if we have a good look around?' I looked around as she said this, to June not yet twelve months old, and knew I had to go on the hard way. But Edna was still at it, in between diminishing sniffs. 'Anyway, there's still your dole. I'm sure we'll manage if we take things very steady... Dick, look at me!'

But I wasn't looking now, for it wasn't as simple as Edna would have it: the clerks at the Labour Exchange would not be amused by a joker who went in and told them he had chucked up his work on his own. This was the unforgivable crime in their eyes, and their damper to stop this kind of lark from spreading was to withhold the scamp's dole for six weeks, which was no laughing matter.

How some employers played on such fears was common knowledge amongst the working class. There was the tale told down our delph of our employer having said he liked to see his navvies going home in the evening holding on to the wall, dragging themselves along in their tiredness, which tale vastly amused most of us – though not me, for it was too near the truth in the first few weeks. My upper legs were chafed red and sore with the constant rubbing of the shovel handle on them, and most every muscle I had was an aching jelly. My boots turned very hard, and I felt as though my feet were encased in iron. My fingers grew stiff and fair creaked when I opened them on waking, and they soon got torn and bloodied from burst blisters rubbed raw with the ceaseless shovelling and frequent picking. I toiled on, miserably hating it all – no conversationalist, yet, amongst the boys, only too glad to throw myself down every moment I could; which moments, I'm glad to say, began coming along more frequently as the hard days went by, and myself 'framing better', as my mates put it.

It took about a fortnight of trial and error, and stumblings-about like a child learning to walk, before I got into a mechanical rhythm of smooth, less tiring movement. I also learned there were shovels and shovels, and that these had different sizes and numbers that signified to a proper navvy. Also, I saw that the old-timers filed a new shovel's edge until it was razor-thin, and I soon had a new edge on mine. Now, I felt there was a kind of poetry about the perfect sweep of shovel to fill, about the graceful, easy swing of a pick, the smooth shaft sliding through practised hands, hands that were never jarred with the impact. It seemed amazing how I could have suffered so in the transition and, typical of me and my mercurial nature, I passed from deep dejection to an almost arrogant sense of sweet triumph. I gloried in my new-found strength and know-how – though, obviously, it was strictly for home consumption, for my mates did not wear attitudes like that. I began moving the mountains of food necessary to stoke up fresh reserves of energy every day. I was now getting down to a good night's sleep with no sweating, no lying awake, no fearing the morning. Very importantly, I took pride in being a real navvy, in deed as well as name, with a very satisfying reaction to my being accepted as one of the boys. The happiest omen was the way things were shaping at home, with Edna tailing off with her cries for me to quit, and with a look of peace and content coming back into her erstwhile troubled eyes.

Every day at noon, we dined in a scruffy little wooden hut thrown up against the haulage-way. Our tea – a *must* – was scalded from a blackened Woolworth kettle that sat on a crude fireplace built by the boys, the fuel being liberally laced with brick oil stolen from out of the yard. Brick oil was very good at promoting a quick blaze, but it also brought clouds of thick, choking smoke bellowing out from the open bottom of the fireplace, which I found pretty acrid on the lungs. Yet we sat through it all, relaxed and very hungry, sandwiches on our knees, and each a thick stone jam jar filled to the brim with boiling hot tea. One huge young chap, Big Cyril, whom I always admired for his strength and ability, also fascinated me with his infinite liking and capacity for 'shirtlifters', his own name for the then all-important, universal brand of tinned baked beans. He had a big tin of these most days. Some days he ate them sizzling hot, taken from the fire ledge with the help of his grimy cap; other times cold, all depending on the caprices of the fire. Nevertheless, the beans, hot or cold, went down the same appreciative way, helped with a couple of thick slices of bread and great swigs of tea, strong and black enough to make the ordinary stomach belch for hours after in righteous sufferance.

Talking of drinking reminds me of the curious habit, to my way of thinking, of my new mates always seeking their ale in a herd, they being very gregarious creatures. Every Saturday dinnertime (for we worked Saturday mornings) would find us in the taproom of the Stag's Head first, studying the form of the gee-gees whilst shifting foaming pints; second, shifting an ample supply of meat pies and relish always on sale at Saturday's noontime. We would stay quite some time (though it bore hard on our wives) dominoing and darting; then, in the last dying moments before the towels fluttered onto the pumps, about three pints per man would appear before my jaundiced eyes. It was an old custom, they uproariously insisted, but it was a custom that daunted me. It was grim going tackling still more beer, with the feeling strong on me that it was already oozing out of my ears, but honour demanded I drink the unwelcome, unwanted pints. Come Saturday evening, and Sunday night, they would gather somewhere else, nowhere in particular, really – but minus me, for Saturday's swigging was quite enough: neither my stomach nor my pocket could stand up to this weekend soaking. But nothing – not rain, nor breakdowns, nor bad filling – stood in the way of their seeking ale in a convivial group every weekend. I suppose it was a navvy ritual amongst Lefty and Dinah and Big Cyril and the rest of the boys.

We could be screamingly funny down the delph; in rough jokes played and in things said – never very flattering, and definitely deflating to one's ego. Tales were told in the hut whilst we sheltered from weather for brief spells: of misadventures, as when I took my very wet clogs off, put them under the fireplace to dry one lunchtime, fell asleep, then woke to pull them out desiccated and breaking like thin pot in my dismayed hands. It was a huge joke, thought the others, but Big Cyril did dash home on his motorbike to bring me a pair of rubber boots to see the day out. Mostly, it was all good fun and taken in good part, choose how hard the humour bore on victims – though, mind, once or twice I saw fists raised and brief squalls darken our skies.

It was about this time that Walt Disney had made a full-length film called *Snow White and the Seven Dwarfs*.[41] The little men were seen, and heard, going to and from work in a very colourful diamond mine. They walked in single file, carried picks and shovels on their shoulders, sang and whistled a merry ditty that extolled the virtues of physical labour. Of course, one slap-happy after-lunch, we seized on this as an excuse for a grand march from the hut into the delph, and it was a sight for sore eyes to see us navvies coming down the slight incline, picks and shovels on shoulders, singing and whistling until the hillside rang with echoing 'Heigh hos', and Walt, the foreman, rushed down from his hut in great alarm to see what had gone amiss with his bloody lunatic navvies, as he so eloquently put it.

Yet he got his bricks, despite our barmy sessions, for we had glorious weather for that job, all that summer of sun and heat. It was the summer Hutton[42] knocked 364 off the Aussies in a Test at the Oval. It was the time Edna, with June in her pram, came to tell me the grand news of that deed. Of course, all this was on the cards the night

41 *Snow White and the Seven Dwarfs* premiered in London in February 1938.

42 Len Hutton, Yorkshire and England opening batsman. His 364 for England in August 1938 remains the highest individual score by an England batsman.

before, when it was evident that if Fortune smiled he would be given a chance to go after the record, and Edna had been briefed to listen in – and, when he did get it, to hurry along to the brickyard and let me know straight away.

'Hutton's rrrrrrrrrrr!' came the sound of Edna's voice, lost in the noise of a ropeful of empty tubs rattling down to us.

'Y' what?' I yelled back, at the same time stumbling up the bank to the iron gate that separated us.

'Oooh! Are you deaf?' yelped Edna. 'I was saying Hutton's got the record!'

And I gave a little dance of joy and shouted the glad news back to the boys down the delph, and they all gave a great cheer, for Test fever was at its highest even amongst folks not normally interested in cricket.

'Well, look at your daughter,' scolded Edna a moment later as I still drooled over Hutton's feat. I mumbled an apology and offered some grubby fingers, through the rails, to the eager ones of June, smiling from her pram.

'I've got you some liver and sausages for your tea,' Edna now informed me, and my cup of happiness was, indeed, filled and running over as I hooted a delighted 'Champion!' of surprise and pleasure and backed away down the delph – for neither Hutton nor the prospect of liver and sausages for tea must keep empty tubs, or impatient mates, waiting too long.

Then, it seemed almost overnight, the long summer was gone. An early hard winter set in. One day's quagmire was the next day's sheet of ice, and snow fell early, to boot. Week after week we worked harder than ever – though previously I would not have thought this possible – and for very little money. Frost and deep snow cut deep into our filling time, problems multiplied, and a good day's filling came very rare. As Christmas approached, we crossed our fingers and hoped we might manage a good week before it was on us, but even that was denied. On the Christmas Eve, we drew just over thirty shillings apiece, for which we had wallowed in a sea of mud from melting snow on one day; and battered another day, with pathetic ineffectuality, at muck ironbound with black frost. It was a miserable holiday for us married men with family; in the words of Big Cyril (single), our pay did not even make beer brass – though he still managed to get his share, I noticed!

After that shocker of a Yuletide, I decided I'd had enough down the delph. It took me seven weeks to find another job whilst I still kept working at my navvying, though one might have been better off on the dole most of those winter weeks. Even then, it was not much of a job I did land, financially or otherwise, and it was introduced with the usual opening gambit: 'It's a lad's job, really… Naw, thur's not a right lot of wage… Still, it's there, if you want it?'

I did want it, and I got it. It was inside, for one thing; it was regular, inasmuch as the boss could be relied upon to give me until the end of the week if I ever did get the push, instead of going at the end of the day, as could – did – happen down the delph. Regular, unless some fresh economic blizzard swept me out again, but that was an occupational hazard that ran with all casual labour just then, and a worry not to be unduly dwelt upon in a world of mounting neuroses.

Yet it was with a twinge of regret I laid down my brightly gleaming, sharpened shovel and left the hole in the hillside. Not about the job, for 'hole in the hillside' about sums it up; it was the thought of leaving grand pals – rough, ready, but real genuine – who left one in no doubt what they thought, for they soon expressed such, often, and with plenty of invective as their octave of emotion. I also left the delph a wiser man, for I determined never to cross swords again with Mother Earth in search of a hardily scratched wage at tuppence ha'penny a tub. I reckoned there were easier ways, if one looked very hard, of earning a living.

CHAPTER SEVEN

ON THE HOME FRONT

The Sunday that war started, Bill and Claire were with us over the weekend, having brought little Patsy to stay awhile because of the prevalent fear London would be bombed within hours of hostilities commencing, though it transpired she was not to stay with us long. Before many more months, Patsy had gone to live with our aunt Jenny and cousin Evelyn for the rest of the war, in a small village called Darton, just outside Barnsley.

It was a very solemn Sabbath, with everybody waiting on Neville Chamberlain, the prime minister, to announce over the radio what must be a mere formality: namely, that because Germany had not answered our ultimatum, we were at war with her, and Hitler, and his taking-all-before-them armies – a grim prospect. It was an unenviable situation we were plunged into, and it was anybody's guess what form the war would take, though most of us feared the worst, by way of immediate air attacks of a frightful nature. And it looked as though we were not far wrong when, that same night, with Bill and Claire on their way back to London, a siren started wailing about midnight and had us all out of bed, undecided what to do for the best. The confounded alarm never stopped its banshee cry until many hours later for, apparently, 'the pea had got stuck in the whistle'.

It is history now that those first six months were called the 'phoney war', though this was a shocking libel on the many thousands, like Arthur, who were busy at sea in a grim war all of their own, for the U-boats and surface-raiders were out sinking merchant shipping the very first night. During this time – slowly, surely – Britain was building up a conscript army, age group by age group; and, towards the end of winter, Bill had already gone for his medical and passed fit for military service, though he still waited to be called upon. When my age group came along in the spring, I don't know what I thought I was doing, but I went along determined not to let on about my murky medical past (though I had not told Edna of this intent). Perhaps I was being vainglorious, or plain daft, or maybe I really knew they would not have me, but I was not for letting on. Howbeit, I didn't get far when I fronted a series of doctors who whipped through us waiting prospects in fine style; the MO who did chests soon had me floored into admitting about my second-hand lungs, and my past, and that was that! I had expected then to get a real old bawling-out for wasting their good time, but they were decent about it all and sent me home, reconciled to my war on that same Home Front.

After that reverse, I told myself I would not volunteer for a Christmas Club in future, and neither did I, not for a while. My awakening, our awakening, followed the April invasion of Norway by the Germans, to stem which the Allies could do little beyond sending a token force that could not hold them. And then came the blitzkrieg! And that was the very first shocking impact the war made on me – when German armies raced through the Low Countries with indecent haste, dive-bombing and smashing all opposition into impotence, sweeping the British army off the continent via a long shallow beach at Dunkirk, and the panzer divisions speeding towards Paris as fast as mobile armour was capable of. That was a sickener, an almost unbelievable sickener, a tragic tale unfolding over the radio every evening. I had been brought up on, and still was pretty steeped in, the legend that we never lost; the whole nation was numbed into a dull stupefaction despite Churchill, hastily made prime minister, trying to stir us out of our lethargy of despair with brave words – though he did not, at that day, offer anything but blood, sweat, toil and tears. But worse was to follow of France's rapidly deteriorating plight. We were to hear that she had capitulated, with the Huns before the gates of Paris, on June's third birthday, a singularly unhappy day on which little things like a birthday, and a surrender, got fixed forever in my memory.

Between these two shattering blows, the war minister Anthony Eden had appealed over the radio for citizens of spirit to band together into local defence volunteer groups in readiness to repel what looked very likely now: an invasion of our country. The next Sunday, I went along to a defunct bowls clubhouse[43] in the village, where a meeting was to be held with the idea of getting such a group together out of our own community. When the meeting was over, I found myself waiting my turn to be one in, lining up to give the organisers a clue, militarily, as to what one could do. And that was the best day's work I did in a long time, for I entered on a phase of activity more satisfying than anything I had ever done before.

I had, of course, been an infantryman, with a ready knowledge of drill, and pretty handy at weapon training; in fact, just the sort of chap the volunteers were badly needing but finding hard to come by. There was but a miserly flow of instructors being earmarked for our movement, bearing in mind the imminent task, and first priority, of rebuilding a new army from the remnants that had come back from Dunkirk. For the most part, the veterans of '14–'18 formed the backbone of our new force, with the undoubted fact emerging that most had, naturally, forgotten what they ever knew some twenty-odd years before, and thus needed teaching all over again. And, despite the comedian-type jokes of us using pikes, sticks-and-bladders, bows-and-arrows, we were kept very busy – feverishly busy, because

43 The bowls clubhouse was next to Front View on Halifax Road, Shelf

of the fear we had no time to spare in learning even the rudiments of defending ourselves before they would be on us, some time in that grave summer of 1940.

Shelf Home Guard, Richard (far left) Albert Scaife (far right) another Pepper Hill resident.

Two, and sometimes three, nights a week were given over to weapon training. It might run everybody a guard apiece per week, with nothing more lethal than a walking-stick to hand the first couple of these; it ran every Sunday morning, getting stuck into platoon training and a spot of foot- drill. We had our fun – the odd round going through the guard-hut roof the first time we got ammo... Which reminds me of a personal tale, all bound up with the issue of rifles. These had come straight from some American armoury, in sturdy cases and smothered in Vaseline, and we all keen as mustard crowded round to reach, grab, as they were handed out. As I got mine and straightened up to get clear, another chap, with a smart bowler hat on his head, stooped forward and got a blob of Vaseline on his hat from my rifle before I could warn him. As he remained blissfully unaware of his misfortune, I, rather meanly, decided to let sleeping dogs lie as I crept away. It might have been a warped sense of humour, of the ridiculous, made me get a quiet chuckle out of it, and I never did let on, even when I heard him creating afterwards. Yet we were a matey lot, for we were a self-contained village platoon, with everybody soon getting to know everybody else by his first name, except on parade. Every Sunday noon, after parade, we would repair to The Bottomleys Arms for liquid refreshment and light talk on 'shop', for all were dead keen on the job in hand, from the platoon commander down to the very old 'uns, toting their new rifles with difficulty, for turned-fifty was no age for the military game, choose how young the heart, how game the spirit.

By this time, at home, we had an Anderson shelter in our little garden where, on an alarm being sounded, my family, plus Benny, plus a couple of neighbours, would retire to await the all-clear whilst I hurried down to the now-styled Home Guard post (though, later, priorities of alarms were arranged so that one was not dashing down to the village for every Tom-Dick-and-Harry sirening that came along). We were very fortunate, throughout the war, in being only on the fringe of things violent, with none of the dreadful air raids that more important places attracted. Our humble share was a bomb dropped one night in an empty meadow, which only made a big hole in the grass for all its noise. And, one other night, there was a stick of firebombs, believed jettisoned, that straddled us without doing any material damage. This lucky treatment stood out in vivid contrast to a friend of Edna's; she had been in blitzes on Croydon, then had gone to Sheffield with her small daughter and caught it again there. She and her daughter came to our house to stay a few weeks, until they could go somewhere else with a bit more room.

As the war went on, my activities grew. I remember attending a course of St John's first-aid lessons, and with no mean interest. I always faithfully carried out my homework, and many times I had June, now rising five, act as my dummy if I was punching up on my bandagings, or slings, or on splinting broken limbs. Many times she was encased like an Egyptian mummy, and she loved every minute – nay, asked for more! She was not amused, poor baby, when I dropped the butt of my .300 rifle on her fingers once whilst practising a rifle movement at home – but we did laugh heartily over it all when she grew up.

One parade night, the platoon commander buttonholed me with a query. Did I know anything about machine guns?

'Do I know anything about machine guns, sir?' I echoed with a joyous laugh. 'I'll say!' And I then told him how I had been a Vickers machine-gunner for three years, and had taken to the gun very firmly.

'Good!' remarked Freddie (Lieutenant Wood). 'Then you'll go attend a machine-gun course starting in Halifax next week, for the Americans have let us have some Brownings… Yes, Brownings. Y'll soon pick up the threads, I should think… The higher-ups say we can have one in Shelf if we can use one… I'll let you have half a dozen volunteers for a team, after.'

We got our Browning.300, and I got the grandest set of chaps as a team to go with it: two textile executives, a marine engineer, a weaver, a coal miner, and a brickyard lad for good measure. We built up into a very happy, efficient team, though my face was very red one black Saturday night, on a training stunt with other units, when I led my team into an ambush, and this within one hundred yards of the building we had left, and with all our kit. My lads were all for having a bash, but I insisted on playing the game, and that took some living down afterwards.

Meanwhile, Bill had come to see us once, on a very brief day's visit whilst he was billeted in Yorkshire and before taking himself off to the Western Desert by way of the Cape, though Bill did not then know where he was going. (As a matter of passing interest, his commanding officer was Sir Mortimer Wheeler, later a famous TV archaeologist, who took Bill's battery out to Egypt and El Alamein, across North Africa, and into Italy). Bill was away the best part of four years with the Eighth Army of redoubtable deeds, finishing his service in northern Italy with a cushy job of corralling hordes of German prisoners. Arthur varied shore leaves between us at Pepper Hill and Edna's relatives in County

Durham, where he was always ensured of a good time – more to his way of thinking than anything we could hash up. Wherever he did go, everybody smoked his Canadian Sweet Caporal cigarettes, or rolled their own from the big tins of shag tobacco he always brought along.

Dad kept turning up plenty these days – and by plenty, I mean once in a while in months. He had not been long at nosing us out after we got wed but, latterly, his wartime preoccupation was trailing up and down the country, on the many new government building jobs now mushrooming all over. These days, he was content to make the teas or odd-job it about the sites, for he was getting older, though he was still as liable to fly off the handle in a rage, or soak in a drinking 'do'. Unannounced, unexpected, he would walk in on us, but only when he was broke, in between jobs. He would have a good meal (always disturbing Edna with his repeated starchy reference to her as 'missus') then go with me to the local for a couple of pints, adding colour to the general conversation with his salty observations, and always ending up with a fair tale of his latest meanderings, which could be so embarrassing for me at times, who had never gone out of my way to boast of our past life. At partings, he would touch me for a few shillings – if I had any to spare – then disappear Bradford-wards, to a Salvation Army hostel for a night or two before setting off once more.

We might not see him again in a long time, but he would turn up, in some outlandish gear he had acquired on the road. He always remained rather wary of Edna (for she was not his greatest admirer), and he was rather shy of his little granddaughter, but he was never one wee bit ashamed of his moochings; rather, he was proud of them, always maintaining a chap need never wallow stuck in the mud of some job he hated, not while ever dear old England had its open roads, and folks who were so kind to the ragged knights of the highways. He was very much a realist; on first hearing of my being in the navvying lark and my assuring him I was coping because the job was getting easier, he remarked, 'Navvying never gets any easier, mate – it's bloody hosswork.' On quiet reflection, I was inclined to agree with the old man.

One Friday afternoon, whilst I was at work, Edna brought me a telegram. It was from a Bradford hospital, advising me that Dad was very ill. I went along at once and saw he was desperately poorly: thin as a reed, huddled up, a mere shadow of his former self, and only rational at odd moments. It was going to be a losing battle, I was told. By Dad's demeanour, when he recognised me, he knew he had reached the end of this road – but he had no moans, no repinings, no whining as he sank. He died in his sleep on the Sunday whilst I was alone with him; Bill in Africa; Arthur somewhere at sea, on *his* last voyage as it transpired. When Dad went, and despite the gulf that had widened between us, I wept bitterly, howbeit briefly, in a side room, for blood was thicker than water. And that was the start of an exceptionally cruel winter, for Dad died in November, and Arthur – named after him –was lost at sea in the following February.

Following these sorrows (and I do not want to appear to be moaning), in the autumn of '43 my old chest complaint started plaguing me again with disquieting manifestations, warning me to stop acting the goat. Prudence, and my doctor, urged me to drop out of the Home Guard, which I did and which was a terrible wrench. Still, at this time, the war effort was at its highest peak – the USA was now fighting on all fronts, Africa rid of the enemy hordes, Russia absorbing all the punishment the Nazis slung at her, and the Second Front slowly building up – and I vainly comforted myself with the thought that, after all, I would not be sorely missed.

During all these stirring times, I worked for a firm of knitting-wool people[44] who had come up north from Walthamstow at the outbreak of war. I had a steady job, though I was not killed with wages; yet neither was I killed with work, as was very apparent by the way I had been able to tackle my quasi-military matters for such a long time.

44 Robert Glew and Co, Ltd, at Robin Mills on Deanstones Lane in Queensbury. Richard worked there from February 1940 to January 1946.

After that, I took things quiet – though not too quiet, as became increasingly evident later on. I was reminded how there had been a domestic joke, just before the war, between Edna and me concerning one of our neighbours who had blamed her baby's conception squarely upon the upset occasioned by the Munich crisis of ill fortune. Now, it would seem, Edna and I had been hoist by an identical petard springing from the dramatic opening of the Second Front – for, in the last few weeks of the European struggle, Edna had a son who was named, spare my blushes, Richard. And, as Richard came into this world, President Roosevelt died within sight of victory.

Bill (on leave from the army), June and baby Richard

Then the war was over. The peace had been with us some few weeks; a peace come on us suddenly, though not unexpectedly; a peace people resolved should amply pay for the five years of total war undergone in defence of liberty and its inherent freedoms for righteous expression amongst free and freshly freed nations. And, because we had been denied this great privilege through the pressure of strife, Winston Churchill and his coalition government resigned as soon as was possible, the party truce was dissolved, and all went to the country to seek fresh support for their respective policies of building the peace.

They went to the country in every sense of the word, as shown by the day I saw Mr Churchill in Queensbury. He was on an electioneering tour of the provinces, whipping up support for the local Tory candidates with his own personal magnetism, putting new life into a tired dog of a party, lately rampant in war but not now so much in favour to lead us in the ways of peace, not now the war had been won! Their policy looked stodgy and dull beside the glitter of socialist new-world promises. 'Now is the chance to rub the slate clean!' cried the Labour Party. 'To have done with the old order, to get on with creating the new Utopia.' And, they went on to ask, what better time to start than now, with everything in the house due for putting back into another rearranging? Clement Attlee and Aneurin Bevan, of the silver tongue, asked that of us, and most of us were minded to cogitate: what better time, indeed?

When Winston left his car, one of a long cavalcade passing through cheering crowds down the main street of Queensbury, it was for the purpose of addressing us locals who had gathered in front of the Stag's Head public house, for years a gathering point in Queensbury (that also went for the many times the same crowds had welcomed their local musical heroes, the Black Dyke Mills Band, back from joyous victories in the brass band world). The crowd now went wild with an enthusiastic welcome as the PM stepped into our midst, taking the arm of the candidate he was asking us to support. Probably because of the stress and hurry of this whistle-stop tour, he did not look very well to me. He appeared to be very old (in truth, he was over seventy then!) and, somehow, I felt disappointed on seeing him in the flesh. I had expected seeing a big man, physically big – probably legend had built that image of him in my mind – and it just shows how wrongly one can evaluate at second hand. Here, I was looking at a rather small chap, with an impish grin on a round face, but looking very tired, sallow, round-shouldered, showing to the full the terrible burden of responsibility he had borne throughout the war. He also seemed to be wearing his oldest clothes, fingering a stove-pipe hat that was green with age – or was green its natural colour? And if *I* thought he looked so fatigued, so ready for taking a long-earned rest (and let others take over), surely thousands and thousands of others who saw him on that exhausting tour must have thought the same – which could explain the terrible let-down he suffered at the subsequent election.

He talked a few minutes in support of his fellow, now beaming at his elbow, whilst the mill folk milled to get nearer, some to actually touch him, to have him shake their hands, to have an aside directed to them, and it was cheers, cheers, all the way – or nearly so! An army truck had edged its way along the side of the crowd, and about half a dozen soldiers standing in the back recognised Winnie and started shouting, 'Vote for Labour!' They were quite good-natured about it all, despite the fact their war job was finished and they were impatiently waiting to be demobbed and sent home for keeps. Churchill, himself now a man of peace, grinned across at them and muttered something I did not catch, though it vastly amused those nearer; and, still shouting slogans from their high vantage point, the troops passed up the street, probably then on the way to some dull, time-killing 'fatigue duty' that would put in one more day of waiting to be a civvy once more.

Churchill, meantime, shook hands with a few more, quipped with all and sundry, then followed a wedge making way for him to his car and, fingers flexed in his now famous V-sign of defiance turned to victory, was whisked away down the main street to Bradford and still more, and much bigger, more exhausting crowds.

It was a red-letter day, that lunchtime we took from work to stand and see Winston Churchill, but we did not put him back in power, which is quite a humbling thought, now. But such is the whim, or the will, of the people. He got back personally, his popularity still as high as ever, but his party was out of office. I can only suppose the price we voters were asked to pay was too high: Churchill versus Labour – a Labour Party that was pledged to reinvigorate the peace with all the good things we working class were supposed to have fought for over decades. So we exercised to the full our rights as a democratic, free-voting nation. It was ironical that Churchill, champion of democracy, fell a victim to the very principles he had so long, so doggedly, fought to uphold in a world that had been ready to cry 'Enough!' at the behest of the evil men who almost won the day, had not Winnie stood where he did.

Yet he was to spurn these latest arrows, barbs, slings of misfortune with a telling phrase and a sly grin, though he was deeply hurt. He was to win through again, to be prime minister again, to live a very long time after that day I thought him past it, to become a living legend, to go to his final resting place with the whole world paying homage to this unique man. It was my privilege to be near him that noontime in our village street in the West Riding; it was my misfortune to be too near him to see him in his proper perspective as the greatest Englishman I would ever know.

Richard and June

'UNCLE' TOM

It had been years since I had last seen 'Uncle' Tom Jolley – in point of fact, the best part of thirty. He was no blood relation. He was a brother to Aunty Jenny[45] and, because of my brother Bill's small daughter, Patsy, staying with this lady almost throughout the war, Bill had formed a more personal connection with the Jolley family than had been the case with me over the latter years. Claire, Bill's wife, had also got to know Uncle Tom very well, for she had travelled to Yorkshire a lot in the troubled years and had corresponded with him and, of course, Aunty Jenny. Claire had also formed the habit of swapping books with him, for he was an avid reader and piled Claire up with these whenever he saw her. When I went along to see him with the others, we were returning books. It must have been pretty close following the war, and I would not have known the old man by sight; nor did he know who I was, at first.

Originally, the Jolleys were a happy family of some five or six living in a back-to-back house that was reached through a wide ginnel that gave on to a backyard. The passage of years, with their share of marriages and goings-forth and death's inevitability, had finally left the old man in the house on his own, and a confirmed bachelor.

Years before, when I had visited, there had been ferrets in shallow box-cages in the small backyard, and a lively fox terrier that was noisily suspicious of my presence, though I was only a kid and with no unkindly intent. There had also been more ferrets in a joiner's yard up the street, deadly-looking creatures with furs so smooth and white, and horribly menacing faces and teeth; they looked out all day at piles of

45 See 'On the Home Front'.

timber, and floor baulks, and coffin boards – yes, coffin boards – and went hunting rats at night, as a way of earning their keep. Uncle Tom, by the way, had many irons in his business fire for, besides being a jobbing joiner by apprenticed trade, he was also an undertaker in a small way, and a catcher of rats. It all followed in a family tradition, for I could remember his father being in charge of this varied business, with Tom and another brother juniors in the concern.

Snooping round the joiner's yard was very interesting to my young eyes, but the mere thought of the rat-catching – even the sight of the ferrets, safely caged – sent a chill up my spine. I don't know which I feared the most: the rat with its natural antipathy towards man, or the ferret whom I could never bring myself to trust – most certainly not to the extent of putting my hand into a cage and 'yarking one aht' on the promptings of Uncle Tom and company, then being laughingly pronounced 'a flayed ha'porth' for shrinking from this unsavoury act. Yet I was always excited about it all, and would have loved to go with them on their rat-catching rounds in the city of Bradford. But I never was privileged to be taken on the nocturnal prowlings and vigils inside the vast wool warehouses, or down in the blackness by the Mucky Beck, a filthy stream that ran (and still does) under the centre of the city, which bubbled up in flood under heavy, sudden rains at that time and housed rats as big as cats, I had heard it said, though not from the Jolley family. Oh, what wouldn't I have given, despite my compulsive squeamishness, to go with Mr Jolley, and Tom, and his brother – was his name Harry? – and the little fox terrier, and those sinister slinking creatures that insinuated themselves into holes and pipes I would not have thought even a wee mouse could have crept into.

And that was all so long ago. This very last time I was to see Uncle Tom, I had gone with Bill and Claire, and Edna tagging along with me. The old man still lived in the dark house with heavy, faded curtains, an old-fashioned fireplace, and bursting at the seams with furniture and knick-knacks that were very much Victoriana. It lacked fresh air and smelled of piles of dusty, shabby books, and of musty plants that raised themselves, gaunt and withering, out of red pots on cracked saucers that took up a low window bottom letting in but little light, situated as it was at the back of the street, and frowned on by another terrace of houses.

Gone now were the fox terrier, and the ferrets, and their cages, and the whole rat-catching business of other days. Tom was retired now. He rubbed up some dark cut from a tobacco pouch made, years before, from a cured rat skin. It was from the biggest rat he ever caught, he said, though I silently thought it did not look as big as all that, you know, to warrant perpetuating; I was thinking in terms of monsters reputed to leap at a man's throat when cornered. Uncle Tom must have read my thoughts. He asked me what I had expected; I told him. With a huge chuckle, he exploded a myth I had cherished for years. 'Nay, lad! Rats nivver wor as big as cats, an' nivver did jump at fowks, nawther… Leastways, Ah nivver saw one that did, an' Ah wor at t'game long enough.'

At that time, Aunty Jenny came from Darton once a fortnight to 'do' for him, but it was a thankless, unsatisfactory 'doing', for the old man would not let Jenny 'side' anything, not even the paperbacks that piled up and up and threatened to topple from the horsehair couch that held them as overflow from the small bookcase on the back wall. Aunty was lucky even to be allowed to dust them, conglomerate heaps in which a dog-eared Edgar Wallace jostled Silas K Hocking's novels, a paperback Nat Gould racing thriller lay stifled under a heavy Conan Doyle, and Emily Brontë turned a stiff spine on Ethel M Dell.

The plants had also been a bone of contention, it was said. Uncle Tom always insisted they be left well alone – he would watter 'em when they wanted wattering. 'Them plants is same as cammils 'at nobbut want watter abaht ivvry fortneet,' he would comment.

Aunty Jenny would snap back with, 'This place would smell sweeter if they were chucked aht, Tom… I'm stalled of 'em.' But she always went back to Darton wasted in purpose, and Tom sat at his plush-clothed table, happy in his great untidiness.

He had a pal, Jimmy, come in two or three nights a week. Indeed, he came the very night we were there, and was not in the least put out of his stride with our being in the house, for the old men quickly managed to quarrel, as was their usual habit. Mostly about politics, for Jimmy was a Labour man and Uncle Tom a staunch Conservative and, in their differing, neither pulled a punch.

'Y' daft beggar!' Jimmy insulted him once. 'What you get to conserve? Y're as poor as a craw.'

'Poor, be blawed!' snorted Tom. 'Ah've allus bin me awn boss, moar or less. In fact, a man of independent means compared wi' you chaps. You! an' yur ruddy Bolshie pals, allus wanting to spend somebody else's brass.'

'Sithee, if it wasn't fur us,' piped up Jimmy – but Tom cut in, 'Aw, get to hell! Afoar Ah lowse me temper.'

As we listened with mixed feelings – wondering whether to be alarmed or have a good laugh – Jimmy assured us that this was only fun, really. They had always agreed to differ and leave it at that for, by the time Tom had got the pots out for their suppers, and scraped some beef dripping on a few slices of bread, they were peaceful enough. After, beslippered Tom would set Jimmy on his homeward way through the dark passage, then slowly let himself back into the kitchen, back amongst his many well-thumbed books, his withered plants, his relics of Victoriana. He would charge his pipe from the rat-skin pouch, sit for a long time and smoke, for he had no occasion for getting up early next morning; with reluctance he would go to bed, pulling his little, lonely world tightly about his muffled head.

He passed away quietly, without a fuss, many years ago. Aunty Jenny later took herself off to Australia to join her daughter Evelyn, now married and gone with her soldier husband to New South Wales. Of the former Jolley house and the nearby yard, nothing now remains but heaps of rubble, where once Uncle Tom joinered, and undertook, and sported rats with his frisky fox terrier and the sinister ferrets, and lived on to fairly substantiate his simple, but just, claim to being a man of independent means.

GALE WARNING

Wh-h-ew! Wh-h-ew! Wh-h-ew!
Shrill the wind blew.
Chased the massed clouds thru black sky,
Hurled them past the moon on high.
Snatched loose boards up from the ground,
Drowned all speech in gusty sound.
Shrilled most vile at wires abroad,
Pulled them almost to the road.
Set shopsigns in crazy swing,
Smashed them down with vicious sting.
Wh-h-ew! Wh-h-ew! Wh-h-ew!
Shrill the wind blew.

ECHOES FROM THE HILLS

And memories borne on waves of sweet sound,
Pushing aside the hurt, and petty round.

As I wrote these words, I was feebly striving to put into my own language just what I feel about music, though I cannot read a note, nor play even a mouth organ. Yet, after my own fashion, and with a taste very much up and down the scales of selectivity, I love music with a deep and abiding passion.

***

Whenever I have wanted to get on to the moor tops, it has been a simple matter of catching the hourly bus that passes within a few hundred yards of my house and riding out to the fringe of the Brontë country. I have gone so often, and it costs but coppers in bus fare, plus a short walk along a country lane, and there is the moorland stretched out before me. One is, right away, off the beaten track – although, if I cared to walk as far as the horizon, a full mile away, I would be looking down a very steep hill on to Haworth. In doing so, I would first of all skirt several worked-out shallow quarries, all of which, at one day, fed a derelict sand-and-gravel workings that stands on the side of a rutted track leading from the lane. Some folks would have it these old quarries and the collapsed staging despoil, but I would rather say they'll tend to blend as the years give the harsh contours a softer line of all-conquering heather, and bilberry, and juicy reeds.

One afternoon, I had walked past the old staging, and was following one of the many paths that lead out to the quarries and the open moors. I could hear music, which was all rather puzzling, for I could see nothing to account for it – not until, turning a sharp bend round a small mound, I almost bumped into a small car pulled in halfway on the path, halfway on the heather of the moor. Inside were a middle-aged couple; the windows were open, the music was coming from therein, and I was beaming with exquisite pleasure, for I had recognised it as something of Sibelius's. I told myself this was nothing short of a minor miracle as I went past the car a little way, then paused so I could listen without embarrassment to this wonderful music in this wild, yet suitable, setting. Here was I, stood in the middle of nowhere, listening to the *Karelia Suite*!

It was fantastic. It was the long arm of coincidence playing up to me for, whenever I had heard most anything by Sibelius, my thoughts had flown straight out here, to these very moors. *Finlandia*, *Tapiola*, *The Swan of Tuonela*, and this suite all mirrored the same picture to me. As the music went on, I gradually heard the wind mounting and shrilling through the few stunted thorns that hung on like grim death to Mother Earth, and whining through patches of fat reeds in the many soughs[46] of bogland. The timpani rattled, rolled away, reverberating and thundering, crashing to echoes far above the valleys that sheltered Oxenhope, and Cullingworth, and Haworth on the hillside. In my imagination, a vast gloom settled over all this land of bleak wildness, the skies boiled with black, wet clouds, and the wind still shrieked like a demon to snatch a fat sheep as it wobbled to the lee of some stones. Outcroppings of black rocks, breaking through the heather and coarse grass, and strands of pebbled sandstone, with scarred, ugly little man-made depressions, were all vying, in their humble way, with Finland's vaster wastes; there were little swollen streams rushing down quarry-sides, and adjacent, silent, icy reservoirs that strove to match the mighty lakes of Karelia, though they could never quite recapture the full majesty of Sibelius's conveying the gobbling-up of ice, and sleet, and the rain of winter's tempests, in far-off Finland.

46 A drainage channel or trench.

Suddenly, and because they are never far away from my thoughts when I am up here, I thought of Emily Brontë's Heathcliff, and Catherine Earnshaw, and of what Sibelius could have made of the two lovers. The savage, white-hot flashes of lightning, the sulphurous cracks of sudden thunder, and the long shaking aftermath, from a hundred musical instruments, to express the black, savage, half-wild Heathcliff; for Catherine, the quixotic glimpses of fitful sun, the petty stinging fury of hail in a lambing storm, the sulk of a morning mist, the cry of a lamb seeking sustenance. All this, and much beyond my ken, the master could have given the temperamental lovers of *Wuthering Heights* on his mighty canvas of sound. I felt an intense, positive desire to shout that Sibelius was one of us; that he had a definite affinity with the Brontës because of his amazing powers of giving us harshness, bitterness, brooding melancholy, virility and fight, all tending to stress the more his great passion for his native land. It seemed to be the first cousin to the rugged affection (we shrink to call it 'love') that we little folks hereabouts felt for our seemingly inhospitable mixture of moorland and dam, and bleak hills, and henhole and pigeon cote, and countless pigholes, and scores of drab villages, and numerous little hamlets stuck on hillsides, without any set pattern, each with its chapel, of Bethel, or Nazareth, or Witnesses, or Gospellers, all sure *they* had God's ear. Some had their quarries to justify their existence, though many looked more worked-out than working; lots more huddled under the economical lee of woollen mills, and weaving sheds, and dye-houses – and all within hailing distance, if one had a loud hail, of this heritage of moors and near-moors, the very salt to add savour to our strong meat of existence. Though, mind, they are not to everybody's taste – which same, I believe, goes for Sibelius's music.

But the music on the moors was not finished yet! And now, as I still listened, I fell to wishing the composer had been a Yorkshireman – a West Riding man, best of all, for somehow a Hull man, or a chap from York, wasn't 'us', if you see what I mean? How we would have made such a fuss of him, in our own rough, hard-to-express way!

Sibelius could be so gentle and happy, for he was not always invoking the storm gods, or the strife, or the wrath of Nature. He could be so moving in the fatalistic sadness of a dance of death, and so happy when invoking an April evening in the far north. He hints of springtime, and I follow the suggesting; the earth heaves to give forth sustenance to the sparse grass, and the heather tufts, and the still-green very young brackens and ferns as they unfold to light and air. The lambs are thriving and have not yet lost their look of snowy whiteness, and icy water lies still and clear over the sands of the pebbly beds worn down though the bogs. In the quiet sky a sparrowhawk poises with deadly intent, watching, with a balancing flutter, some stupid small creature timorously creeping out to a point where – swoosh! – death attends with steely talons and tearing beak. An old gimmer nibbles sweeter grass at the bottom of a tumbledown stone wall, originally shaped long years ago in a letter L that shelters from the teeth of sudden gales and deep, drifted snows. In reality, I hear a shepherd's dog bark from far away, and the sharp noise ricochets off the rocky outcroppings and the tight spoil-heaps of sandstone. In the profound silence that follows, I become aware all is still; I look around, and realise that the music has stopped. Even the car has gone. I am left alone and, as I step out, my still-warm mental picture of my moors is pushed slightly skew-whiff on sighting an old bed-mattress in one of the many shallow barings.

***

Within blowing distance of any of our moors, you can bet there is a brass band flourishing, putting in its two-nights-a-week rehearsals between engagements, humble or otherwise, with many more practices (and Sunday mornings) when they're getting ready for a big contest in Manchester or London. It would seem that hilly districts have always been good breeding grounds for brass-bandsmen who go to London every October for the Big Blow, with high hopes of a celebration big blow amongst themselves when, the contest over, time allows. Maybe if one is born and thrives on the hills, then he has a strong pair of lungs, and as soon he can find his way to the band room along the dark passageway, he stands a real chance of emulating his now resolved idols of the brass band. This, of course, is always depending upon one of the old-timers running the rule over him, seeing he measures up, telling a proud, but anxious father, 'We-ell, Ah might mek summat of the lad... But he'll hev to work hard, mind... Believe me, Ah'll mek a bandsman aht on him, if anybody can... He'll be blawing yon cornet straight aht into a post-horn afoar Ah've done wi' him, mark my words!'

Black Dyke Mills[47] Band foregathers not a mile from our hamlet, and is amongst the most famous in the world. They're part and parcel, flesh and bone, of the traditions and history of the brass band world, with honours over the past hundred years hung thick and heavy around their modest necks; yet every practice night will find at least one or two old 'uns at the back of the room – not necessarily ex-players – sat listening in stolid silence whilst the music lasts. They'll say nothing out of turn but, if invited, they will not be backward at telling exactly what they are thinking, and choose who it may concern. Nothing, nobody, is immune from their honest, blunt tongues, and over the years they have collected the very curious nickname of 'pondashers'. How, why, or what the name means is something I have never fathomed, but there is a suite of music named after them that was composed by a famous conductor of some few years back.[48]

One of the grandest treats we locals enjoy is to be able to sit in the village hall when the band gives a concert, possibly twice a year. To hear them play 'Crimond' or 'Abide With Me' is a humbling, sacred experience, for you really feel you walk with God. Slowly everything, everybody about you is hushed as the music starts. The very hall is hallowed as the rich, deep tones swell out to every corner, out even

47 Richard worked at Black Dyke Mills from the late 1940s to the early 1950s.

48 *The Pondashers* was written by Major George Willcocks, bandmaster of several well-known brass bands (including Black Dyke itself), in 1959. He dedicated it 'to those loyal supporters of "Dyke" in times good or bad'.

into the main street, and we simple folks sit there and feel privileged, exalted as though we are in the presence of the Almighty. We join in with our humble words of song, we shed our burdens on to somebody else's shoulders – a Somebody who is always at our side, though many times we doubt it. We know we are in some other's care, that the 'help of the helpless' is here with us, each and every one, and we feel we'll never want again, nor fear to walk in that valley we so involuntarily tend to dread. We are lifted above the trivia, the trials; and Heaven seems just above as the music draws to a finish. Nothing moves, no one makes a sound for a few precious moments, then there is a slight stir and the spell is broken. But what an uplifting experience, even though it does last but a few minutes, and the band soon away on a cornet carillon, bringing back the froth of light-heartedness to a rapt audience. Yet the memory of Black Dyke playing 'Abide With Me' – or any hymn, for that matter – lasts a long time. Their playing has a bell-like tone, deep, solid, ringing, and it echoes and re-echoes long after that aspiring young lad of earlier has almost blown his cornet straight in his enthusiasm, long after he makes the big band, long after – following a firm tradition – he has left the Dyke for more exalted, more genteel musical circles – aye, even the Hallé!

***

In a different way, one piece of music, Dvořák's 'New World' symphony, holds a dramatic appeal, a mysticism, for me. It has a haunting quality and fills me with a great melancholy, a sadness occasioned by something having gone from me, and never again to be brought back. It makes me feel, and I know it sounds droll, that I have had a previous existence. I have a very strong sensation of having lived in this new world of Dvořák's. I can almost see the great trains of 'prairie schooners' slowly moving across the American continent in quest of a home, of a place of one's own. I am with them as they make heavy work of fording the wide rivers, and enduring the crossing of great tracts of wilderness where nothing grows, where all is rock and choking dust, where heat and cold are hell and the landscape never varies for hundreds of miles.

I glimpse the clumsy-duck paddle-steamers chuffing along wide rivers, so wide at times we peer hard to see the other side; sometimes we are borne swiftly along with a rapid-flowing current, other times we're battling hard upstream. Sometimes the river moves sluggishly, and is the yellow of liquid clay (why this clay, I know not). There are times when we sing and dance; many emigrés come this way, seeking a new life in a new country, yet never forgetting their old songs and dances. Sad, merry, drunken, savage, they sing in a score of outlandish tongues, yet the music is a common interpreter of our mood, with everybody literally in the same boat, seeking our new world together.

We come across many Negro slaves, with their own style of hymns, simple songs, and snatches of pure gibberish. They sing of the Lord and they chant about Uncle Sam all in the same breath, for they have no fine distinctions. As they sing of their simple faith, we press on to the Golden West, as folks back east phrase it when they are selling the idea of going west to simple people who thirst for a chance to start afresh. We trudge across the rolling prairies, their tall grasses waving like seas, then out to where the foothills of giant mountains are sighted. These, our guide tells us, are the gateway to that promised land, to be the final test, the proving point of whether we are worthy of what we seek. Even at a great distance we can see they are snow-capped, though we'll seek a pass on nearer approach, but *now* the mountains look so austere, cruel, forbidding, impassable, that the thought rises, willy-nilly, in many minds: 'What further hardship, suffering, lies in those hills?'. But not many are really daunted, for we all knew from the start, of others' retelling, just what lay along the hard-won trail before the Promised Land was reached.

And, there I am again – dreaming away under the hypnosis of lovely music. Only, this time, I was taken into the great mountains, as a change to the footling hills I climb and descend every day of my workaday life and which, most times, limit my horizon to the next footling hill, some couple of miles away: a mere nipper of a hill, not high enough to warrant showing on any map, yet nevertheless effectively blocking my view to the infinite. Who knows but what this frustrating factor may be the prime reason we folks who live on little hills have such vivid imaginations, are ever restless, ever given to picturing dream worlds at the drop of a cap – or the raising of a baton!

WINDS OF CHANGE

'Wheww! Shrill the wind blew!' – and it is blowing fiercer than ever before – a cross, contrary wind, a wind with an 'R' in it, that has us West Riding folks in a very maelstrom of deep doubting about this guessing game of who-goes-with-who just now. It is a regrouping wind that is at work and, so far, our village has been variously rumoured to be going in here, there, everywhere. It would not surprise me if we finished up one better than the celebrated fictional 'Cleckheckmondwike' in a sprawl of nearby villages. Brrrrhhh![49]

Yet we are used to winds, and from every point of the compass – the adverse, the cutting, the wet, and at rare times the balmy – and they all come the same. Some use us ill, even go berserk at times, as witness one wild November night the very first year we came up here, when a screaming-mad wet west wind blew the chapel down.[50] It looked a substantial stone chapel, but down it came in the terrible madness of that awful night; yet, fortunately, it happened in the night with nobody there to get hurt, for it looked a complete write-off with but two end walls left standing. Perhaps I exaggerate – there was a small kitchen untouched, a place where they had made the teas and washed up, for the social evenings then were more frequent, and the refreshing of worshippers who travelled long distances to come to service on a Sunday. For twelve months the Unitarian chapel centred round this small room – indeed, somebody got married from there; in the meantime, such was the spirit to the awful challenge of Nature, a new

49 Shelf joined with Queensbury for local government purposes in 1937 after rumours of take-overs by both Halifax and Bradford. In 1974, Shelf joined Calderdale and Queensbury joined Bradford.

50 See 'Youth's a Stuff'.

shell was rising from out of the old, a stronger bastion to withstand the worst of weathers, and it stands there yet, a silent witness to man's resolve. Quite frequently this same miscreant blows successfully at drystone walls, sends ill-anchored hen huts flying, has our electric supply winking and blinking bemusedly in this fiercest of blasts, has us leaning against it whenever we venture out to face its lashings of rain that pepper one with flurries of stinging darts.

His opposite number, the east wind, is none of this. He is a mean one, a skulker, a menacing bag-o- bones chap who is so thin he blows straight through anything that stands up to him. He runs swiftly along the ground, his high-pitched whine gradually fills the air, and his frozen breath whistles through every crack that has the misfortune to face east. He creeps through doorways, chills the family hearth, puts ice into one's veins. Outdoors again, he shrivels the very sun and dehydrates the earth, turning it to black iron; and, depending on the season, makes malicious play with new-fallen snow, more especially the dry, powdery kind, the sort that flies easy before this searching wind and scours our faces red and raw ere seeking final lodgement in the narrow lanes and, at last, forces our reluctant feet to take to the open fields in seeking the long high ridges swept bare by the withering gusts.

This icy fiend probably had his finest hour in the late winter of '47, after a mild season that had lulled us all into the false, cosy feeling that winter had let us off lightly, by way of a change! We were disillusioned early in February, when the snow started and kept on well into March; it was heavy, almost continuous, and the east wind danced attention most every hour. Almost every morning we would waken to fresh-fallen snow and the cruel whine from the east. Again and again we would wearily take to the trampled tracks across the fields, and leave the exasperating piled-up snow to time, a hard pressed council plough, and a gang of German prisoners-of-war[51]

51 Both German and Italian POWs were housed at Shelf Hall during the war. Richard's son Richard remembers a friend, who was a child in the war, telling him that 'the Italians used to love playing football with the local kids. Not so the Germans, who were a very dour lot!'

still living in Shelf Hall and sent up, at least three times, to dig us from out of our white isolation.

In the midst of all this, we were also facing a national fuel crisis, with every pound of coal dearly prized; so dearly that, one bitter night, we menfolk trudged home to hear how the women had spent a great part of their day at home sledging – that is, sledging coal to our houses. These gallant ladies had brought every cottage two bags of coal from the main road, where it had been left by the coal wagon that couldn't get along the snow-packed lane to our hamlet. That morning, when the news of the awaiting coal had reached them, our women had not wasted any time wringing their hands and wishing we men were at home to cope; they had got themselves a youngster's sledge and a couple of stout clothes cords, wrapped themselves up like balls, and by dint of pushing and pulling, and struggling and stumbling, over and through the humps and ridges of snow, all the coal (precious little though it was) had reached our homes. It would see us over the worst, we optimistically told ourselves every succeeding day, for it was the end of February, and the weather was sure to pick up.

But it did not! After a few days, we were anxiously phoning the coal people again, and they were promising to do all they could, though it was to be a repeat performance of their wagon leaving our coal at the lane end again. But this time we were organised, and the women left well alone until we menfolk got home in the evening, when we borrowed a horse and cart from a farmer and moved the coals that way.

It was a savage business, for the frost was keen, the wind terribly cutting, and the young horse too frisky from insufficient working at this deep of winter. We met several near-disasters on the four trips, for the cart was of the light two-wheeled type and threatened to topple sideways every time it took the many hardened snowhills, with the horse plunging and putting a terrific strain on the dried-up harness leathers, and we attendants yelling and yipping like apparitions on the night air, shoving and heaving at snow-bogged wheels, dragging and yanking at the horse's bit – though, brave lad, he was putting up a better job than us. At last it was all over, the last bag had been cleared from the laneside, and everybody was happy, with a deep, silent satisfaction that spoke louder than any words; I doubt if we lost above a bucketful of the coals, and the fires roared hot and fierce that black night.

Come to think of it, would this 'joining-up' with whomsoever make any difference to us whenever February blizzards howled again? Whenever the wind skulked and whined and the white menace silted into every slit and crack about the house? I supposed not; we would still be wise to have a couple of dozen candles put away in the top of the big cupboard by the back end of every year. Candles kept indefinitely and they never ate anything, and our smelly paraffin lamp rusted away a long time ago. It went along with the old float-cart in which Irvine Scott had brought round the paraffin years ago, and the battered former milk churns filled with the oil he toted around, and his filling funnel, and measures down to the pint and even gill for those who could not afford a whole gallon in those less palmy days before the war. I chuckled as a whimsical thought struck me: we still had a sledge handy in the coal place – the one my son, Richard, had used as a boy. I found myself heroically dwelling on the fact that our present milkman had a horse eating his head off in comparative idleness, having yielded his former job of bringing round the milk to a more handy jeep – so we would get through again, if 'getting through' had to be, although I would quite possibly delegate my responsibilities to Richard in the active role that might spring from any act smacking of putting back the clock.

June and Richard 'Baby Temps'

***

And, as proof of how one thought begets another, that remembrance of 'getting through' puts me in mind of the time a neighbour and I went for water with a borrowed horse, a cart, and a big tub, in the days before we had got piped water into our cottages.

That year, the east wind had plagued, off and on, all spring, drying everything up and with hardly any rainfall, and this unsatisfactory state of affairs regarding our weather had continued with long weeks of hot sunshine well into June. With long faces we watched the precious water, spewed up by the overworked pumps, change slowly from sparkling clear to clouded grey and peopled by wick things that, normally, would have been happy to lie undisturbed at the bottom of the well – and we should have been happier to let them! Then, one by one, the pumps had gurgled to dryness, without even the traditional 'mouth under the spout' trickle issuing forth, and we had all joined the thickening trek to the public well.[52]

52 The public well is on Blackshaw Beck Lane, next to Queensbury Golf Club.

This well was – is – a deep stone trough set in a wall at the bottom of a long hillside, and bears the graven inscription 'Public Well 1864'. It is fed by a pipe let into the hill behind. This well was veritably perpetual, inasmuch as choose how we drew on it, coupled with the much heavier drain on it of farmers for their stock, it never showed any signs of going dry. Water was to be had for the mere dipping of a bucket, but – our individual snag – the well was the best part of half a mile from our place, and one could hardly carry a full bucket all that way. The farmers fended with great tubs and barrels and churns on carts, and we envied them, in these moments of drought, and wished we also had tubs and carts. However, the next best thing was to cultivate their friendship – many times, a shared drink across a taproom floor could work wonders. As it so happened, at that time we had as our milkman (though he was a teetotaller) a smallholder/ farmer named Moses, and Moses (long since dead) had recently got himself an extra-large water tub, almost as high as a man, at a farm sale. And what nicer than he should say to my wife, one dry-as-dust morning, whilst measuring out a pint of milk (which, incidentally, he brought round twice a day), 'Aw, missus, tell yer hubby Ah've bowt a reyt watter tub – if he wants to borry it, he can.'

My wife murmured a pleasant, 'Oh, thank you.'

Moses cleared his throat with a meaning *rhmp*, then went on, 'Of course, Ah s'll want him to fotch me a tub o' watter, mind.'

'Understood,' smiled my wife, and left it at that, after a parting 'Thank you!'.

The following Saturday morning found a neighbour and myself at Moses' farmhouse door reminding him of his kind offer of the tub, 'etcetera'.

'Aw,' grumped Moses, sounding as though he had thought better of his magnanimous gesture, 'trouble is, y'll hev to fend fur yersens cos Ah'm varry threng[53] this morning. Can y' manage to yoke t'hoss up baht my help?'

53 Busy.

'Certainly!' I hastily assured him – perhaps rather foolishly, for I knew very little about the mysteries of horses and harness, but I did so badly want that fresh water. With that, Moses made no more to do than place a frayed rope halter into my hands, with the information 'Y'll find Bob [the horse] in yond far field,' and shouting over his shoulder, as he went away to a barn, 'He's a bit fresh, mind, so tek him steady.'

How right Moses was! Bob was a lot fresher than us. We coaxed, we chased, we swore and sweated and puffed, and all for nothing. Two or three times we got him into the corner of a field, halter poised to slip over his head, when he would suddenly swivel like a ballet dancer, up would go his hind legs in most unfriendly fashion, and we would dash out of range to allow him to thunder away with an angry neighing. We were in a pretty pickle and might have been there some considerable time if Moses' wife, old and rheumy, had not come out to the field carrying a crust of bread and muttering some incantation to the horse (as distinct from the oaths we had uttered). No sooner did the beast sight and hear her than he walked straight up to the good lady, nuzzled her hand for the bread, and received a commiserating pat on his head and soft words of sympathy. We must have cut a very comical figure going back to the cart-shed, the old lady leading Bob, and us two non-horsemen shamefacedly shuffling along in the rear.

As we neared the shed, Moses shouted, 'What's up, lass? Couldn't they catch him?'

'Catch him!' she shouted back. 'Ugh! They've freetened the poor lad into a mucksweat wi' thur hallocking abaht.'

We looked discomfited whilst Moses chuckled hugely. Then, turning to my companion when we reached the shed, he bade, 'Nah then, mate! Let's see if tha can manage to pull these cart shafts dahn.'

I grinned treacherously, but I grinned too soon, for Moses turned to me with an old, straw-shedding horse collar in his hands and invited me, 'Here y' are… Sam this on him – Naw, Ah mean Bob!'

Bob was not a big animal, really, but what a swollen head he appeared to have. I looked from Bob to collar, from collar to Bob, received no inspiring revelation, searched frantically in my mind's eye for instances when I had witnessed collars going on horses' heads. Unhappily, I had not watched closely enough, and now I was paying the penalty for not being very observant. I turned the collar this way and that, but could not get the darned thing beyond his ears. It all reminded me very much of childhood's 'twisted nails' puzzle – so easy when one knew how! I twisted, turned, pushed and pulled, grunted and swore, got very hot under *my* collar, but Bob just gazed dully before him, and still standing minus his first essential trappings of harness. I caught sight of Moses grinning, a little sleeve-waistcoated devil he looked, and that made me flummox even worse, and I was now rapidly losing my temper, for a chap could only stand so much, water or no water!

'Ah thowt y' knew summat abaht hosses?' asked the grinning Moses, stepping forward to my side.

'Ah don't remember saying Ah did,' I snapped back, testily.

'Naw, maybe nut, but y' wanted me to think soa. Onnyway, get aht o' t'road – Ah'll fettle it.' And Moses had that collar on with one vigorous move, had the whole turnout ready in a couple of minutes, and was regarding me and my fellow unfortunate with a twinkle in his eyes, telling us, 'Well, it's all yours but tek Bob steady – an' mind he doan't treyd on yer toes. An' doan't furget to bring me a full tub back.'

We got our water, though we spilled plenty on the way back – and Moses got his full tub. He still had the Indian Sign on me when I unwisely remarked how pleasant it would now be to get a good wash for a day or two, by way of a change.

'Wesh!' he howled. 'This stuff fur blurry drinking, nut weshing, mate. Wesh? What next!'

***

It was about this time that our horse-drawn ambulance gave way to the march of the motor, for the County Authority was now taking care of such things with its fleet of motor vehicles. Up to then, our local council's horse-ambulance had taken all the infectious cases to a nearby isolation hospital. It was driven by a chap called Bill Cawkwell[54], a local farmer who sat atop of a wooden, square-box, iron-tyred vehicle, coaxing a heavy draught horse on its occasional errands of mercy. For these jobs, he was provided with his sole badge of office, a big dark greatcoat that reached right down to his calves, big man though he was. Other times he would be emptying middens, or leading road chippings for the council, all this in between his farming work. But Bill, his horse, and the ambulance all dropped out of the picture when the West Riding Council took over, with the old square box, after being what was thought 'honourably retired', falling a victim to the vicious, contrary winds as it stood in a hillside field, serving as a makeshift hen hut, and lightened of its large iron-shod wheels. In about three short years, all that remained of the former ambulance was a collapsed skeleton of whitened spars and warped plywood, with no one bothering even to clear up what was left.

Pretty soon, as I saw it, our little hamlet would be like that. The winds of change would be on us with a vengeance when this game of amalgamating, absorbing, swapping-about caught up with us. They would sweep far beyond the modest wall letterbox proclaiming 'Pepper Hill 9 a.m.' that the GPO gave us as a compromise to our request for a telephone box some time back, ignoring our hint that the phone was now mightier than the pen. *Swoosh* would go our remoteness, our stark bleak individuality, our grim much-too-much-for-most way of living, all gone before the piles of new bricks, breeze blocks, slates and pebbledash, with the cross winds making a great sport of the shoals of hand-delivered soap coupons, football pools letters, empty ice-cream cartons – and, especially, the brand new asbestos-sheeted garages, not anchored down with a full respect for our special winds.

If all this did come, I only hoped they would build everything strong enough to take the brunt of that wester with its howling wet

54 William Cawkwell lived at Upper Fleet Farm in Queensbury.

bluster, and to be sneak-proof against the low cunning of the icy east wind. I also hoped they would not build new houses between our cottages and the brow of the hill, where one saw the lights that ribbon, varicoloured, to Bradford and Halifax and Huddersfield. But it must come to something like this if we wanted that sorely needed bit of plumbing, and a bus or two past our croft. It was all going to cost a price – no doubting that!

Then, all at once, an appalling thing occurred to me. Supposing they cleared us all out? Supposing the missus and I got dumped into one of those cliff-flat dwellings in a big town? Supposing this did happen, and we were never again to see black hill upon black hill rolling away into Lancashire on an April evening! Or never more to hear the late lark trilling high up above, and me peering hard to get a glimpse of this speck in the evening sky. Never again to walk slowly on the lane, tired out after every workday's close, gradually reviving in the clear air, and feeling I had all the time in the world on my hands. Not again to see smoke rising lazily from a dozen chimneys and full knowing one of these to be mine, waiting to bid its unspoken 'welcome home' as I crossed the threshold. Nor to feel the antiseptic winds blowing away the insidious cobwebs of ill, and filling me with an intense sensation of being recharged with relaxation and quiet happiness, and being wholly at one with my bit of world, despite its many failings to conform. Oh! the sheer serenity of all these foregoing things that I had always taken for granted. Surely, it would never come to such a parting?

I chewed a mental cud of all these blessings, regarding them as a reward vouchsafed we humble folks by the near miracle of spring following winter's ill-using; these, and the first flushings of light of day brightening the way to work again in late February, and the stirrings of life at six o'clock cock-crow, and the bark of a dog on the air as he races, stretching his legs in a far-off field. I tried to comfort myself with the crumb of hoping that this 'integration' stuff would never get beyond the talking stage – that it might easily be stillborn after the first hot, fevered flush of conception. I scratched for more comforting crumbs, but slowly became aware Edna was drawing my attention to drops of water west-wind-driven through a back window, a window that had long suffered this defect. I shrugged it all off with a promise of doing something when the weather picked up – though I knew, and Edna knew, that when the weather did pick up I would be out stretching my legs towards the moors, or else gawping around on Chapel Lane[55], or busy cutting my bit of grass on the lawn out front, and probably telling the tale, in between runs, to my next-door neighbour, an ex-army man of the old days, with his own line of talk very much to my liking, or being interrupted in my perambulations by one or other of my two grandsons, Baby Temp's babies, who almost live with us, being resident in the other next-door cottage.

And mention of children brings me to the most exhilarating breeze of all – the one that, clean- sweeping, and starting to blow long before the boys were born, had brought such great changes into their young lives. These lads would never be subject, as we kiddies had been, to so many distressing ailments; the winds that now blew were cleaner, unladen of the terrible muck and ills of yore. No longer did I see children with horribly sore or squinting eyes, with bow legs or knock knees, shaven ringwormed heads hidden in caps of shame (as we regarded them), and all the rest of the plagues that once beset childhood. Nor were children now heirs presumptive to mornings in the mill at twelve years old, with the compensating surreptitious dozing whilst sat at a school desk in the afternoon, the drone of teacher's voice, the buzz of a bluebottle acting as a soporific. Nor would they set off to school fortified with a couple of slices of bread thickly spread with sweetened condensed milk – or fail to set off for school because of having nothing to put on tiny feet.

God must, indeed, have blessed us innocents of those latter days, for nobody else did, family excepted. And we kiddies really believed we lived in one whale of a great country, specially placed under the wings of the good Lord's guardian angels, and pernicious poverty accepted

55 Chapel Lane is a local nickname for Cross Lane, site of Pepper Hill Unitarian Chapel.

as our inevitable lot, as some kind of contribution to the industrial sinew of Britannia. Thank heavens, winds of change had blown all that away! Nowadays, youth was much more realistic in its outlook; it took in situations with calm, assured gaze; it spoke easily, and with grace. Even the tinies' belief in fairies was tinctured with common sense. Early on, I became aware of the three cardinal assets, the ones that I had learned (though bitterly and latterly) sustained one best in life: the three Ts of Trust, Truth, and Tolerance. Youth would do well to hang on to them, for the Ts will always stand them in good stead, this loftier race than ever the world has seen before! It might not come amiss for them to keep alive the old-fashioned adage: it's a very ill wind that blows nobody any good.

Richard with grandsons Ian (left) and Philip Langford, with neighbour Pat Mason

STARLINGS[56]

T'city cahncil in solemn conclave did sit,
To tackle t'sore point "wheer t'starlings could flit?"
An' offered rewards if owt could be heard
'At would rid ahr fair city o' this fahl bird.
Then, humbly, one mornin' to t'Tahn Hall thur came
An old character, known only bi' t'name
o' t'piper who makes all pipe dreams come true.
Said, "Ah'll clear t'Tahn Hall, an' t'environs, too!"
He tewk out his pipes an blew… lahd an' clear;
An' off ivvry perch t'birds flocked to him theer!
Then he marched 'em on t'valley, reyt out to Saltaire,
An' telled 'em, "Nah, birds… yew mek yer muck there."
Beamed t'council, "Weal done, lad," but gev him noa pay,
Said t'rates wodn't run to a piper this day.
Soa he browt all t'birds back, wi' one pipin' trill –
An' theer th' still sit, scatterin' largesse at will.

56 Richard wrote this poem in response to a plague of starlings that hit Bradford.

ACKNOWLEDGEMENTS

I would like to thank the following for their help in producing this book, without them it would not have happened:

Richard Langford
Chloe Novak
Charlotte Mouncey
Philip Langford
Alison Birch
Ben Stables

Richard William Tempest 2025